Virginia Woolf

Virginia Woolf

a portrait

Translated by Jody Gladding

VIVIANE FORRESTER

Columbia University Press   New York

Columbia University Press
Publishers Since 1893
New York   Chichester, West Sussex
cup.columbia.edu
Copyright © 2015 Columbia University Press
Original French edition © Editions Albin Michel—Paris 2009
All rights reserved

Library of Congress Cataloging-in-Publication Data
Forrester, Viviane.
[Virginia Woolf. English]
Virginia Woolf : a portrait / Viviane Forrester ; translated by Jody Gladding.
pages   cm
Includes bibliographical references and index.
ISBN 978-0-231-15356-0 (cloth) — ISBN 978-0-231-53512-0 (electronic)
Woolf, Virginia, 1882-1941. 2. Novelists, English—20th century—Biography. I.
Gladding, Jody, 1955- translator. II. Title.
PR6045.O72Z63513   2013
823'.912—dc23
[B]
2012045644

∞

Columbia University Press books are printed on permanent
and durable acid-free paper.
This book is printed on paper with recycled content.

Printed in the United States of America
c 10 9 8 7 6 5 4 3 2

COVER IMAGE: Victoria and Albert Museum, London, UK
© The Wyndham Lewis Memorial Trust/Bridgeman Images

COVER AND BOOK DESIGN: Lisa Hamm

TITLE-PAGE ART: *Dahlias*, illustration from a volume containing woodcuts by
seven artists, published by the Omega Workshops Ltd, London, 1918 (woodcut),
Bell, Vanessa (1879-1961)/Private Collection/The Stapleton Collection/
Bridgeman Images

References to websites (URLs) were accurate at the time of writing.
Neither the author nor Columbia University Press is responsible for URLs
that may have expired or changed since the manuscript was prepared.

CONTENTS

Virginia Woolf

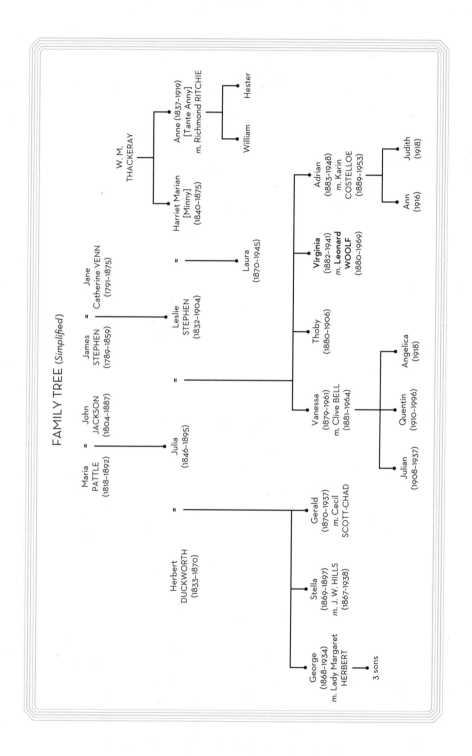

FAMILY TREE (Simplified)

Part 1

HEARING the breath issuing from another body as it brushes against the skin: this can and does endlessly result from the pages brought to life by Virginia Woolf.

There she is. In these signs. Virginia, so distant from herself, as is each of us, but ever relentless in her attempt to assemble, to feel the scattered mobility, the multiplicity that constitutes her. Worried as well about responding to the "impossible desires to embrace the whole world with the arms of understanding."[1]

And endlessly failing in this, having failed, having admitted that "no, no, nothing is proved, nothing is known,"[2] having rejected such proof or knowledge and retained the uncertainty of achieving the exactitude beyond the silence that surrounds words, having above all and endlessly repeated her quest: this makes it all the more real, quivering with what she does not know but senses, trembling with what cannot be written down but what she knows how to indicate.

Here she is, passionate, ever watchful for what is always escaping, although she manages to capture its transience; here she is demanding, a little weary, impatient: "Why is there not a discovery in life? Something one can lay hands on & say, 'This is it'?"[3]

But can we say of her novels, which are so many live beings, her letters, her personal diaries that reveal her in all her states, sparkling or fragile, that make us convulse with laughter or tremble with emotion, that make us detest her too, can we say, "That's her"? Thousands of pages overflowing with thrills, gossip, angst, and so rich as well in detailed analysis of her battles with the text, exposing the very core of the science of writing, of being a writer—the very wound, the miracle, the disaster not only of being alive but also of becoming life's stunned, sensual, greedy, and desperate witness.

Around her, a constellation of men and women, of bodies, of destinies, all interwoven and, if fickle, also faithful to one another throughout, we discover. Telling their own stories, or each other's, most left their marks . . . which shape her. So many elements that more or less corroborate one another, each protagonist revealing himself, his circle, much more than he thinks. So many elements of which Virginia is usually unaware, whereas, of her own existence, she registers even the least tremor.

And thus the sensation of opening and, yes, of rummaging through drawers that even she does not know about, but also of living with her in the places, the homes, the landscapes that were hers; of knowing the climate accompanying each of her encounters and what impressions the hours of a day left in her; what impulses pushed her to the limits and to expand the limits, regardless of danger; what laughter enchanted her.

We do not know anyone, much less ourselves and those closest to us, as we are able to know her, not only her but also her circle and all the entangled lives, the secrets, the lies, the dramatic misunderstandings that ensued. Through those convolutions runs the work that cuts its way, that churns, unyielding. The body that perceives it.

But surrounding the woman who was the site for that work and who managed to shatter the frozen tongue, opening it to other languages? So many countertruths. She submits—entrusts?—to us so many clues about herself and the conflicts and accords, the quest and doubts that she comprised. So much information long kept secret was leaked by her circle through their memoirs, autobiographies, diaries, and letters. Throughout the innumerable "moments of being" offered us, we will discover beings bearing little resemblance to the perceptions they had of one another and often of themselves, who often differ fundamentally from their well-known profiles.

Without Virginia knowing it, most of those closest to her, in particular, her father, sister, and especially her husband, differed sharply, and in vital ways, from their reputations—which often still endure. In their own and in others' eyes, so many equivocations fixed them in roles that were not theirs but that they performed as such, creating serious misunderstandings that Virginia labored under, equivocal as well, deceived by the false appearances that are often still accepted, even confirmed, today.

Some examples? They abound throughout her life, surround her self-inflicted death. The death that Mrs. Dalloway called "an embrace."⁴ Perhaps the only one possible for Virginia, all the more alone the more she was surrounded.

"How is one to live in such a world!" she exclaims at fifteen, before making Clarissa Dalloway, once again, say how "very, very dangerous" it is "to live even one day." But she has the answer: to become someone who could write, years later and shortly before her end, "I feel in my fingers the weight of every word."⁵

And that was the essential thing.

But was it?

What is the weight of a life?

What we absorb from a work born of the torments and delights experienced by another, thrown naked, raw, into the worst indecency, utterly entangling us: does it compensate for the exploration of loss that sometimes devastated, ravaged as much as intoxicated, that other—in our place and to our profit?

What entangled Virginia?

But, before launching into whole new aspects of her trajectory, one more remark: outside of any religion, Virginia recognized the point at which life itself (a fortiori the life of a human being) cannot be grasped, discerned, much less explained, and how reducing it to narration, to plots, an outline, or worse, conclusions, denies its very being—and how pinning it down to some configuration of conventional reality would destroy the shadow of its passage, its tenuous tie to a conventional reality.

Nevertheless, that is exactly the reality that she summons and interrogates in her novels, that she seizes in its immediacy, as though to better strip away its masks, extract its pulp, watch for its lapses, take it by surprise: the moment of a fleeting apparition of the present captured in its very disappearing.

The world as palimpsest, whose original text poets, painters, musicians, thinkers of all kinds struggle to perceive: it is at the level of appearances that this world subjugates Virginia. From the age of thirteen, with her mother's death—then in an incestuous climate created primarily by her father, but also with the pattern of early, successive bereavements—yes, from childhood, the landmarks of the habitual, habitable, acknowledged world threatened to elude her, to lead her astray. She quickly perceived other directions, stemming from the loss of all direction, a universe exploding with other possibilities. To return to the everyday, to the commonplace, rational, predictable world, must have seemed as strange, tenuous, and dangerous to her as those chaotic terrains approaching distraction. Coming back to the banal must have seemed more unusual and enigmatic, more charged with magic than the exploding boundaries. And certain coherences more fantastic than chaos. Hence, her fascination for the mysterious effervescence of the moment in its plenitude, its fragility, in that reality, however trivial, briefly fused to the real, that represents, perhaps, dangerously, beauty. That substitutes for the divine: "there is no God; we are the words; we are the music; we are the thing itself."[6]

* * *

Actually, we are it. She was it. She expresses it throughout. But beginning where? Let us go back to the domain of the traditional account (truly, the most impossible), the story of one life lived among other lives, silhouetted against them, and let us find the distortion between what we know of her and what the images of her journey, in all its multiplicity, complications, entanglements, and enigma, seem to reveal.

The first example of such discrepancy? Well, the primary one that focuses on Leonard Woolf, that fascinating, passionate man who nevertheless had to and immediately learned to develop a shell, to construct for himself the persona behind which he hid the rest of his life. Strange, perhaps, this first choice, as Leonard only entered Virginia's life to marry her. He was thirty-one years old, she was thirty.

However, a quick glance backward to this man's youth (he was, among other things, an exceptional, if castrated, novelist), and we discover someone wholly other than the man we know, than the man he wanted to be recognized as: a Leonard who uses Virginia to better hide himself and who officially attributes to her his own troubles, his own vertigo in facing the risk of his own alienation. His own hells. If Virginia endlessly seeks her own identity, Leonard, perhaps more painfully, conceals his.

Behind the persona known to be austere, solid, supremely rational, regarded as a pillar—overshadowed by that being of strict reason and moral rectitude, rather cold but ever dynamic in his wisdom—appears another Leonard Woolf, fragile, neurasthenic, deeply despairing after having been mad with hope, and broken. A discouraged, ruined man, as he says, who struggles fiercely but without confidence in the mire of defeat that seems to him inescapable. A man he never ceased to be, who never left him even at the height of success, but whom he considered banished, whom he learned to repress throughout his life, with such vigilance, and such subdued violence as well! And so successfully! In the midst of devastation all around him, unconsciously or rather instinctively wrought.

To encounter this unexpected Leonard, passionate, vulnerable, mired in defeat, forever disappointed, and with suicidal tendencies, we only have to read his agonized, shattering letters, sent to Lytton Strachey from Ceylon. They attest to a past, the traces of which Leonard learned to blur, even if many documents remained. Just as he later learned to promote his own version of his wife's life, to frame Virginia's portrait so as to serve his own memory. Thus diverting attention from what could be self-revelatory, exposing him as he was.

Without convincing her of it, he made Virginia accept his view of her. But he was able to convince their circle. And even to convince posterity, thanks to the first well-documented biography of Virginia, not only authorized but ordered, practically dictated by him to his nephew Quentin Bell. Not actually dictated: it appeared, with much fanfare, in 1972; Leonard, who had died three years earlier, had only read the first chapters of this work, though he had been slowly, patiently weaving the material for it for decades, from the early days of his marriage to Virginia.

The most revealing aspect of this biography? Bell's condescending tone, speaking of his aunt while scotomizing the writer, whose work, as he was fond of admitting coyly, he did not know very well. Instinctive revenge (which we will find often) among Virginia's survivors, in this case, Vanessa, her sister and beloved rival, who was also Quentin's mother: to be able finally to dispose of Virginia Woolf, to summon her respectfully, officially discredit her, and disguise it as familiarity; to compare her indulgently, ironically (here good-naturedly) to the supposedly "normal" image she did not present. Separating the writer from the woman to avoid one and disparage the other. Above all, trivializing and ridiculing her alleged lapses with regard to the trivialities from which she stood apart. And thus, inversely, marginalizing her with great authority. In short, putting her back (or rather putting her publicly) in what, it had always been hoped, was her place. And would partly remain so—once Leonard's fixed ideas, justifications, and conclusions were definitively sanctioned, ratified as legitimate.

She, a genius, and thus all the more eccentric and naïve, intermittently mad, always mentally fragile, a bit of a mythomaniac, and moreover, frigid. The timelessness, the power, the marvel of her work all becoming secondary.

And he, the backdrop, playing the serious, stable man, the protector, the husband sacrificed sexually to his wife's inhibitions, devoted to her salvation, watching over and enabling her work.

Quentin's account (that is, the inventory of all his uncle's theses and versions) has been debated, criticized, contradicted ever since—often brilliantly, movingly—but according to Leonard's obsessive vision. Even today, those who no longer accept this account remain dependent upon it, adopting it as their premise, either unconsciously or in order to contradict it.

There is a way to escape this stranglehold, one that leads less to knowing Leonard's life, already so well recorded, than to discovering *who* he was. *Whom* Virginia Stephen married. Virginia, whose childhood and then entire life we will explore only afterward, Virginia, battling so many errors, so much ignorance regarding those who surrounded her—living or (too early) dead.

Virginia, whose legend we will examine, the legend that holds her captive still and that Leonard instinctively wove, controlled, throughout their marriage; which was possible because he managed to forget and to make others forget the parts of him and his past that could expose his strategies, the explanations, the versions of their life, as it unfolded, that he provided. So many scenes in which he gave Virginia the same role, conforming to the rigid pattern in which his own role was to present an impassive front and make others and especially himself forget the wounded, vulnerable, offended Leonard Woolf.

So let us meet this forever overshadowed, clandestine Leonard. The one who, at twenty-three, despairs: "O le sale monde! O le sale monde!" Or, as a leitmotif: "The fetid, sordid world!" The one who wonders "why one doesn't commit suicide, except that one is dead & rotten," but who is also mad about literature, who asks of Henry James, "Did he invent us or we him?" and who rereads Madame Bovary, "the saddest & most beautiful book I had ever read . . . One day I shall sit down & read straight on to the end: I don't think one would ever reach the end, I think one might die with Emma." The one who believes, hopes, knows himself to be a writer, and whose youth is misspent in exile, a civil servant in the colonies.[7]

A tormented, romantic Leonard, offended socially, close to defeat, resigned and bemoaning the hardships, the impasses, his ruined future. A Leonard whose true reasons, or rather, whose need for marrying Virginia Stephen we will discover.

His childhood? His adolescence? His father, Sydney Woolf, died at forty-nine years old, a successful, prosperous lawyer, his career already among the most brilliant, but as Leonard writes, "we had only recently struggled up . . . from the stratum of Jewish shopkeepers."[8] Leonard, born November 25, 1880, was then twelve years old, with eight brothers and sisters, and a mother who, much impoverished by her widowhood, would descend the social ladder but would manage to enroll her children in the most prestigious English universities. At Cambridge, Leonard spent the most fulfilling years of his life; he fascinated the other students, among them Thoby Stephen, Virginia's brother. There Woolf was elected "Apostle," thus becoming part of an envied elite, to which belonged, among others, John Maynard Keynes, Lytton Strachey, and E. M. Forster, as well as his professors, the philosophers Bertrand Russell and George Edward Moore, and later Ludwig Wittgenstein.

He had found his niche. He lost it. And quickly.

His failure: "the crash has come &, by God, it is a crash. It came just an hour ago. I'm 65th!"on the final examination. Without financial resources, his only choice, he said, was to depart for the colonies or become a college usher. "A battered usher of 50, among filthy boys & people with whom he cannot talk, on 150 pounds a year when he wants 15,000? Good God, what a farce, for it might, I feel, so easily be true."[9]

It would be the colonies. Exile. Permission to return to England for one year out of six: "very yellow & silent—but I should be making 600 pounds a year! . . . This is a sordid letter, but I feel so." He is annoyed with himself for having written it, but his addressee, Lytton Strachey, protests: "Oh! No, no, no. Say what you feel at any & every moment. How could I bear anything else?"[10]

Soon after, on November 20, 1904, Lytton, whose homosexuality Leonard did not share, writes: "As I watched your ship in the Channel last night, I thought that all was lost. You have vanished and the kisses that I never gave you, and your embraces that I have felt—they are all that remains."[11]

Leonard had just embarked, equipped with ninety volumes of Voltaire's works. Responding to Lytton's protest would sustain him through six long years of trials: he would pour out his feelings without restraint to his friend in letters that show him tormented, demeaned, shattered in the midst of frantic activity; overwhelmed with work, garnering local successes and promotions, but lost, suffocating outside the circle of his Cambridge friends and struggling, often filled with impotent anger: "You think I shall be in a position to forgive God one day?"[12]

Cornered.

And why not stuck in this trap forever? To Lytton: "I feel that, in a way, you are lost to me already; you at any rate will be here, & there are other people, but I shall be rotting in Ceylon. I shall be out of date after 6 years." He knew nothing now but regret, longing, nostalgia: "It was always one of our supremacies—our poor dead blighted supremacies—that we could laugh. I think too I can remember them all; how we laughed [at Cambridge] for hours in that dingy old attic of mine & in the Goth's[13] green room & Turner's yellow barn, in your rooms & the cloisters & all over Richmond Park. I haven't laughed like that since Nov 19th though I was hysterical often on the Syria, & I suppose I shan't again for 6 years, when I expect I at any rate shall be dried up." The disorientation persists, the uprootedness, the sensation of a waking nightmare: "You *can't* exist, nor grey old Cambridge, nor Bob Trevy nor the Yen. I can't believe I have ever spoken to you, or rather I shouldn't if I did not want to so much now."[14]

The idea of a definitive return faded. Foundering, Leonard anticipated a life of constraints, engulfed in a destiny he abhorred. He envisioned himself incapable of ever escaping, suffocated by financial need, lacking qualifications, in a kind of social paralysis that isolated him where he loathed to be: "One thing you must understand & that is that I am done for as regards England. I shall live & die in these appalling countries now. If I come back for good now I should do nothing but loaf until I died of starvation. What else could I do? And as for happiness—I don't believe in being happy even in England."[15]

Throughout the six years he lived in Ceylon, his letters reflect him actively depressed, overwhelmed with discouragement. Three years before he returned to London on leave, Lytton suggested an escape to him: marry Virginia Stephen. Leonard, who was very close to Thoby Stephen at Cambridge, had only met his two sisters, Virginia and Vanessa, twice, over tea and at a farewell dinner. He immediately latched onto the idea, but not without concluding: "To think of existence at all fills me with horror & sickness; the utter foulness, the stupid blind vindictive foulness of everything & of myself."[16]

This is the man, the man of Ceylon, who, returning to London three years later, would marry Virginia. And this is the man of Ceylon, as we know him, as none (except Lytton) knew him, who would forever claim ignorance regarding all notions of neurosis, neurasthenia, depression or melancholia, any personal thoughts of suicide.

But it is he, the socialist Jew, who in 1940 would propose that he and Virginia, also on Hitler's blacklist, should asphyxiate themselves if the Nazis landed. And it is he whose suicidal tendencies, melancholia, neurasthenia, and neurosis run as a leitmotif through the letters he wrote from Ceylon, confiding to Lytton: "I sometimes wonder whether I shall commit suicide before the six years are up & I can see you again; at this moment I feel as near as I have ever been. Depression is becoming, I believe, a mania with me, it sweeps upon & over me every eight or ten days, deeper each time. If you hear that I have died of sunstroke, you may be the only person to know that I have chosen that method of annihilation." And again: "Damn damn damn damn damn I took out my gun the other night, made my will & prepared to shoot myself. God knows why I didn't; merely I suppose the imbecility of weakness & the futility of ridiculous hopes. Whores & vulgar gramophones, fools & wrecked intellects. Why am I caged & penned & herded with these. I laugh when I read that San Francisco is wiped out & weep over the wreck & ruin of my existence."[17]

Strangely enough, that is where Leonard's strength resides: in the power of his tragic ardor, as later, in the energy, the endless energy required to keep from expressing it, to hold that ardor in check to ensure his decisive status, never again to find himself an outcast, forever to be respected above all (even if it meant being cowardly sometimes in order to maintain this; even if it meant feigning ignorance of the anti-Semitism to which he was often openly subjected, even among his close friends).

Only his correspondence with Strachey still tied him to the Apostles, to the life that was running its distant course among his friends. Lytton remains passionately faithful to him and finds his letters "Wonderful. . . . Why are you a man? We are females, nous autres, but your mind is singularly male."[18]

Lytton's writing is more brilliant, more spirited than Woolf's. He overflows with dynamism, ambition, humor, and beneath his light dandy-intellectual façade, he reveals a keen capacity for observation and lucid sensitivity toward his friends. A boundless enthusiasm—this was written in 1904, when he was twenty-four years old: "We are greater than our fathers; we are greater than Shelley; we are greater than the Eighteenth Century; we are greater than the Renaissance; we are greater than the Romans and the Greeks. What is hidden from us? We have mastered all. We have abolished religion, we have founded ethics, we have established philosophy, we have sown our strange illuminations in every province of thought, we have conquered art, we have liberated love."[19] Up until then, they had only good intentions!

Strachey's only difficulties come precisely from his love affairs, among them his rivalry with Maynard Keynes over the irresistible young painter Duncan Grant, before the latter became the lover of Adrian, the younger brother of Virginia. Who, in their eyes, was only the sister of her other brother, Thoby, so revered at Cambridge. "Oh but the Goth! Don't you see that if God had to justify the existence of the World it would be done if he could produce the Goth?" exclaims Lytton, who, less than a year after Leonard's departure, would have tea with "the Gothic at home" and this time would find Virginia "rather wonderful—quite witty, full of things to say, and absolutely out of rapport with reality."[20]

Lytton and Leonard had in common their desire to become and knowledge of being writers. Lytton was already imagining readers for their correspondence. And a publisher. Which also explains his flair. But it is Leonard who reveals himself to the fullest, as he is, hyperactive and broken. Devastated. Something died in him then, for good.

Although, if he considered himself a banished, mortified failure in Ceylon, foundering in dereliction, he held sway in the villages there, in the ever increasing regions that fell within his jurisdiction. People bowed down to him. There he dealt with, directed, judged men (natives) destabilized by a triumphant order that was foreign to them, managed by a civilization that was not their own.

Leonard slipped easily into the colonialist role. He was restive only with regard to his own fate, so different from his expectations, falling so far short of his hopes. It is true that the Empire was taken for granted at that time, that colonialism was everywhere accepted, even among those who tended, as he did, toward what would become the British Labour party.

Nearly sixty years later, in his autobiography, he would mention some qualms, a growing uneasiness he felt in Jaffna; a belated awareness of the imperialism that ruled and his own role in it as proconsul. His letters hardly mention it. Nor the reprimands of his superiors, however disinclined they were to condemn their administrators for applying too stringent measures with too zealous rigidity—as they would do themselves.

To be fair—and his first novel, *The Village in the Jungle*, testifies to this—he was dazzled by the landscape and moved by its inhabitants, whom he preferred to the unthinkable vulgarity of his colleagues. He learned Tamil and Sinhalese. Nonetheless, he was a White Man, civilized, triumphant, brutal: "The Arabs [!] will do anything if you hit them hard enough with a walking stick, an occupation in which I have been engaged for the most part of the last 3 days & nights."[21]

In each of his posts, he assumed multiple responsibilities: secretary, accountant, administrator, police officer, judge, tax collector, even veterinarian: didn't he inspect the herds? He inspected . . . everything everywhere in the ever vaster territories for which he was responsible. He endlessly made the rounds, grand tours in old vehicles, on horseback, on bicycle, grappling with malaria and other diseases; the insects swarmed, the climate was unbearable, his colleagues insipid. The work (an average of sixteen hours a day) became an antidote: "I work, God, how I work. I have reduced it to a method & exalted it to a mania."[22] That would be true, and could be the motto, for his whole life.

One of his responsibilities was to attend hangings; he even had to give the signal for them:

> I had to go (as Fiscal) to see four men hanged one morning. They were hanged two by two. I have a strong stomach but at best it is a horrible performance. I go to the cells & read over the warrant of execution & ask them whether they have anything to say. They nearly always say no. . . . I have (in Kandy) to stand on a sort of verandah where I can actually see the man hanged. The signal has to be given by me. The first two were hanged all right but they gave one of the second too big a drop or something went wrong. The man's head was practically torn from his body & there was a great jet of blood which went up about 3 or 4 feet high, covering the gallows & priest who stands praying on the steps. . . . I don't know why I have written all this to you except that whenever I stand waiting for the moment to give the signal,

you & Turner & the room at Trinity come to mind & the discussion in which Turner enraged us so by saying that he would not turn his head if anyone said there was a heap of corpses in the corner by the gyproom [college servants' pantry]. I don't think I should any more.[23]

In fact, he adapted and the "appalling spectacle" soon became part of the routine:

My only news is that I had to shoot my dog yesterday & that I had to be present at an execution on Friday. It was really more unpleasant shooting the dog than hanging the man. . . . The man himself did not care at all. He walked up the scaffold smiling. I heard the priest say to him on the scaffold, when he was waiting with the handkerchief over his face & the noose round his neck, "Are you frightened?" & the man answered in the most casual of tones, "Not a bit."[24]

Upon his return, Leonard would be able to exploit these stories of tortures and the role he played in them. From their first meeting, Adrian, Virginia's younger brother, would remember especially that his "descriptions of hangings were very interesting."[25]

"He has ruled India, hung black men, and shot tigers," Virginia would write her friends a few years later, perhaps to compensate for the announcement (the "confession," she would call it) of her engagement to "a penniless Jew."[26]

Colonialism! It went without saying among the Europeans, particularly the British, in all circles, whatever the political or emotional sensibilities of its protagonists or witnesses. Fundamentally, racism. Unconscious, insofar as it was then considered natural, obvious to the point of going unnoticed, much less judged. And isn't that still the case? So many present-day forms of reprehensible, even criminal ostracism will be recognized in retrospect.

One more remark: there is no question of idealizing anyone here, much less Virginia. To conceal or temper the known facts would mean sacrificing accuracy, acquiescing to a concern for appeal. It would mean despising Virginia Woolf to present her other than she was in order to preserve her memory.

But one thing is unassailable: her work. A body of work does not require its author to be an ideal or even a decent human being: only a person for whom life is not sufficient as is. It is not incumbent upon this person to offer the reader a gratifying reflection, a model or an example, but, among other things, she must endure her own self and somehow extract something from reality. However sublime, the work of a writer grows from composite, sometimes unpleasant (a euphemism) ground, and does not aim at the sublime, but at the least accessible, most reticent thing: accuracy. And the miracle of its creation often derives from its link with the general turmoil, indeed even its deep roots in failure, decay, or worse. . . .

And then no life offers a clear outline. We lack the words and expressions for capturing what animates, what circulates, multiple and inaccessible, within each of us in our "moments of being." And we each live only within ourselves: whether conflicted or extroverted, devoted to others, we can only inhabit ourselves, live within the first person throughout the fits and starts, the ups and downs of our journey.

"Even in the wickedest man there's a poor innocent horse toiling away, with a heart, a liver, and arteries in which there's no malice, and which suffer."[27] In the words of Marcel Proust.

But let us return to Leonard, who would rather become a man who no longer suffers, and who would soon put on his impassive, legendary mask.

Return to Leonard and Virginia? To their marriage? We aren't there yet. And neither is Leonard. Until the time of his engagement, what was his relationship to women, to desire, to sex, to being in love?

Still back in England, he believed Lytton had fallen in love with a woman—but no, he realized, because, with regard to a woman, "you could not be or at any rate would not—with women. I never am either with any individual of the species—yet—except perhaps for a moment with some face or form—only it is more than that—that I see in a carriage or a bus or gutter. But at any rate I know I have the ability if not the inclination."[28] An inclination that would not develop in Ceylon—but rather a growing repulsion, almost a hostility toward women and especially their bodies.

Nevertheless, it was in Ceylon that he experienced his first sexual relations. 1905. He was twenty-five years old. A prostitute, of mixed blood. A night of "degraded debauch. . . . The ridiculousness of existence never reaches such heights—the elaborate absurdity made me almost impuissant from amusement." In Ceylon, he would have sexual relations with prostitutes and would experience them with a kind of horror and fascinated guilt, in denial of "these degradations—their lasciviousness or their ugliness."[29]

In that narrow colonial environment where everyone watched everyone else, it was difficult, it is true, to maintain a personal life, but Leonard considered all female proximity, no matter how chaste, as sordid. He happened to confide to Lytton that "among other things," he had fallen in love with a young girl in his circle, whom, as a gentleman, he had to respect (lacking intentions of marriage), thus congratulating himself for acting as though there was nothing between them and deploring what was "none the less unpleasant & filthy. I am beginning to think it is always degraded being in love." "Degraded" is a term he often pairs with "in love." In his poems, lovers exchange a "cancerous kiss," and a woman doesn't recognize a "dead man's lips," unaware that she has kissed a corpse.[30]

Let us not forget that he would marry Virginia Stephen immediately upon his return to London. It is this lover who would become her partner. The one who in 1907, five years earlier, related how, at the classic invitation from a man ("Would you like a woman?"), he entered a house to find himself face to face with "a half naked woman sitting on a bed. But I was too utterly bored really to feel even the mild disgust which was my only feeling (if there was any). I just sat down on a chair dumb with dejection & finally, without doing or saying anything, gave her all the money I had on me & fled." It is this lover who declared, three years before marrying Virginia: "Most women naked when alive are extraordinarily ugly, but dead they are repulsive."[31]

Upon his return to London, did he suddenly fall in love with Virginia, to the point of being transformed into that man so often portrayed as a skilled, duped lover, who would selflessly sacrifice his passion for women, his ardent sexuality, for an utterly inhibited wife?

Hardly! That widely accepted version, whispered discreetly during Virginia's lifetime (she accepted it), repeated decades later by Leonard in his autobiography, is decidedly false. First of all, their meeting had nothing to do with chance. It was a matter of two trapped beings, each of whom appeared to the other as a last resort.

Virginia, so firmly rooted in the social set that enthralled him, represented the solution for Leonard, who dreamed of leaving Ceylon and reentering, for good this time, the only environment in which he could breathe.

And Leonard, a man of quality, unencumbered, could save Virginia from the dreaded label of "old maid." "No one has asked me to marry them," she wrote in 1908, when she was twenty-six years old. Virginia, despite her beauty, was hardly sought-after; without a partner and the status of a married woman, her solitude was a burden to her. A Virginia full of yearning, prey to long, silent grieving due to those wounds of the past that we will soon meet.[32]

At thirty years old, Virginia Stephen, who was, in fact, truly supreme, had had two vague, belated proposals, and only one serious one. From Hilton Young, who took quite some time to declare himself and whom, in the end, she turned down. Through the many letters exchanged with her sister, Vanessa, we can follow their anxious, often vain hopes for rendezvous with potential, yet fleeting suitors. "Am I to have no proposal then? If I had had the chance, and determined against it, I could settle to virginity with greater composure than I can, when my womanhood is at question." Vacationing in Somerset, she worries about Hilton Young: "I have heard nothing from H.Y. [Hilton Young]: and it strikes me that I probably led him to think that I should be here till Saturday week. . . . I may have been too cold, or too hot, or he may have thought better of it. Anyhow, my chance of a proposal dwindles." He is the only one (apart from Leonard) to actually declare himself—and she would refuse him.[33]

The two other proposals? One from a man already married, Sydney Waterlow; the other from the pusillanimous Walter Lamb, who asked her to wait and could not make up his mind. "Marriage is so difficult. Will you let me wait? Don't hurry me." And she: "What am I to do! Am I such a d——d failure. We talked for two hours."[34]

Adrian was amused by Virginia's eagerness to seduce Leonard upon one of his first visits.

> It was too funny, after coming in she went up deliberately and changed her costume in spite of the fact that it was pelting with rain put on her best Turkish cloak and satin slippers and so on. Saxon, Woolf and I were kept waiting while she did all this and then we had to take a taxi. She made great eyes at Woolf whom she called markedly Leonard which seems to be a little forward. Her method of wooing is to talk about nothing but fucking and [illegible] which she calls with a great leer copulation and WCs and I dare say she will be successful, I hope so anyway.[35]

A few weeks before Leonard's return to England, Virginia seems almost to scream when writing, in the depths of depression: "Did you feel horribly depressed? I did. I could not write, and all the devils came out—hairy black ones. To be 29 and unmarried—to be a failure—childless—insane too, no writer."[36]

Yes, they could each provide the other the status they lacked.

Of course they would discover that they had more in common with each other than with most of their circle. They also had Thoby in common, who had recently died at age twenty-five. Thoby, Leonard's close friend and Virginia's favorite brother; among her long list of bereavements, her most persistent ghost.

It was Thoby who first mentioned Leonard to Virginia, she would remember, as "a man who trembled perpetually all over [Leonard's right hand had a permanent tremor, as did his father's]. He was as eccentric, as remarkable in his way as Bell or Strachey in theirs. He was a Jew. When I asked why he trembled, Thoby somehow made me feel that it was part of his nature—he was so violent, so savage; he so despised the whole human race. 'And after all,' said Thoby, 'it's a pretty feeble affair, isn't it?' Nobody was much good after twenty-five, he said. But most people, I gathered, rather rubbed along, and came to terms with things." Thoby thought it sublime, Woolf did not: "I was of course inspired with the deepest interest in that violent trembling misanthropic Jew who had already shaken his fist at civilization and was about to disappear into the tropics so that we should none of us ever see him again."[37]

Of course Leonard and Virginia would not have married each other if they had not in some way "recognized" each other, and the lukewarm prelude to their marriage did not prevent them from becoming a true couple, based on an enchanting, permanent, potentially fulfilling attachment—undercut by uneasiness, lies (those one tells oneself), and especially, growing contention.

Nothing is ever Manichean, nor often simple. In the smallest fraction of the most tenuous moment, only indistinct, simultaneous, confused elements; whereas composing an account of them, making something of them, requires choices and development. Virginia knew that: to a large extent, it serves as the basis for her work; the moment, which she makes ring like crystal, intercepted as is, unresolved, sprung from, drawn from the real, but issuing from a world at odds with the false compartmentalizations that mask reality.

It was not the facts that were detrimental to Virginia, but the carefully constructed tableau imposed by Leonard. It was his trafficking with immediate memory that led her astray. We can trace it in Leonard Woolf's autobiography, which recounts his life, beginning with his return from Ceylon, as he told it to himself, his own version, which he needed to achieve the life he chose. He had to forget the humiliated, nearly destroyed young man who already thought of Virginia Stephen as his last hope and, regarding Ceylon, for example, he had to remember only the competent, steady civil servant, too refined for such work, destined to a great and fascinating career in the colonies.

But Woolf seems to have forgotten that his letters to Lytton might appear in print, testifying to a more personal and entirely other reality. No doubt he had repressed all memory of their tone and content, so different from the self-portrait he would leave. He did not foresee how comparing them would refute the long-established legends.

Like the one of Leonard falling suddenly in love with Miss Virginia Stephen and only then deciding to ask for her hand in marriage, which required him to renounce the brilliant colonial future opening before him. "What a career you're ruining!"[38] Virginia would sigh, moved and flattered.

But how can we forget Leonard struggling in Ceylon, suffocating, trapped, mortified, with no way out, and Lytton suggesting that his friend marry Virginia in order to extricate himself, and how can we forget Leonard realizing immediately that it was the "only thing to do"? That was in 1909, three years before the long-awaited leave, which Leonard would convert into a definitive return and his reentry into the only circle compatible to him. It all became possible thanks to his marriage . . . with Miss Stephen in August 1912.

His response to Strachey three years earlier in Ceylon? Marrying Virginia? "The final solution. . . . It certainly would be the only thing." It is as if it were done: Leonard lived perpetually, he said, "on the principle that nothing matters." He concludes: "I don't know why the devil I don't." All the same, he adds later: "Do you think Virginia would have me? Wire to me if she accepts."[39]

Lytton's perversity: he is the one who proposes to Virginia! She was under the spell of his deep originality, his importance or the importance he audaciously claimed, the charm and mordant intelligence that, without knowing it yet, still too shy, she shared with him, but to her own share she added . . . all that Lytton lacked. He would long impress her, often as a rival: she was sure (and jealous) of his literary worth and imagined him, mistakenly, destined to magnificent, lasting renown. She would always be pleased and flattered by their exchanges. Above all he was someone very dear to her. In 1924, she would write again, after he had come to dine with her and Leonard: "Oh I was right to be in love with him 12 or 15 years ago. It is an exquisite symphony his nature when all the violins get playing as they did the other night."[40]

Immediately terrified, horrified by his own move—and the idea that she might kiss him—then, to Lytton's great confusion, Virginia accepted the proposal. The next morning she retracted it—or was led to do so by her panicking neo-fiancé. She confessed to not loving him, allowing him to make an honorable retreat, as he wrote, still trembling with fear, to his brother James Strachey.

But can't we imagine his pleasure at promptly informing Leonard, and again urging him to court the woman he didn't want? Panic-stricken, upset, he claims that she would have been his for the taking, had he been "greater or less. . . . You *would* be great enough," he adds, before turning to the chief cause of his distress: Duncan Grant. Duncan with whom he has just "copulated . . . again this afternoon, and at the present moment he's in Cambridge copulating with Keynes." The letter then turns to Woolf's poetry. Oh, what trials![41]

Leonard is still suffering in exile:

> You cannot imagine the effect of your letters in Hambantota. They make me laugh & cry out loud. To imagine that really Sanger & Bob Trevy & MacCarthy & Virginia exist! I suppose they do in some dim existence move vaguely through life. I suppose everything isn't jungle & work. But it's damnably difficult to believe it. . . . I believe in the reality of you & (the reality of the unreality) of Turner, because if I didn't I suppose I should cease to believe in my own.[42]

Such lines make him so endearing (in my eyes, at least) that we mourn the brevity of his career as novelist—only two novels. Never would he confess (and especially not to Virginia) what Lytton alone knew. Never in Leonard Woolf's life after that time, much less in his autobiography, would there be any sign of the suffering, simultaneously faltering and confident man he had first been.

Yet what a strange suitor he would make!

Lytton persisted: "You must marry Virginia. She's sitting waiting for you." He knew, he guessed how much she wanted to be married, which he insinuated and which Leonard understood. A miracle that she existed, so "young, wild, inquisitive, discontented, and longing to be in love," continued Strachey. The only woman intelligent enough for Leonard. Dangerous to wait, he warned; Woolf risked missing "the opportunity."[43]

And Woolf once again acknowledged that "the one thing to do would be to marry Virginia." What stopped him? "The horrible preliminary complications, the ghastly complications too of virginity & marriage altogether appall me."[44]

How not to think here of the reputation for frigidity that would haunt Virginia Woolf, and of the sexual prowess, expert and sacrificed, that would be credited to Leonard?

I remember my first meeting with Quentin Bell in 1973. He was participating, with his delicious English accent, in a series of radio programs I was producing on—guess who! In person the most exquisite and jovial of men, Quentin spoke with kind indulgence about his aunt, whose importance he considered to derive primarily from her relationship to Clive and Vanessa Bell, his parents. Vanessa possessed the wisdom, good sense, and social integration that her sister lacked (as we shall see later). And in 1973, little or nothing was known of Virginia herself, of her life, of those close to her, except what her nephew wrote about her, with great charm and liveliness, but with even greater unintentional bad faith, for he was writing atavistically, out of his fidelity to the family tradition. His biography of Virginia Woolf had just appeared in French.

I remarked: "You show her to be a very complete, very intellectual woman, who loved life in all its forms." At which point he immediately interrupted: "From the perspective of sexual life, one cannot call her a complete woman. She was cold. She was not normal from this perspective. In other relationships, yes, she was normal."[45]

"Not normal!" That was exactly the label Virginia dreaded and bore; Bell's account testifies above all to her circle's more or less implicit rejection of Virginia as she was: the brilliant, famous Virginia Woolf, often arrogant, even fierce, irresistibly funny, as well as the uncertain one, so vulnerable to suffering, to the horrors that often assailed her. Of Virginia the writer, accessible only in her work, who, in order to accomplish it, had to draw on her torments and to renounce the defenses that would have allowed her to avoid them, but only by forfeiting her direct access, harsh as it was, to what she desired.

Virginia Woolf, invincible and disarmed.

In 1973, Quentin Bell's word was law, yet I had to ask him if that "abnormality" hadn't sparked in Virginia her sense of nature, of life, and influenced her writing? Above all, hadn't she experienced her own sexual "normality," which was not restricted to the sexual organs, neither to condoned patterns of sexuality nor to those considered forbidden? With which she was familiar?

Appalled, Quentin let out a pained, indignant protest: "That coldness!"[46] Before sighing, conciliatory but no less reproving, and saying that she "saw the world in a very unusual way." He then recounted the lovely remark made by Clive, his father: "For the rest of us, life's great business is the adventure of love. For her, it is when a butterfly comes through the window." And that was true. As well.

Dear Quentin! He did not even need to say the word to make it heard: "frigid," and frigid, Virginia disappeared into the ridiculous. Invalidated. She became a writer, but was deprived of the right to speak of sexuality. She could write novels brimming with sensuality, not a word lacking sexual potential? No matter. Hers is an alternative view of the libido's distribution? She's an outlaw. She doesn't adopt or conform to the common cliché? She's cold. She derives pleasure directly from her writing? You could say she's dreaming, she's sublimating. She expresses negation, frustration? Well, you can see that! She's not a real woman—since she does not embody a disembodied woman.

"That coldness!" groans her nephew regarding a woman whose every sense was perpetually on alert and who lived forever permeable to the world—which was a living organism for her, entirely erotic, in which she participated, eagerly, attuned to and awaiting all its pulsations.

The wild sexuality that runs through her work, that cannot be reduced to one conventional act and never focuses on a bed, can be disturbing and even terrifying, but especially can take us aback. Lytton reproached Virginia for including not a single scene of coitus. Indeed. But did Strachey believe he could thus defuse the subversive sexuality that underlies these pages, so diffuse that it is indistinguishable from the text? "I'm sure I live more gallons to the minute walking once round the square than all the stockbrokers in London caught in the act of copulation."[47]

Sensual, yes, the work of Virginia Woolf, but sexual as well, in the sense that the tension, potentiality, and genius of sexual pleasure and its orgasms are everywhere invoked, coveted, attained. Suggested in various ways. Physical as well is the need to induce the writing to become a corporeal, connected, joined being, capable of experiencing and inciting rapture. The orgasm.

Sexual beings, Virginia Woolf and her work, but not according to a binary model. Few authors have written as she does, starting from an atmosphere imbued with sexuality, determined by sex or the lack of it. Of the Holy Grail, the forbidden, the sexual divide, few have written as she does, restoring sexuality intact, not named but permeating the moments, destinies, the scenery, and encompassing as well the frustrations, disappointed or rejected passions, the distances, the impotence that are all part, a significant part, of sexuality.

She is aware of an immense, general coitus, of the throbbing orgasm within which each human orgasm flutters and moves, and it is with each detail, each minute, each living organism of whatever species that these pages attain sexual pleasure, it is with absence that they couple. The erotic presence is distributed throughout multiple neural networks of infinite complexity. The exchanges do not take place where we normally observe them, but in the language itself, in its intervals and interstices, "between the acts," in short, the title of her last work.

Or rather, they do not take place at all and desire prevails, unresolved, maintained in abeyance—in the state of desire. "The old horror come back—to want and want and not to have."[48]

In *To the Lighthouse*, it's the living presence of Mrs. Ramsay, dead for years, that Lily Briscoe desires in vain, straining against the intractable and, like Virginia after so many early losses, confronting this loathed finality against which she is endlessly shattered. "To want and not to have—to want and want—how that wrung the heart, and wrung it again and again."[49]

But what Virginia desired was something else too, something else that she still lacked desperately in 1923, four years before the publication of *To the Lighthouse*, when she wrote in her diary: "And as usual I want—I want—But what do I want? Whatever I had, I should always say I want, I want." But what? The impossible, of course, the dead coming back to life; the work under way finished, of course, and the next one already . . . , and then, and then. . . . But also, and perhaps above all, the carnal closeness, denied her, of other desiring bodies, mutually enacting, fulfilling those desires—in a word, coitus, Lytton Strachey would mock. Yes, but not only that. But that as well. Perhaps above all, an embrace that would not be death's, but equivalent to the power of death, which Mrs. Dalloway also thought was "an attempt to communicate."[50]

Yes, because ironically, in everyday life, even in the narrow sense that her nephew understood it, it does not seem that Virginia was so hostile to the everyday forms of sexuality. Unlike Leonard. Of the two, he is the one who finds sex repulsive, she the one who safeguards him from it.

Evidence shows that sexual rejection was not Virginia's doing, but her partners'—Leonard and also Vita Sackville-West—given their equivocations, their frightened retreats not from the "coldness" Quentin Bell names, but rather from her fervor, her anticipation. Her "excitement," as Leonard says. "Ça lui dit trop," worries Vita.[51]

Unwitting testimony from Woolf, who hopes, on the contrary, to demonstrate the stubborn unresponsiveness of his companion: he confides in Gerald Brenan, a writer friend of Lytton, in March 1923, the very year when Virginia wrote: "I want—I want. But what do I want?" The Woolfs, on vacation, stopped to see him in the small Spanish mountain village where he lived, and Brenan remembers: "Leonard told me that when on their honeymoon he had tried to make love to her she had got into such a violent state of excitement that he had to stop, knowing as he did that these states were a prelude to her attacks of madness. This madness was of course hereditary. . . . So Leonard, though I should say a strongly sexed man, had to give up all idea of ever having any sort of sexual satisfaction. He told me that he was ready to do this 'because she was a genius.'"[52]

There it is.

Brenan hears it before Bell.

As far as genius goes, Leonard was one too, for turning situations to his own advantage, as here, for acquiring over Virginia an influence that he would let be known within his circle, so that each of its members would subsequently attest to it. He provided an intimate portrait of Virginia Woolf, which he created, he believed, in the liberated Bloomsbury style, as we will see. Quite a dirty move, actually, revealing one of the ways he will use Virginia's alleged ("of course hereditary") "madness." Throughout their marriage, Virginia would have to adapt to the version of her own life continuously invented by Leonard, in real time. Just as she would have to submit to the consequences he inferred from it, sometimes very serious ones—in particular, being deprived of children.

Most importantly, it is not a cold, passive woman, nor one adverse to sexual pleasure, that we discover in the confidences shared with Brenan. He does not call her disinterested, repulsed, but "excited"—in what sense? That of a potential lover, expectant, responsive, easily aroused?

A disaster for Leonard!

And he does not persist, fears her eagerness, hopes against hope for the opposite reaction. He is more terror-stricken than she is by how "ghastly" the undoubtedly clumsy "preliminary complications" might be. She is not the one he wants to protect by interrupting the act; it is he who withdraws and flees, terrified.[53]

He does not speak to Brenan of Virginia's frigid behavior, but on the contrary, of an "excitement,"[54] which could mean that she resisted (not necessarily irrevocably, of course), but also that she responded to this lover, hopeless as he might be, that she expected him, endowed with some capacity for that pleasure which he would rather consider harmful to a wife he termed mentally ill, continually threatened by madness.

Now, at the time of their honeymoon, he could not have "known" of a single "state of excitement" signifying "a prelude" to what he calls "her attacks of madness." He hardly knew her, they had not lived together, he had almost no experience of her—he would often insinuate that he was not adequately warned about his fiancée's fragility. He had yet to imagine the rituals he would later perform, constantly watching over his wife with ostentatious discretion, playing a role generally perceived as that of protective, dominant guardian—interrupting her in public when she spoke with too much passion, according to him, limiting her engagements, managing her time to avoid all forms of "excitement." Excitement that he would decide, once and for all, provoked the attacks from which he would protect her. So many conspicuous arrangements would persuade their circle, would convince Virginia herself, of her state of suspended madness, forestalled by the devotions of a providential benefactor.[55]

Virginia's fragility was obvious, but what made her more fragile, what endangered her, was the continuous, surreptitiously spectacular fuss made over her throughout her life, even though, beginning in 1916 and over the course of her remaining *twenty-five years*, she experienced not a single real attack. Perhaps (although nothing is so simple) in part thanks to Leonard and his fanatical precautions!

Leonard's constant vigilance would serve as a screen for his own troubles, allow him to project them onto a woman and tend in her what worried him about himself, what he feared, repressed, tried desperately to forget through the strict protocols and routines necessary to the obsessive personality he was. Like the daily glass of milk that he brought her and made her drink—in short, suckling the woman whom he would deny children. In fact, he distracted himself from his own neurasthenia, from his existential anxiety, evading them by transferring them symbolically to a skittish Virginia, whom he would nurse for life. "I begin to despair of finishing a book on this method—I write one sentence—the clock strikes—Leonard appears with a glass of milk."[56] A glass also emblematic of his influence over her.

What he describes to Brenan is his own neurosis, his phobia, his terror—among others—of degradation, his dread of the "horrible preliminary complications" and, just as "ghastly . . . of virginity and marriage," provoked by a honeymoon, the very idea of which repulsed him in Hambatota. Caught in that situation, he is the one who feels threatened and who blocks, interrupts, "stops" what viscerally alarms him.[57]

For Virginia, that part of life was done for. Maybe she had hoped that Leonard could show her the way to it; what was forbidden her had to be turned into another loss.

Thanks to Leonard, it was decided that she was frigid toward men and the sexual act, under the pretext that her experience—if it could be called that—with her husband had not delighted her. The opposite would have been rather surprising! It is easy to imagine the immense disappointment of her honeymoon, such a failed, curtailed initiation, for which she would accept sole responsibility.

But upon returning, to a woman friend: "Why do you think people make such a fuss about marriage and copulation? . . . I find the climax immensely exaggerated," before adding: "I might still be Miss S . . . ," and "Don't marry till you're 30—if then."[58]

Writing to Lytton, casualness and crude expressions were due. From a letter written during the honeymoon, this most romantic account—we are in Venice: "The W.C. opposite our room has not been emptied for 3 days, and you can there distinguish the droppings of Christian, Jew, Latin and Saxon—you can imagine the rest." But there is a certain (resigned) bitterness between the lines:

Several times the proper business of bed has been interrupted by mosquitoes. They bloody the wall by morning—they always choose my left eye, Leonard's right ear. Whatever position they chance to find us in. This does not sound to you a happy life, I know; but you see, that in between the crevices we stuff an enormous amount of exciting conversation—also literature. My God! You can't think with what a fury

we fall on printed matter, so long denied us by our own writing! I read
3 new novels in two days: Leonard waltzed through the Old Wives
Tales like a kitten after its tail: after this giddy career I have now run full
tilt into Crime et Châtiment . . . [Dostoyevsky] is the greatest writer
ever born: and if he chooses to become horrible what will happen to
us? Honeymoon completely dashed. If he says it—human hope—had
better end, what will be left but suicide in the Grand Canal?

Much to be heard here under the chatter that is trying to be pert, and
then, as throughout the letters, the diary, and the work, water to throw
oneself into.[59]

There remains the loss of a love life more or less consciously awaited
for a long time, thus refused her, out of reach. "To want and want and not
to have."[60]

And the legacy of this fiasco: the role of the wife promptly pronounced
"frigid." Never did the illusory masculine archetype or Leonard himself
come into question. The lover's prowess went without saying? Like Brenan
and the Bells, didn't everyone perceive Leonard (he saw to this) as "strongly
sexed"? No one was privy to what we now know about him at the time
of his marriage, through his letters to Strachey, except the cynical Lytton.

And so, "masculine frigidity, reluctance"? You must be joking! A het-
erosexual male's aversion to the female body? You must be delirious! Leonard, the couple's male principle, obviously embodied the "norm." Virginia
herself didn't deny it. From which arose a sense of deficiency regarding her
own body, of indebtedness to her husband. But also a feeling of doubt, perhaps, and resentment over what went supremely unspoken, for no doubt
she was aware (more or less consciously!) of what that was. What had
determined for her—reflected in her—his justified withdrawal.

Virginia was never clear herself on those grounds, but it seems certain
that Leonard led her into sexual failure, which he made almost public and
attributed to her, and which was his doing. And which would not have had
such significance if Leonard had not sacrificed his wife in order to exoner-
ate himself and even derive benefits, boasting of his victimization, playing
the hero. If he had not thrown his wife's reputation to the Brenans and the
Quentin Bells, thus allowing them to discuss Virginia Woolf's sexuality
and to conclude that she was "abnormal."

Their failure might have strengthened their bond, henceforth founded
on less fragile relations, but not without favoring a certain domination

on Leonard's part, not without justifying his tacit demands, not without nurturing and solidifying the image of a wife so far outside the norm as to be "abnormal." And not without giving the husband power over his deficient wife.

And truly, what could be better than the alibi Virginia offered? Henceforth, it would allow her husband to escape all women, including her, even as it secured him the reputation of a frustrated Don Juan, with a martyr's halo.

What a blessing!

Virginia "frigid"? No. But the opposite, deprived by others of what she had hoped for.

In any case, why not let Virginia Woolf be her own model? Why hold her up to convention and be shocked that she doesn't conform? Her "norm" would have us consider "normal" her own sense of the erotic: a raindrop sliding down a window, say.

Which is true, as well.

But there is more.

Let us listen to Rhoda, also assumed to be frigid, and who clearly speaks for Virginia in *The Waves*, where six voices tell of six lives at every age and over time. Is this voice silent on sexuality?

> There is some check in the flow of my being; a deep stream presses on some obstacle; it jerks; it tugs; some knot in the centre resists. Oh, this is pain, this is anguish! I faint, I fail. Now my body thaws; I am unsealed, I am incandescent. Now the stream pours in a deep tide fertilizing, open-ing the shut, forcing the tight-folded, flooding free. To whom shall I give all that now flows through me, from my warm, porous body? I will gather my flowers and present them—Oh! To whom?[61]

To whom?

With Leonard, Virginia can act in concert, with him she can gather flowers—but give them, receive them?

Oh! To whom?

And of whom is she thinking when Septimus Smith, in *Mrs. Dalloway*, attributes his own feelings to Shakespeare? "Love between man and woman was repulsive to Shakespeare. The business of copulation was filth to him." Or: "How Shakespeare loathed humanity—the putting on of clothes, the getting of children, the sordidity of the mouth and the belly!"[62]

Oh! To whom?

One oasis in this desert, in this wasteland of sexual desire: Vita Sackville-West, gifted with a love for women, as Virginia was attracted to them. Virginia, who fell in love with Vita in 1925. Passionately, and it was reciprocal. But on her part, she offered herself totally, without the least reservation, overcome with well-being, sensuality, and physical pleasure. There for the taking. And almost immediately rebuffed. Soon Vita would beat a retreat with regard to sex. Her pretext? It would be . . . identical to Leonard's!

She confided in her husband, Harold Nicolson (they were forever linked to each other and, in principle, forever without jealousy; he as captivated by men as she was by women and some men as well). Vita, coming from an aristocratic lineage that made Virginia dream, was a writer, often successful, but she was thrilled (and flattered) to be loved by Virginia Woolf, so prestigious and whose value she measured, which did not prevent her commentaries, even more boorish than Leonard's confidences to Brenan.

Virginia's reputation prompted Vita's boasting, flattered as she was by such a conquest, even as she reassured Harold. Like Vita, he was under the influence of the legend, started by Leonard, accepted by Virginia, according to which the latter was frigid and would be mad were it not for her husband's vigilance. Vita remarked in her a "funny mixture of hardness and softness—the hardness of her mind, and her terror of going mad again."[63]

A radiant Virginia, believing she was experiencing the natural sensuality of a shared passion, did not stand a chance. Vita declares to Harold,

> I am scared to death of arousing physical feelings in her, because of the madness. I don't know what effect it would have, you see; and that is a fire with which I have no wish to play. No, thank you. I have too much real affection and respect. Also she has never lived with anyone but Leonard, which was a terrible failure, and was abandoned quite soon. . . . Besides *ça ne me dit rien;* and *ça lui dit trop,* where I am concerned. . . . So you see I am sagacious—though probably I would be less sagacious if I were more tempted. . . . I *have* gone to bed with her (twice), but that's all; and I told you that before, I think.[64]

A true chauvinist!

Virginia frigid? No, dangerous: "*Ça lui dit trop.*" Once again, she is too "excited."

Harold was reassured, which was the aim of Vita's letter, at least part bluff; it ends there. Of course he considered Virginia "beneficial" for his wife (as well as for her literary reputation). Nevertheless he warned: "I do hope that Virginia is not going to be a muddle. It is like smoking over a petrol tank." Then, recovering his composure: "It's a relief to feel that you realize the danger and will be wise. You see, it's not merely playing with fire; it's playing with gelignite."[65]

So there it is.

The game is up. Virginia is judged. A perpetual candidate for madness. Inaccessible. Taboo. Kindness means that she be spared what she desires—what she wants and wants and cannot have, "protected" from all bliss of that order, from all supposedly harmful excitement—but according to what decision, what decrees, if not the scenario concocted (in all sincerity, he believed) by Leonard? No one thought at the time—or since, really—of the contradiction between a woman judged as simultaneously frigid and too "excited." Both grounds for rejecting her.

It was not her lover's coldness that fazed Vita Sackville-West, but her seemingly excessive ardor, her desire, no doubt heightened by her long-standing frustration and her frantic hope. Virginia tries to reassure Vita: "Please come, and bathe me in serenity again. Yes, I was wholly and entirely happy. If you could have uncored me—you would have seen every nerve running fire—intense, but calm."[66]

Vita, as seen by Virginia: in her eyes, all pearls and cashmere, castles and prestigious ancestors. Vita, in love with her for a time, but forever fickle, only briefly the physical lover of the long-awaiting Virginia: "Remember Virginia. Forget everybody else. Should you say, if I rang you up to ask, that you were fond of me? If I saw you would you kiss me? If I were in bed would you— . . ."[67]

Awaiting, often in despair: "Talking to Lytton the other night he suddenly asked me to advise him in love—whether to go on, over the precipice, or stop short at the top. Stop, stop! I cried, thinking instantly of you," she wrote to Vita. To Lytton she wrote: "I do feel that love is such a horror I would advise anyone to break off." [68]

Virginia: then incandescent, singularly passionate. Anything but frigid. Rejected, "interrupted" here as she had been by Leonard.

As for him, surely the most awkward of lovers, reluctant, incapable of engaging his partner except in his own denial—perhaps the hint of

passion, even of sudden wonder, might let him successfully shift their relationship to another register? But if we search her husband's autobiography
for signs of Virginia, he seems immune to any such enchantment.

Let us watch her surface in these pages and memories, their author's
life, let us watch for signs of emotion. He has returned to London, on leave
from Ceylon. The trouble is . . . she does not come up. Leonard mentions
other thrills, as the young poet Rupert Brooke appears to an enthralled
Woolf, passing through Cambridge: "When I first saw him, I thought to
myself: 'That is exactly what Adonis must have looked like in the eyes of
Aphrodite'. . . the red-gold of his hair and the brilliant complexion. It was
the sexual dream face not only for every goddess, but for every sea-girl
wreathed with seaweed red and brown and, alas, for all the damp souls of
housemaids."[69]

Let us turn the pages. Virginia? Still no sign of her. Then here comes
one by way of her sister: "Vanessa was, I believe, usually more beautiful
than Virginia." This belated, inferior Virginia, whose sole function is to be
compared to her sister, who outshines her since

> the form of her features was more perfect, her eyes bigger and bet-
> ter, her complexion more glowing. If Rupert was a goddess's Adonis,
> Vanessa in her thirties had something of the physical splendour which
> Adonis must have seen when the goddess suddenly stood before him.
> To many people she appeared frightening and formidable, for she was
> blended of three goddesses with slightly more of Athene and Artemis
> in her and her face than of Aphrodite.

As for her voice: the most beautiful ever heard. Ah, and her tranquility! Which did not at all detract from her depth, because in addition to
extreme sensitivity, there reigned in her "a nervous tension," indicating
"some resemblance to the mental instability of Virginia."[70]

The first glimpses of Virginia, recollected: less beautiful than her sister
and mentally unstable.

Let us read on. Here is Woolf, overcome with admiration. For Virginia
this time? No: for Thoby, who so embodied his nickname, the Goth. And
whom Vanessa embodied in turn . . . his female double. Six years earlier in
Ceylon, when Lytton announced that Vanessa, Thoby's double, was going
to marry Clive Bell, Leonard acknowledged his bewilderment:

I always said that he [Clive] was in love with one of them—though strangely I thought it was the other. . . . You think that Bell is really wildly in love with her? The curious part is that I was too after they came up that May term to Cambridge, & still more curious that there is a mirage of it still left. She so superbly like the Goth. I often used to wonder whether he was in love with the Goth because he was in love with her & I was in love with her, because with the Goth.[71]

But what about Virginia, so rarely and belatedly encountered in these pages? Ah, there she is! And, at last, defined: "a very different kind of person beneath the strong family resemblances in the two sisters." But Virginia? Virginia herself? Well: "She was, as I said, normally less beautiful than Vanessa." Nonetheless, Leonard continues, "when she was well, unworried, happy, amused, and excited, her face lit up with an intense almost ethereal beauty," and also "when, unexcited and unworried, she sat reading or thinking." Otherwise, tension, disease, or anxiety did not erase her beauty but rendered it "painful."[72]

All the more so because Virginia was, alas, a genius, the only one Leonard acknowledged knowing personally. A genius. Is that even reasonable? And what can be done about it? "One has to call it genius because the mental process seems to be fundamentally different from those of ordinary or normal people and indeed from the normal mental processes of these abnormal persons."[73] A bit convoluted, even vague, but how disturbing! Though it's reassuring finally to encounter here the "true" Virginia Woolf: Quentin Bell's Virginia Woolf.

After such an enthusiastic description, Leonard immediately moves on to the essential thing: poor Virginia makes passersby laugh. She seems "strange to the 'ordinary' person." The word "ridiculous" appears three times in two pages, and the word "laughter" repeatedly: people "would go into fits of laughter at the sight of Virginia." They "stop and stare" and "giggle" and "roar with laughter."[74]

And note especially that, to their eyes, Virginia represents: "some monstrous female caricature."[75] According to Leonard. This is not innocuous. What he claims here is what he himself imagines; what he claims to interpret and convey are his own assumptions, originating with him.

These are Leonard's spontaneous memories of the past; this is how Virginia appears in the book that is his witness.

Now, among any of their contemporaries who mention her, no such portrait emerges, nothing even close; and Virginia, who records daily whatever assails her, troubles or joys, does not mention a single incident (much less recurrent ones) of hysterical passersby; on the contrary, she is continually delighted by her happiness, even her intoxication, wandering the streets of London, walking there for hours. "London is enchanting. I step out upon a tawny coloured magic carpet, it seems, & get carried into beauty without raising a finger. . . . One of these days I will write about London, & how it takes up the private life & carries it on, without any effort. Faces passing lift up my mind."[76] Her photographs testify to her beauty, which increased, and did, in fact, vary with her moods. Her contemporaries bear witness to . . .

No! That's not the question, no need for such testimonials. Why does Leonard's judgment even matter?

The real question concerns his choices, his priorities, his selective memory; the dryness of his account when it involves Virginia, in contrast to his relative enthusiasm for his other subjects; it concerns the discrepancy between the tone of these pages and Virginia's, the unkindness, intentional or not, in these first references and the mute, unconscious aggressiveness that seems to lie beneath them.

The question? It concerns this almost hallucinatory entry, this initial, so naturally antagonistic approach; it lies in the order, the strange sequence of incongruous memories; the minor place Leonard gives the woman whom, he will announce tersely a few pages later, he has fallen "in love with"[77]; in the grotesque situations attributed to her, in the lack of tenderness, or even sympathy or respect, for her. Rather a kind of revenge, it seems to be an instinctive confession. The expression of a long buried, undeclared contention finally acknowledged. And nothing of all that struck the author in rereading the text, a familiar exercise for the great editor that, among other things, Leonard Woolf had become (as had Virginia).

Such an introduction to his wife, such a preface to his account of their life together, is, at the very least, surprising. Doesn't Leonard's memory include a single image of Virginia that would place her in the company of those idols he so admired, like Thoby, Rupert, or Vanessa, kindred spirits in heart and mind?

And what to think of certain unexpected leaps? For example, from the paragraph that ends with Virginia's death: "On March 28 she drowned herself in the Ouse," to the following one that begins with: "I must return to the subject of our income." And what to think of the single (written) memory of their honeymoon (in which she does not appear): being hungry on a boat carrying them from Spain to Marseilles. They had practically not eaten because of their travel schedule, so: "At 7:30 in the morning I staggered up on to the deck and found the Third Officer who spoke English. I explained to him that I was very hungry and why. He took me up on to the bridge and had breakfast sent to me there; the first course was an enormous gherkin swimming in oil and vinegar. One of the bravest things I have ever done, I think, was to eat this, followed by two fried eggs and bacon, coffee and rolls, with the boat, the sea, and the coast of France going up and down all round me." Then there are three lines about Venice, but only about the weather, describing the wind: "whistling through its canals, [the wind on the Grand Canal] can sometimes seem the coldest wind in Europe. And at the end of November we returned to London."[78]

Strange glimpses, strange memories—especially strange in their selection, the priority certain ones are given. Are they still stamped with the impressions of the Leonard Woolf who still did not like women and chafed against the future destined to him in India, from which only Virginia Stephen could save him? Dependent as he had been on her, on her decision to marry him, on the stability and status she provided him . . . was he ever able to forgive her for it? And between them we will encounter so many other points of contention, even within their deep affinities.

Strange, yes, strange entrances for the actors in this retrospective. Apocryphal recapitulation of his own life by the Leonard we have known as young, foundering, volcanic, at bay, cursing fate, suffering . . . this Leonard who will subsequently be banished. Absent from an autobiography devoted to illustrating an existence entirely balanced, satisfied, scholarly, and centered, never mentioning the tormented, impervious, furious, terrified man that Leonard long continued (or never ceased) to be, whom he hides here again, or has learned to forget.

Ongoing oscillations. . . . Throughout his memoir Leonard furiously erases the place held in his life by what he wants forgotten; his systematic omissions are all that can protect him. Resulting in the version that verifies, through so much exorcism, the deceptions he rehearsed following his return from Ceylon.

What survives in these pages is a path of serene wisdom, certitude, and amnesia, traced to the detriment of the man Leonard had once hoped to become, whose life he would surely have been able to assume, inhabit, lead to the end, but who was evicted: that young man exiled from Cambridge, vibrant with despair, developing through hardships the nervous tissue of a poet, that is to say, the true writer he could have been and whom he had kept mute for decades in the body of this octogenarian who was now recounting his life without revealing it.

And in comparison to Leonard's landmarks . . . the sudden desire, the need to encounter here something precise and tangible, listening to Virginia Woolf not as she appears fixed in her husband's discourse, but as the Virginia who contemplates time and summarizes what is in question, what really does and does not happen, thus: "One incident—say the fall of a flower—might contain it. My theory being that the actual event practically does not exist—nor time either."[79]

Which serves as one example of what Leonard lost along the way: the right to hope to create, beginning from what he alone could say, beginning from what he alone had achieved, apart from the rest. He is left with the ability to listen, to follow, and to publish the kinds of works he would no longer write. And, as a writer, to produce many other kinds of works, essays, political pamphlets, in which he could avoid anything personal. Only Virginia remained free to risk the ordeal of endless self-searching, while he would flee from himself, behind his impassive mask. But did he flee or was he chased?

For he had spoken. Written. Confessed. Risked. He had spelled out his truth, confided it, conveyed it, precisely, in all its convolutions, in all its subtlety, with the simplicity of exactitude. That was after his return from Ceylon, at the very beginning of his marriage, in his second novel, *The Wise Virgins*.[80] Note the initials of the title: reversed, they are Virginia's.

Guilelessly, he had laid out what he would never speak of again. His fury and unease, the anguished spirit, the calm, lucid derision, the indecision, the bittersweet renunciations, the youthful rage, the ultimate numbness of the young Harry Davis, Leonard's double. Which would unleash in his circle, cruelly exposed, such rancor, even such suffering as only the utter failure of the work could make them forget.

The book could only founder. It was to be drowned immediately in silence, rejection, denial, shock: it was to be killed even before the battle. Its publication in 1914 altered nothing. It was ignored. Death by nonreception. Permanent leave. The novel, which naïvely exposed what went unsaid and innocently addressed taboos, had committed suicide. Unwittingly, unintentionally subversive, sincere, Leonard, at his own risk, had given himself away. Unsuspecting, through Harry Davis, he had proclaimed his unresolved differences, his otherness. His weakness. He had shown himself vulnerable.

To let surface in these pages the insignificance perceived by the terrified Harry Davis, the hopelessness of his resistance, the endless oppression of the banal, and most importantly, the sickly, frantic role of sexuality in his life, which finally traps him, he must expose the intolerable, ordinarily eluded: that infinite sadness, which goes beyond the tyranny of sex, which hints at what it may conceal of sexual misery.

But also, by proclaiming through his hero, and in all their violence, the distress, rage, pride, embarrassment, challenge of calling oneself and feeling oneself to be a Jew (without the least religious allegiance, the least pious sentiment), he is stripped of the armor that allowed him (and would allow him henceforth) to appear deaf to insult and takes refuge in indifference, so as to consolidate and affirm his place among those who offended him.

From Lytton, even from Lytton, he had concealed those wounds. It was understood between them that they could discuss anything without scrutinizing it. The casual tone of Cambridge and the Apostles, which Bloomsbury would inherit, elegant and supple, cynical when need be, would sweep him along. When Strachey described to him a successful playwright, a Jew, whom he had met among Bertrand Russell's friends, as "utterly vulgar with the sort of placid, easy-going vulgarity of *your* race," and was outraged by "how many thousands roll into Sutro's circumcised pocket per year," Leonard had answered from Jaffna: "Your Jewish parties with Mrs Russell are nothing to my perpetual existence here." But *The Wise Virgins* exposes his distress at such insults and injuries, suppressed, as here, in complicit silence.[81]

In this book, he betrays this silence that authorized the habit of insult, anti-Semitic cracks taken for granted. He reveals a presence, his own, constant and conscious. Suffering and targeted. He imprudently reveals himself as vulnerable, fragile, vehement. For the last time.

With the work soon forgotten, his circle could speak in his presence once again and yet remain "among themselves." In 1930, Harold Nicolson, a diplomat, would nevertheless express doubts; in his personal diary, regarding a meeting on the social qualifications necessary for entering the Foreign Office: "The awkward question of the Jews arises. I admit that is the snag. Jews are far more interested in international life than Englishmen, and if we opened the service it might be flooded by clever Jews. It was a little difficult to argue this point with Leonard there."[82]

Had he read this private document, would Leonard have reacted, defended his obvious right to exist, the same as Nicolson's, as an Englishman? It seems unlikely. Henceforth, he would remain impassive toward what perpetually hung in the air, apparently benign. Woolf, the leftist, the influential Labor Party figure, would overlook the political content of such discrimination, all the more perverse for being unconscious. When Virginia announced to friends at dinner that "the Jew"[83] would answer their questions, he protested mildly that he'd speak only if properly addressed. That was the height of his rashness; no fear of him causing any scandal. But in his professional and private life, his authority prevailed. Respect, great esteem, even admiration surrounded him until the end. A reasonable trade-off?

This much he had understood: nothing more would be heard from him of his inner life, that very exile from which the impulse to write and to confide derives. Any record of rejection, of his own enigma, of his singularity would be banished before having been considered. Scotomization. Woolf would never again be that writer; he would forgo awareness of his isolation and focus on remedying it, and in order to do so, keep quiet about it. No more states of the soul, reports, confidences; nothing of his truth, his desires, or lack of them.

He would no longer approach that which was intimate, since his unconventional sexuality would be taken as utmost indecency, an aggressive obscenity, not even to be considered. Above all, in order to retain his place among those he had chosen (which would partly form, around him and his wife, the Bloomsbury group), he would pretend to ignore that exotic status they would secretly grant him. To make them forget it, he would seem to stand with them, taciturn, when Jewish specificities (usually derogatory) were discussed.

He kept quiet. Virginia spoke.

"Then the curtain rose. They spoke."[84] Isa and Giles, at the end of *Between the Acts*.

But Leonard and Virginia?

Countless exchanges between them. Endless affinities. Unshakeable foundations. But what did not have a place, what separated them, what they did not mention, weighed more heavily still—too heavily.

The curtain had not risen.

Unless . . .

Unless they had done away with it unknowingly, unintentionally, instinctively, at the end of a long journey. Poignantly: the first lines of *The Wise Virgins* come to join the last lines of another book: the last book by Virginia, *Between the Acts*.

"In the beginning," writes Leonard Woolf in 1913 or 1914, on the very first page of his second and final novel, "he and she lived in a cave . . . or they burrowed holes in the earth." Huts and caves will become houses where we discover the man "jealous for the woman who has come to him, despite the clergy man and the gold ring, as she came to the cave, to be possessed by him and to possess him and to bear him children in the large brass bed."[85]

"Before they slept, they must fight; after they fought, they would embrace. From that embrace another life might be born," writes Virginia in *Between the Acts*, in 1941, in the last line of the last paragraph of the last book that she would ever write. "The house had lost its shelter. It was the night before roads were made, or houses. It was the night that dwellers in caves had watched from some high place among rocks. Then the curtain rose. They spoke."[86]

Let us leave them together.

* * *

Because they were, together. Inseparable.

She, often in love with their life, enchanted by their marriage, by its song and its security. "'Are you in your stall, brother?'" is how she describes their coexistence, and she delights in their divine solitude one day in October 1938, at Rodmell, their country house where they so often stayed:

> I said to L. as we strolled through the mushroom fields, "Thank the Lord, we shall be alone; we'll play bowls; then I shall read Sévigné; then have grilled ham and mushrooms for dinner; then Mozart—and why not stay here for ever and ever, enjoying this immortal rhythm, in which both eye and soul are at rest?" And for once, L. said: "You are not as silly as you look." We are so healthy, so happy, and I returned, I put kettle on, took the stairs four at a time, looked at the almost neat room, beautiful fireplace, logs in a bad way, but I was still soaring on the wings of peace. Prepared the tea, took out a fresh loaf and honey

and I called L. from high up the ladder against a big tree—where he looked so beautiful that my heart stopped for pride at the idea that he had ever married me.[87]

He, more secret, stubborn, having achieved his goal, faithful and constant, eminent, clinging fast to the prudent stability he has finally won. And she, transfixed with happiness when one day he declares her to be the most beautiful of women or slips into her bed one anniversary morning (they don't sleep together) to give her a green handbag and sweets, or if they enjoy taking off to Brighton for the afternoon to buy those chocolates they adore and all the newspapers before he takes her to a movie and then to a tea room. And especially if he admits his helplessness at the idea of being separated from her, even for a few days, and she decides not to leave for Paris: "You see it is enormous pleasure being wanted: a wife."[88]

Bound.

But let us go back to their beginning, years earlier in London, when Leonard returned on leave from Ceylon in May 1911. He was constantly afraid. Afraid of asking Virginia Stephen for her hand, and even more afraid of not winning it and having to return to Ceylon. The year's leave was coming to an end.

In November, he wrote to Lytton this last item in their exchange:

I saw Virginia yesterday. They have taken Brunswick Sq. [Virginia and her younger brother Adrian]. I am going to see it tomorrow as they can give me rooms there. I shall decide then. I see it will be the beginning of hopelessness. To be in love with her—isn't that a danger? Isn't it always a danger which is never really worth the risk? That at any rate you of all can tell me. I expect after two weeks I shall again take the train not to Morocco but to Ceylon. It is something to feel that it is always waiting there for one at Victoria.[89]

Virginia, with her sister's support, seems to have considered and greeted Leonard as a potential and welcome suitor. It was Vanessa who first invited the young man to dinner; it was Virginia who then invited him to the country, and who suggested that he take rooms in the residence she shared with Adrian, who was by then Duncan Grant's lover. Duncan, also a boarder, as was Maynard Keynes.

Leonard moved in that fall. Since his arrival in London six months earlier, he had hardly encountered her, but those months he would remember as the happiest of his life. He would marvel at having led then an existence of "pure, often acute pleasure," as he had never known before or after, in this rediscovered England, reunited with his friends. The six most beautiful months of his life came to an end as 1911 ended, and it was then, in January 1912 (the enchanted months forever over), that he fell "in love with Virginia" and asked for her hand in marriage. They were wed that summer.[90]

She hesitated, in enough distress to warrant a rest cure. "I only ask for someone to make me vehement, and then I'll marry them!" Leonard did not make her vehement. She does not hide it from him, says she is vexed by "the strength of your desire. Possibly, your being a Jew comes in also at this point. You seem so foreign. . . ." She asks him to wait and warns him: "Again, I want everything—love, children, adventure, intimacy, work. . . . I sometimes think that if I married you, I could have everything—and then—is it the sexual side of it that comes between us? As I told you brutally the other day, I feel no physical attraction in you. There are moments—when you kissed me the other day was one—when I feel no more than a rock." Perhaps, without knowing it, she thus reassured him, seemed to offer what he hoped for—or feared—something less degrading? But most importantly, she admits to her surprise sometimes at "being half in love with you, and wanting you to be with me always, and know everything about me."[91]

Woolf makes his wager, resigns his post. Waits.

And Virginia accepts him.

Then the series of letters from Virginia on the topic announcing, as to Violet Dickinson: "I've got a confession to make. I'm going to marry Leonard Wolf [sic]. He's a penniless Jew."[92] A penniless Jew who is giving up a great career for her.

To Lytton, a card: "Ha! Ha!"[93] signed by the engaged couple.

Eighteen years later, she would confide in a new friend, Ethel Smyth, a composer and conductor, eccentric, elderly, in love with her and perhaps her only true confidante: "How I hated marrying a Jew—how I hated their nasal voices, and their oriental jewellery, and their noses and their wattles—what a snob I was." She reproaches herself for it . . . but not excessively! She admits that Jews of course have an "immense vitality, and I think I like that quality best of all," but, valued or scorned, they were for her, before all else, "Jews," defined by their ethnicity. In that same letter: "They cant die—they exist on a handful of rice and a thimble of water—their flesh dries on their bones but still they pullulate, copulate, and amass . . . millions of money." That certainly had not been the case for poor Mrs. Woolf or for her children.[94]

Virginia is unrelenting. "I do not like the Jewish voice, I do not like the Jewish laugh,"[95] she writes in her diary three years after her marriage, regarding her sister-in-law Flora. To the point that her visceral hatred leads to hysteria, nervous attacks, and delirium, brought on by her frantic, almost superstitious physiological horror, gone entirely unexamined?

Leonard? For her, he was an exceptional Jew, hardly labeled, hardly exotic. Labeled all the same by his circle, in that refined environment famous for its progressive ideas, its open-mindedness and free morals. Intellectuals who would be horrified by Hitler's rise, and wouldn't realize the extent to which they and their kind throughout the world had cleared the way for him.

Harry Davis, provocative and wild, beside himself, at the end of his rope, screamed: "I'm a Jew, I tell you—I'm a Jew!"[96] Leonard protected himself, silent, "nothing matters" having become his motto. In his last interviews he liked to claim that he had never suffered or even encountered discrimination. Maybe he did not suffer any longer, once the Harry Davis in him had been killed.

In 1939, Virginia notes that Leonard told her he had trained himself to completely avoid all personal feeling.

Did he feel anything the day of their marriage? He records the sober celebration in just a few lines, with no mention of Virginia. What did he remember of it? The registrar's office opened onto a cemetery. Standing facing the windows, he had looked at the tombstones and thought of the expression: "Till death do us part," not included in the civil ceremony. That's all, except for the moment of comic relief: Vanessa (in true Stephen-esque style) had interrupted the service: how was she to officially change the name of her son Claudian to Quentin? "One thing at a time,"[97] had been the answer.

But what Leonard does not mention: his mother was not invited, nor anyone else from his family. Only a dozen close friends . . . of Virginia.

He would be careful not to mention it in his very adaptable memoirs.

Conjuring away a suppression, an insult, an offense. Accepting them.

If her son passes over the event in silence, if Quentin Bell feigns surprise and assumes this absence had something to do with the wedding date, a letter has been published addressed to Leonard from Marie Woolf, written three days before the marriage; he must have informed her that she was not invited.

> My dear Len . . . To be quite frank, yes, it has hurt me extremely that you did not make it a point of having me at your marriage. I know full well that neither Virginia nor you had the least desire to slight me, why should you, but it has been a slight all the same. You are the first of my sons who marries, it is *one* of *the* if not *the* most important day of your life. It would have compensated me for the very great hardships I have endured in bringing you all up by myself, if you had expressed the desire that you wished me before anyone else, to be witness to your happiness. . . . It has been the custom from time immemorial that one's nearest relatives are paid the compliment of being invited to the marriage ceremony; to ignore that custom & to carry it so far as to leave out one's Parent, must strike one as an unheard of slight. A wedding entertainment no one asked for, you're wise in discarding it. However, I will not say more; you have missed a great opportunity of giving me some happy moments—I have not had many lately! With very much love.[98]

Leonard had let himself be castrated.

All his life he would keep quiet in that way. But all his life he would respond to it, unrelentingly, unconsciously, after the fact.

Instinctively, he would restore the balance, without saying as much. He was "Jewish"? Labeled as such? Declared marginal? Then Virginia would be declared "mad." Each of them marginal and a step away from disgrace. He would suffer in silence. She would struggle. Their captivating, harmonious life, filled with work, with plans, abundant with warm friendships, perennial gardens, cozy rooms, public recognition, would be undermined on both sides by resentment.

A silent one.

And first, the question of children. Forbidden.

Virginia hoped for them, was sure of having them. "My baby shall sleep in the cradle,"[99] she wrote confidently to her friend Violet Dickinson, who offered her one in an anticipatory gesture. She was pleased with her new home, with its lawn where her "brats" could play.

But they did not.

A few months after their marriage, alone and *without informing his wife*, Leonard consults several doctors: isn't it dangerous for Virginia to have a child?

The pretext: she suffers from insomnia, headaches . . . no doubt largely the effects of unexpressed disappointment and feelings of loss over the marriage that now holds her captive, the paths that have closed to her. "Marriage," she would confide later to Ethel Smyth, "what about marriage? I married Leonard Woolf in 1912, I think, and almost immediately was ill for 3 years."[100]

But Leonard insists, clandestinely: isn't it dangerous for her to have a child? Sir George Savage, Virginia's doctor, considers, on the contrary, that it would do her "a world of good, my dear fellow, do her a world of good!" Leonard promptly dismisses him as a mere socialite and seeks the opinions of many other doctors, whom he always visits alone and none of whom has ever met Virginia. Some of them confirm Leonard's fears. He also consults Jean Thomas, director of the rest home where Virginia stayed, and whose conclusions—conveyed by Woolf and conforming to his own—surprise Vanessa: "I am rather surprised at your account of Jean's opinion, for she certainly told me the opposite. Why has she changed? I hope you will get something definite from Savage. After all he does know Virginia and ought really to be the best judge. I suppose Craig can't tell as much without having seen her or knowing her at all." But Savage's opinion is not taken into account. Woolf considers all the other diagnoses, Thomas's among them, to support his view. "They confirmed my fears and were strongly against her having children. We followed their advice." We! He would say no more about it. The question was settled. Or rather the edict.[101]

Without the least participation of his wife, who never saw a single one of those doctors, who was completely ignorant of those consultations, without the slightest discussion, the briefest exchange with her, the decision is made. Leonard imposes it upon Virginia: she will not have children. But "We followed . . ."

For her, a bell tolls. A verdict. An affront. A new loss, to which she would not be resigned.

The status of mother denied her, which she immediately sublimates, in which she locates her deficiencies, defeat, guilt, failure. It would represent a major verdict toward denying her "normality."

Aside from the warmth, love, the tenderness, sensuality, and intimacy associated with maternity, to participate in it would be to merge with that "normality" radically called into question here. All her life, Virginia's encounters with children proved delightful, a joy for both parties. Quentin Bell beamed as he recalled them during our interview session: "I have marvelous childhood memories of her. She took part in our games; she had an imagination that helped her to share our joys and our own imaginations. When she arrived, it was a delight. Virginia is coming today, what fun! She was charming with children."[102] But all her life, she reeled under their inflicted absence.

"Oh, dearest Gwen," she wrote to the wife of Jacques Raverat, a French painter who was very close to death, "To think of you is making me cry— why should you and Jacques have had to go through this? . . . I was going to have written to Jacques about his children, and about my having none—I mean, these efforts of mine to communicate with people are partly childlessness, and the horror that sometimes overcomes me." She is often angry at herself for not having made Leonard defy the doctors: "My own fault too—a little more self control on my part, & we might have had a boy of 12, a girl of 10: This always makes me wretched in the early hours."[103]

Later, in *Mrs. Dalloway*, she would take it out on the omnipotent Dr. Bradshaw, responsible for the suicide of his patient Septimus Warren Smith: "Sir William not only prospered himself but made England prosper, secluded her lunatics, forbade childbirth, penalized despair."[104]

Infertility would not have bothered her so much, so often devastated her, or plunged her into so painful and recurrent despair. But to find herself forbidden motherhood by her partner, to have consented to it, to prove powerless before this edict that denied her mental health. A disaster. A violent aggression, a debilitating blow.

A sentence. A sanction. She would submit to it without a fight, it seems, no doubt taking the pretext for proof. She was also too humiliated. Too weighed down with her past and blaming herself, repressing her distress. At the time of the verdict, she does not mention it in her diary, much less in her letters. She would be close to tears when, at the height of her fame, she joked with Vanessa over the recent success of her paintings: "Indeed, I am amazed, a little alarmed (for as you have children, the fame by rights belongs to me)."[105]

But a strange symptom affected her whole circle (and their descendants): throughout the long, grave crisis that almost immediately followed Leonard's announcement of his decision, and during the subsequent, almost successful suicide attempt, no one, much less Leonard, considered that such a loss, such a dictate, such a shock might be the cause of those episodes.

The cause? Never was it found! Virginia was "mad," that's all. She would never experience another crisis like that over the twenty-five years she had still to live? That was the anomaly, no doubt!

This blind spot regarding the obvious reasons for Virginia's collapse (there are others as well) would support Leonard's theory, adopted by Quentin Bell, of a groundless, purely physiological insanity. And everyone around her would seem astounded to witness Virginia, beside herself, violent, held by hired nurses, screaming her hatred for Leonard for days on end, refusing to let him come near her for weeks. Her outbursts were considered sheer raving, aimed at such a poor, patient, and devoted husband. Such childishness!

Forbidden children? No one except Virginia would consider the matter further, except to assume it was settled and for the best. "In this I imagine that Leonard was right," Quentin would write in the biography of his aunt. "It is hard to imagine Virginia as a mother."[106] The subject was closed.

Anyway, children, what for? Her books would take their place.

Leonard and then Quentin resort to the classic clichés of books having been given birth, and being taken care of, protected as offspring. Leonard's version: "As with so many serious writers, her books were to her part of herself and felt to be part of herself somewhat in the same way as a mother often seems all her life to feel that her child remains still part of herself." And further on, "The mother wants the child to be perfect for its own sake, and Virginia, whose attitude towards her books was, as with so many serious writers, maternal, wanted her books to be perfect for their own sake."[107]

So, why have children with him? She could produce them all by herself!

Of course, those children, those novels, conferred upon her a measure of fame that the ones he had renounced may have offered Leonard, but he expresses no regret, not the slightest bitterness, regarding the work that he would not write. His output of essays and communications would be prolific; his life was fulfilling, and he led it with energy, conviction, success, as publisher (with Virginia), as man of politics, essayist, historian, and . . . skilled gardener. He would become his wife's passionate publisher and the first and only reader of her manuscripts (but only once finished): their trustworthy and feared judge, whose good opinion was never assumed but nearly always won. He would very naturally merge with her, expertly and perfectly in sync with the domains of Virginia that had remained his, even as he practiced other ones.

Nevertheless, she is the one who achieves the success, the destiny that he had wanted and anticipated to be his, and Lytton Strachey's, when he was young, just as possessed, and perhaps just as talented as she was. Must we see, here again, the balance of the marriage restored, a compensation for the dissymmetry? No novel for him, no children for her, except those novels that she can produce without him?

In any case, obstacles, inhibitions, affronts on every side!

"We've had such rows with poor old Mother Wolf, who says she never imagined such a slight as not being asked to the wedding,"[108] writes Virginia to Duncan Grant, who was invited.

Is it nonsense to compare the slight suffered by Marie Woolf, supplanted mother, to the one suffered by Virginia Woolf, deprived of becoming a mother—thus supplanted as well?

For what accounts for Leonard's stubborn resistance to the idea of fatherhood and especially of fathering Virginia's child? The broader answer lies in his letters from Ceylon, in the rejection, discouragement, and pessimism of that not-so-distant time.

But there is also another answer, for which evidence exists: how to reconcile the idea of descendants, who would be Leonard's mother's descendants as well, with Virginia's visceral contempt for her mother-in-law and her line? Here is Virginia complaining in a letter, "9 Jews, all of whom, with the single exception of Leonard, might well have been drowned without the world wagging one ounce the worse."[109] How could Leonard reconcile the presence of a child with the arrogant rejection of his origins by its future mother?

A letter from Clive Bell serves as proof. Most revealing, it demonstrates the distressing but inescapable consequences of such a situation within this social circle, and the subtle but palpable atmosphere Leonard lived in. Timorous as Leonard was, he was pushing the limits here, but he ignored that his future brother-in-law Clive would confirm as much. Clive, a few days before the couple's official engagement, writing to Molly McCarthy, with whom he had a brief affair in May 1912: "Virginia and the Woolf have come to some pretty definite understanding. . . . It is really very satisfactory, I suppose; but it would be rather horrible to think that, most probably, people would feel for one's children what none of us can help feeling for Jews.—Oh he's quite a good fellow—he's a Jew you know—. Don't you think it would be rather painful to get oneself into that plight? And Woolf's family are chosen beyond anything."[110]

Need we say more?

Again it is the dashing Clive who writes to his mistress Mary Hutchinson three years later: "I wonder why the Jews instituted the rite of circumcision [*sic*]. Was there money in it, d'you think, as there is in lambs' tails? Did the Levites traffick in prepuces?"[111]

No comment.

Thus, within a web of increasingly complex factors, for Leonard, it might have been less a matter of revenge than of an impasse, facing up by giving up.

A precision: nothing is innocuous here. There is no hierarchy in ostracism. The anti-Semitism of the salon weighs as heavily as any other, even the worst kind, to which it is prelude. It is already criminal precisely because it reveals the calm conviction, the acquiescence of those considered eminent. Their acquiescence to discrimination, to hatred of Jews, constitutes their support of the principles upon which Nazism and its European offshoots would be founded.

Mockery, shallow complicity, unexamined prejudices establish a complicit norm and authorize racism, or even worse, make it out to be harmless. Whereas the slightest word uttered in this context, the lack of respect, the self-granted supremacy, the arbitrary, narcissistic, and paranoid contempt are auxiliaries to the crimes that may follow, that they have guaranteed. Barbarity also took root in the Bloomsbury salons and their ilk, all precursors of the reign of the arbitrary that spawned such crimes.

The concentration camps, the gas chambers, the deportation trains, the manhunts, the negation of the living among the living did not suddenly spring up out of nowhere. Neither does any tyranny. They emerged first from the same anecdotes that targeted Leonard Woolf, the atavistic manias of Virginia, the presumptuous jokes and self-importance of their friends, their self-satisfied complicity, their certainty of being right . . . because they were certain of being so. They authorized the fundamental principle underlying the horror: permissiveness. Arbitrary scorn.

For Virginia, this was a poison, a vital, most inward factor in her self-destruction.

Another precision: such anti-Semitism had nothing to do with religion. On the Woolf side, the family still vaguely maintained certain practices around Marie. But when the nine brothers and sisters married, none of them married anyone of Jewish origin. If, as a child, Leonard had learned to sing in Hebrew, he had also rejected all religious faith. Devoted to politics and philosophy, he would remain steadfastly agnostic.

On the Stephen side, absolute agnosticism. Virginia's father, Leslie, at one time an ordained pastor of the Anglican Church, had lost his faith, renounced it, and so became a lifelong agnostic . . . as did Julia, his second wife and Virginia's mother, who had lost her faith for good upon the death of her first husband and who was first attracted to Stephen, by then an eminent man of letters, because of his essay on the history of free thinking. Virginia? She was agnostic as well.

What we are confronting here is a matter of "race."

Of course, this anti-Semitism contradicts Virginia's antifascist impulses and militancy, but she is not alone in revealing such contradictions. Although it is particularly surprising in her, gifted as she was with a political sensibility unencumbered with received ideologies. Witness *Three Guineas*, an ardent, thoughtful essay firmly opposed to any obedience to fanatic creeds. Which denounces hatred of the Jews.

Haunted by the Spanish Civil War, by the fatal roles of already triumphant Fascism and Nazism, she addresses the male population of 1938:

> [The dictator] is interfering now with your liberty; he is dictating how you shall live; he is making distinctions not merely between the sexes but between the races. You are feeling in your own persons what your mothers felt when they were shut out, when they were shut up, because they were women. Now you are being shut out, you are being shut up, because you are Jews, because you are democrats, because of race, because of religion.

Throughout the work, which will cause a scandal, she compares the segregation and oppression of women to Nazi anti-Semitism. Let us note that she rejects the "feminist" label and emphasizes that, with regard to men and women, a "common interest unites us; it is one world, one life."[112]

Nevertheless, compared with Leonard, who agrees, she considers herself an "amateur": "But I am not a politician: obviously, can only rethink politics very slowly into my own tongue."[113] In doing so, politics, "rethought," and "slowly," becomes political, attuned to the intelligence of history.

Her unexamined anti-Semitic attitude, in contrast to this text, is all the more paradoxical in that her literary practice, her very act of writing, is grounded in her refusal to accept necessarily reductive, received definitions. She takes nothing for granted, nothing as fait accompli. She requires each thing to be fresh each time it appears. Here is the voice of Virginia rebelling against all fixity, all ossification: "In a world which contains the present moment, [said Neville] why discriminate? Nothing should be named lest by doing so we change it. Let it exist, this bank, this beauty, and I."[114]

And then that parasitic voice that, in everyday life (the life to which Leonard and their marriage belong), hardens into hackneyed racist clichés, inherited from her ancestors, never analyzed or questioned, never the object of reflection. Never "rethought." Accepted as is.

Of that voice, of that anti-Semitic fetishism, here are two examples drawn from among so many others. In 1905, while on a cruise to Portugal with her brother, Adrian, Virginia Stephen complained about finding "a great many Portuguese Jews on board, and other repulsive objects, but we keep clear of them."[115]

In 1933, the year Hitler took power (which she immediately deplored), Virginia Woolf wrote to Quentin Bell of having nothing to wear to her friends the Hutchinsons', who were holding an engagement party for their daughter and Victor de Rothschild, "the richest Jew in Europe," but she refused to go out shopping for "gloves, hat, and shoes, all for a Jew." A few hours later, when Vanessa returned from the reception, Virginia announced to Quentin how much his mother "didn't like the flavour of the Jew. Like raw pork, she said. Surely rather an unkind saying?"[116]

Hard to imagine Virginia's deep contradictions, her incessant inner resistance, the unconscious, instinctive, surreptitious efforts that summoned her to disguise the reflex reactions, probably even physical, that the constant proximity of a Jew must have caused in her, along with the official tie to a representative of the race she abhorred, even (perhaps especially) if he was closer to her than anyone else in the world, except Vanessa.

Hard to imagine as well the social humiliation that haunted her and that she hoped to overcome by pre-empting it, by going on the offensive to defend herself, by casually announcing her husband's Jewishness in the same breath as her anti-Semitism which, in her circle, went without saying—which canceled out the significance of having married a Woolf. For Leonard, even Virginia's anti-Semitism was a trump card, validating and guaranteeing his admission into the only group he recognized as his own.

But it is shame, yes, silent shame that torments Virginia, eats at her, usually without her knowing it. Despite Leonard's quiet, growing prestige, she suspects the reactions of those closest to them, like Maynard Keynes, an intimate friend, who mentions "Virginia and the Jew," and congratulates himself for visiting one day and finding Virginia home, "but no Jew." All this did not mean hostility toward Woolf. He was greatly and increasingly respected in this circle where everyone was bound to the others. Linked to them beyond all amorous rivalries, all justified reproaches, no member missed an opportunity to criticize the others then unaware of it, behind each other's backs. But Leonard Woolf's case was different.[117]

A difference Virginia dreaded facing, before which she shrinks. To the French painter Jacques Raverat, long absent, now in France, incurably ill (and whom she floods with letters in which she exposes her whole soul, breathing with vitality, keeping him alert, persuading him of the significance his life has for her), she answers, when he is surprised at learning nothing of Leonard: "What is my husband like? A Jew: very long nosed and thin, immensely energetic; But why don't I talk about him is that really you are Anti-Semitic, or used to be, when I was in the sensitive stage of engagement; so that it was then impressed upon me not to mention him." And joking in a letter a year earlier: "I make him pay for his unfortunate mistake in being born a Jew by discharging the whole business of life."[118]

Yes, hard to imagine the violence she had to inflict upon herself and her distress at unconsciously having to maintain this contradiction between the constant, indispensable presence of a companion so dear to her, and the innate, congenital rejection of what, in her own eyes, must forever define him, even if she attributes to him the role of the exceptional Jew. Here we are in the perversion of a perversion.

A poison, and it especially affects Virginia. Leonard knows how to defend himself on this point; his pain has consumed his ability to suffer: he perfects his indifference to the ambient anti-Semitism, which he has trained himself not to notice. Thus, within his circle, he never falters in his role as a most eminent member, embraced by them thanks to his tacit, abiding consent to let them wound him again and again.

A secret wound locked away in a part of him no longer accessible, forbidden even to himself, as he retreats ever further into his increasingly rigid shell. But for all of that, never sacrificing his earnest charm, his laughter, his affability, both warm and distant; his energy, his obstinacy, his legendary pigheadedness; his alternately severe, austere, or childish air; his growing infatuation with animals; his prodigious persuasive and decision-making abilities; his natural osmosis with his circle and his ability to withdraw. His passion for gardening, which might also have been a symbolic means to root himself in the English soil. His often hysterical fits of anger, the last traces of the former, tormented Leonard, who, repressed, explodes. His reputation for wisdom, dignity, vigor. And never sacrificing his obsession to "care for" and protect his wife, who so protected him and who was, who remained, his lifeline. He must thus become hers—and above all, he must make it common knowledge.

He would not create work comparable to Virginia's, but would remain convinced that he safeguarded her power to write. And that may be true. In any case, it's clear that he did not impede the work, as often happens in marriage. And a different fate might not have produced equivalent work. And Virginia's life might not have included such rich moments.

On the other hand, neither would it have been marred by what she considered a nightmare: the existence of her in-laws, whom she could not bear for being Jewish and even less for their social status, which Virginia mistook to be much lower than it actually was.

Sydney Woolf died at the height of his career. Suddenly without resources, his widow had to move with her nine children from their elegant Kensington address to Putney, a much disparaged neighborhood.

Virginia's first visit there following her engagement, as she describes it to her beloved Greek teacher, Janet Case:

"A sandwich, Miss Stephen—or may I call you Virginia?" "What? Ham sandwiches for tea?" "Not *Ham*: potted meat. We don't eat Ham or bacon or Shellfish in this house." "Not Shellfish? Why not shellfish?" "Because it says in the Scriptures that they are unclean creatures, and our Mr Josephs at the Synagogue—and—and . . ." It was queer.

Before this exchange: "Work and love and Jews in Putney take it out of one."[119]

How often she would describe to her friends and her sister Marie Woolf's birthdays: "10 Jews sat round me . . . imagine eating birthday cake with silent Jews at 11 pm." To Ottoline Morrell, the refined hostess of those grand receptions Virginia adored and Leonard avoided: "I do nothing but read Borrow, when I'm not dining with 22 Jews to celebrate my mother in laws 84th birthday." The latter exasperates her for considering her children, "these dull plain serviceable Jews & Jewesses . . . all splendid men & women." And when they are invited to Rodmell, she sizes them up: "dressed, like all Jews, as if for high tea in a hotel lounge, never mixing with the country, talking nasally, talking incessantly, but requiring at intervals the assurance that I think it really jolly to have them. 'I am so terribly sensitive Virginia' my mother in law says pensively, refusing honey, but sending me into the kitchen to find strawberry jam." Often Virginia's anti-Semitism merged with a classic aversion to mother-in-laws.[120]

She sometimes felt a fondness for this woman who was always anxious to see her, worried she hadn't come if Leonard entered first. Their visits with Marie were apparently affectionate and courteous. She admired Virginia and, on her deathbed after a fall, told Virginia that she should call her next novel *Fallen Woman*. Nevertheless, Virginia refrained from developing tender feelings for her, and when she found herself feeling daughterly affection one day, immediately the image of a terrifying mother, ready to seize her in her clutches, arose.

That reaction of horror and terror had nothing to do with Marie's Jewishness or Virginia's snobbishness, but with a fantasy of fatal proximity, of threatening, inescapable intimacy, that made Mrs. Woolf the universal maternal symbol that threatens every daughter, in this case, Virginia, even if their connection was only through Leonard: "To be attached to her as a daughter would be so cruel a fate that I can think of nothing worse; & thousands of women might be dying of it in England today: this tyranny of mother over daughter, or father, their right to the due being as powerful as anything in the world. And then, they ask, why women dont write poetry. Short of killing Mrs W nothing could be done!" And again: "How many daughters have been murdered by women like this! What a net of falsity they spread over life. How it rots beneath their sweetness—goes brown and soft like a bad pear!"[121]

Here we recognize the "Angel in the House" from *A Room of One's Own*, which each woman must kill within herself in order to be free. What a strange confusion! Marie Woolf displaces Julia Stephen, Virginia's mother, dead so early on, so sublimated, so equivocal, whom Virginia is "to want and want and not to have." And whose power over her daughters and their father, irresistible when she was alive, remains inextinguishable and more tyrannical after her death. What does Virginia want to kill? The death of her mother, surely; the death of the untrustworthy dead, a pervasive ghost. For whom Mrs. Woolf, alive, must pay.[122]

Poor Marie Woolf, whose great power is reduced to reminding her son of her right to gratitude for never going to bed, as a young widow, without a basket of socks to darn for company; to punctual visits from her children; to celebrations of her famous birthdays—daunting, it is true, if we are to believe an overwhelmed Virginia, who describes plans to celebrate: "And on Wednesday the Jews assemble and poor 80 chocolats in the form of sovereigns into the lap of the Mother Woolf who is 80; and there will be a cheque among them for that sum."[123] All to be followed by parlor games.

But here is "Mother Woolf," whose status of "Jewish mother" changes to symbolic universal mother, the bane of tyrannized daughters; here is Virginia, spellbound, who briefly, passionately, takes her for a maternal symbol. Virginia who is then stricken, disconcerted, and who resists, as when Marie confides to her an unconfessed secret of her adolescence.

A furtive intimacy, which the daughter-in-law dreads, sometimes brings the two women closer over the years. Inhibitions are immediately awakened in Virginia, a wild terror, emotions Marie Woolf is not the true object of, even though she may have revived them by her emotional power and her easy acceptance of the role of mother. Virginia would be moved when Mrs. Woolf confessed to her that, of all her daughters-in-law, Virginia was her favorite.

And Virginia thanks her nephew Julian Bell, Vanessa's oldest son, who paid a visit to Bella, one of Marie Woolf's "unfortunate" daughters: "my mother in law was delighted that according to you I am very fond of her. That was a master stroke—I am, in a way; but how did you know it?"[124]

The old woman's grief over the death of her daughter Clara would, for once, get the better of Virginia:

> Leonard's sister you see . . . died, poor woman; literally was killed by her husband; and I went up to see my mother in law; and really it would have drawn tears from a stone—poor old woman, aged 84, she'd sat up 2 nights with the dying and the husband [George Walker], a cheap American ruffian, with whom she'd quarreled violently; there they sat side by side and the daughter died between them; and my mother in law said, "She asked so little of life"—an extraordinarily good epitaph: "And why am I left alive?"—and then there was the funeral and all the Jews came to Tavistock Square and sat round like prophets in their black clothes and top hats denouncing unrighteousness.[125]

Marcel Proust comes to mind again, and Swann, who "belonged to that stout Jewish race, in whose vital energy, its resistance to death, its individual members seem to share." The narrator goes on to describe the moment of death when "One can see only a prophet's beard surmounted by a huge nose which dilates to inhale its last breath, before the hour strikes for the ritual prayer and the punctual procession of distant relatives begins, advancing with mechanical movements as upon an Assyrian frieze."[126]

But, again, how can Virginia's horror for even the word, "Jew," accommodate the flesh and bone, the very substance, of the Jew who lives and breathes permanently at her side? How can she endlessly express a visceral hostility for what he must represent to her, even as she affectionately calls him "my Jew." "Lord!" she writes to Ethel Smyth. "How I detest these savers up of merit, these gorged caterpillars; my Jew has more religion in one toe nail—more human love, in one hair."[127]

Even as a newlywed, this was her thank-you note for armchairs received as a wedding gift: "my Jew had the one with the green border." At a reception that Virginia found ghastly, "a good deal of misery was endured[,] Jews swarmed," she found it quite natural that Leonard got on very well with Gertrude Stein, the guest of honor, himself being also a Jew. And Gertrude Stein seen as a Jewess, not a writer.[128]

Virginia's alarming masochism, bound to what she detests and what has neither shape nor reality, but for which Leonard serves as her image—and Leonard's masochism in letting her detest what has neither shape nor reality, even as he represents it and accepts her scorn. Even though she respects and often admires him. Unconsciously, perpetually conflicted with herself. Leonard's solution: to be generally perceived as dominating her and declaring the law.

Whatever their alliance, their pleasure at being together, their affection, their oneness, how could they not hate each other, despite themselves, somewhere deep within?

Such underground operations can only erode the apparent peace that unites the couple. In 1937, they surface, resistant and triumphant, in a novel: *The Years*. The saga of the Pargiter family. A book written under duress because Virginia has forbidden herself any spontaneous outbursts. She has planned it to be a traditional, even academic novel, based on straightforward narrative, although "I am writing to a rhythm and not to plot"[129] had been her watchword. Now she would tell a story, neither evoking nor invoking her subject. Her priority for this narrative: *The Years* must differ from her other novels. None of which holds the slight trace of anything having to do with Judaism, much less anti-Semitism, a topic Virginia only addresses in her personal writing, her letters and her diary. Until now: only three or four pages, but there we find the unspoken madness, the nausea Virginia experienced in living with Leonard Woolf, a Jew, who would contaminate their space, as she dreaded. Pages where Leonard serves as a model of what she despises, what she abhors, but which she seems never to acknowledge feeling as a kind of repugnance aimed at her husband. And which seems so at odds with the delightful familiarity, the mental and emotional closeness that will make them come to resemble each other physically as they grow older.

In this novel, which was meant to be objective, realistic, and free of all personal disclosures, where the unconscious was hardly to have a role, the very worst, most repressed symptom appears, elsewhere kept at bay. In pages that are lyrical even as Virginia meant them to be temperate, steady, concerned most with the story, a song filters through and bursts out, barbaric, unbridled, in Sara Pargiter's voice . . . and it is Virginia's song, which she thought she had renounced.

Sara Pargiter, ugly, vacant spinster, eternally puerile, slightly impaired mentally and physically, without purpose, Sara, almost inarticulate but lyrical, sometimes pierces through this determinedly realistic, even prosaic text with her irrational outbursts, unconnected to the story. Scansion animates her voice, litanies carry it, and thus what we hear through her are very much the rhythms, accents, outbursts of the author. And what this voice expresses, in a scene that has no other reason to be there, is her instinctive, visceral disgust for a Jew about whom we know nothing, except that he is Jewish. In 1937, Hitler is in power, and in *The Years*, which has just appeared, Sara's small voice says: "The Jew . . . pah!"[130]

The scene bears no relation to the rest of the novel; there is no need for it—except as a release valve for Virginia. There is no sequel to it, and it could go unnoticed in the thick chronicle. What escapes through Sara is a certain madness, out of line with the conventional saga unfolding.

Sara's cousin, North, comes to visit and is chatting with her; they haven't seen each other in a long time, and the conversation stops abruptly, interrupted by the sound of water. The water that runs throughout Virginia's work, as though pointing the way to the River Ouse. But in other novels, it is the sea, waves, rivers, the water "like a drowned sailor on the shore of the world," or that of "the depths of the sea. . . . only water after all." Whereas here it becomes a matter of plumbing, loud faucets. It is the dirty water of the Jew, the other:[131]

> "The Jew," she [Sara] murmured.
> "The Jew?" he said. They listened. He could hear quite distinctly now. Somebody was turning on taps; somebody was having a bath in the room opposite.
> "The Jew having a bath," she said.
> "The Jew having a bath?" he repeated.
> "And tomorrow there'll be a line of grease around the bath," she said.
> "Damn the Jew!" he exclaimed. The thought of a line of grease from a strange man's body on the bath next door disgusted him.[132]

They share the same repulsion, as if it were a given. They listen to the running water again, the man coughing and clearing his throat while he scrubs.

> "Who is this Jew?" he asked.
> "Abrahamson,[133] in the tallow trade," she said. They listened. . . . "But he leaves hairs in the bath," she concluded.[134]

North feels a shiver run through him, asks if she uses the Jew's bathtub. She nods yes. And he says, "Pah!"

> "Pah. That's what I said," she laughed. "Pah!—when I went into the bathroom on a cold winter's morning—Pah!"—she threw her hand out—"Pah!"[135]

When the Jew first appeared, Sara had thought of a river. She had run outside enraged, stopped on a bridge, amid a crowd. "And I said, 'Must I join your conspiracy? Stain the hand, the unstained hand . . . and sign on, and serve a master; all because of a Jew in my bath, all because of a Jew?'"[136]

Ravings? Revelations!

What other body shares Virginia's bath except Leonard's, a Jew?

But into the water of the River Ouse, Leonard never entered.

He was the first to read these pages where Virginia Woolf, porous to all voices, intercepts the most vile of them this time, which is hers, and which, stifled until now, rises to an outcry. And which denounces Leonard Woolf.

One type of water hardly runs at all through the Woolfian corpus: tears. But, according to Virginia, with this text, tears did run: Leonard's. Virginia is not at all well after five tortuous years of working on this book she considers bad, "an odious rice pudding." So bad, when she entrusts the proofs to Leonard she asks him to burn them unread and flees. "It was cold & dry & very grey & I went out & walked through the graveyard with Cromwell's daughters Tomb down through Grays Inn along Holborn & so back."[137]

She feels "very tired. Very old. But at [the] same time content to go on these 100 years with Leonard." They have lunch, she figures out how to repay the cost of the proofs and falls "into one of my horrid heats & deep slumbers, as if the blood in my head were cut off. Suddenly L. put down his proof & said that he thought it extraordinarily good—as good as any of them. And now he is reading on. . . ." Two days later: "The miracle is accomplished. L. put down the last sheet about 12 last night; & could not speak. He was in tears."[138]

He says he finds this novel better than *The Waves*. But in his autobiography, he admits to having known "that unless I could give a completely favourable verdict she would be in despair and would have a very serious breakdown. . . . I had always read her books immediately after she had written the last word and always given an absolutely honest opinion. The verdict on *The Years* which I now gave her was not absolutely and completely what I thought about it." All the same, "it was obviously not in any way as bad as she thought it to be." But too long and "not really as good as *The Waves*, *To the Lighthouse* and *Mrs. Dalloway*. To Virginia I praised the book more than I should have done."[139] Those tears? They weren't tears of emotion because the text was so beautiful, or even disastrous. So how to account for them? In these pages, he had just read the scene of the foul Jew, staining both the bathtub and the soul of the anti-Semitic Sara, who issues from his wife's very core. Could they be tears of discouragement, rage, defeat, or even of simple sadness? Those tears, which he will not mention. Unless, of course, Virginia was exaggerating.

Epilogue: *The Years*, which does not lack Woolfian charm, although it does lack her magic. *The Years*, deliberately more conventional, stylistically more sedate than her usual work, would be (is it any surprise?) Virginia's greatest commercial success. In the United States that year, only *Gone with the Wind* would outsell it.

Now to a taboo question: where among the countless, often magnificent books devoted to Virginia is her anti-Semitism discussed? So recurrent, spontaneous as a tic, expressed casually and as though a given, in keeping with her circle, why is it almost never mentioned, never or rarely alluded to, and sometimes even denied? For fear of turning readers against her? Because that would seem irreverent? Because no one wants to admit it? Because it's not important, just "one of those things"? Because such disillusioning exactitude threatens the immunity and redemption granted her work? Because no one wants to tarnish its author or question the already suspect illusion of her "purity"? But also, why doesn't it turn me against her and all that she offers?

I have no answer, except that I want to hear it all; I want to be told everything.

And because we neither live nor die in an innocent world. Must all authors be naïve strangers to those damaged places? Exempt observers, preserved from the evil they observe? Never its agents, always its witnesses and judges? The judges of what they do not commit? Or are they especially, above all, uncertain, at the mercy of the very worst that may inhabit them?

Work, life, paths; people must be considered as a whole, all pointing toward consolation.

A life's paths lead in many directions, and Virginia Woolf's paths can be unexpected, without compromising her absolute demand for exactitude regarding her passions and propensities. A demand usually met. She does not misjudge herself in this, or lack the courage to express herself. And her spontaneous, inescapable self-awareness would allow for natural evolution, so that shortly after demonstrating such clear, sane, exceptional political awareness in *Three Guineas*, she would affirm, without the least ostentation or appearance of contradicting herself, "we are Jews," and speak of "our Jewishness" with regard to her marriage. This at the time when Nazism triumphs.[140]

She would take part in antifascist movements, which was always her orientation, though anti-Semitism seemed a given, part of the unwritten family code, almost tribal in some way, and considered a form of savoir faire, proper to her circle—rather than an expression of its perversity and a key to the crimes that were about take place.

Was she truly free from its grip, from the tradition handed down through generations? Yes, with regard to thinking, action, profession of faith—but at the visceral, unconscious level of her physical being?

Perhaps anti-Semitism suited her to the point of becoming necessary to her, so that she never considered thinking about it, applying her intelligence to it, that intelligence that led her, in *Three Guineas*, to a political awareness running counter to such impulses.

In 1940, it was as Jews and Socialists, only secondarily as writers, that Leonard and Virginia Woolf appeared together on the Third Reich's blacklist.

"We knew," their friend the poet Stephen Spender, also blacklisted, told me, "that if the Nazis arrived, we would be sent to the concentration camps: we were on Hitler's blacklist, and if the Germans landed, we would have to be arrested immediately."[141] In May 1940, Leonard who, strangely, never considered resisting, proposed a joint suicide to his wife if the Germans invaded, which seemed imminent.

A suicide . . . by gas. In the garage, he stockpiled gasoline. She immediately accepted. Here is Virginia Stephen included in the fate of the Jews, in solidarity with Leonard. And Leonard: "we discussed again calmly what we should do if Hitler landed. The least that I could look forward to as a Jew, we knew, would be to be 'beaten up.' We agreed that, if the time came, there would be no point in waiting; we would shut the garage door and commit suicide."[142]

Virginia's version, almost identical: "This morning we discussed suicide if Hitler lands. Jews beaten up. What point in waiting. Better to shut the garage doors. This is a sensible, rather matter of fact talk. Then he wrote letters, & I too: thanked Bernard Shaw for his love letter." But a few lines later, this protest: "No, I dont want the garage to see the end of me. I've a wish for 10 years more, & to write my book wh. as usual darts into my brain." She has decided to follow Leonard, but "its all bombast, this war. One old lady pinning on her cap has more reality. So if one dies, it'll be a common sense, dull end—not comparable to a days walk, & then an evening reading over the fire."[143]

The war—the tears it prompted even before it began and which Virginia remembers over the course of those months, "while all the guns are pointed & charged & no one dares pull the trigger. Not a sound this evening to bring in the human tears. I remember the sudden profuse shower one night just before war wh. made me think of all men & women weeping."[144]

The triggers, the guns worked. The garage was ready. France was going to fall, invasion threatened—"our waiting while the knives sharpen for the operation," and June 9: "I will continue—but can I? . . . A sample of my present mood, I reflect: capitulation will mean all Jews to be given up. Concentration camps. So to our garage. Thats behind correcting Roger, playing bowls. . . . Another reflection: I dont want to go to bed at midday: this refers to the garage."[145]

Nine months later, she would end her life, alone. Leonard would survive her by twenty-eight years.

A suicide results from a network of factors, not a single cause. It is not yet the time for us to go all the way to the River Ouse. Only to remark that because of his (justified) anxiety, Leonard, the pillar, the rock, proposes a joint suicide to a woman who has already attempted it and whom he considers fragile, verging on madness. The idea of suicide is thus introduced to her, very concretely and precisely, by the champion of reason within an arena that has turned tragic, and into which Virginia resolutely follows him. She very simply enters with him into the Jewish fate, without a shadow of theatricality and despite her desire to live.

From anti-Semitic fantasies she moves to the reality of inhuman history. She shares the ordeal of the marked victims, those most threatened. Body and soul. She engages fully. With her whole being. "We are Jews."[146]

She seems unaware of the evolution she has undergone, on a personal level, in her marriage, and regarding antifascism as well. She may not necessarily have forsworn the hackneyed litany she unconsciously recited to condemn the Jews, but what pleasure would it give her now? Even Marie Woolf, her favorite target, has been dead and buried almost two years.

The disorder, the unvoiced part of that disorder, the physical disgust, the fantasy of the Jewish body and the word "Jew," that specific disease that surfaces only in *The Years* as the irrational, instinctive repugnance expressed by Sara, must have always lain beneath the deep understanding and harmony Virginia and her Jewish husband shared. And at this point the disorder itself becomes disordered, part of an imaginary construct.

Or rather, with the war, this disorder alone remains, irrational, visceral, screened by its public expression, the blatant, hackneyed anti-Semitism so commonplace in their circle: the unwitting insults, the clichés automatically linked to anything Jewish. These stereotyped, knee-jerk reactions mask and in some way banish a certain irrational, hallucinated terror. For now, labeling Leonard "Jewish" is innocuous. But that label's effect on Hitler cancels any other effect, makes it truly bad form.

Without the store of insults, the anti-Semitic clichés, the physical presence and raw substance of a tangible "Jew," of Leonard, remain. And everything they evoke of what is invisible and disturbing, disguised or even exorcised until then by the hackneyed anti-Semitic repertoire, aimed at stereotypes, not live bodies. The atavistic loathing remains, perhaps, but goes unvoiced now. Impossible to express henceforth. To consciously feel.

Will Virginia's perception of Leonard change now that she cannot set him apart from other Jews? Might she lose some of her authority over him, now that he is freed from the label that allowed her circle to judge him . . . in a case already decided against him, since Leonard Woolf was a Jew. "We are Jews,"[147] says Virginia Stephen now.

Perhaps renouncing her racist fantasies, or banishing them, made her more fragile? A whole network of unconsidered landmarks collapses with them, a solid structure, a part of her personality, a familiar hysteria upon which they may rely. That exhilaration of acquired dominance, being in league with her circle, the arrogance of a kind of condoned cruelty punctuated her life, and perhaps she felt protected in the narrow, rigid corset of arbitrary certitudes and spitefulness. But especially in the stasis of fixed beliefs, within a space constricted enough for doubts and anxieties to fade, without room for oscillation; in holding racist positions whereby the pain and dreaded humiliation are blindly inflicted upon others, while personal rejection shuts them out.

It will not be gas that will do in Virginia Woolf ten months later, but water. The water that runs throughout the work, that calls, drowns, surrounds, attracts her from all sides and toward which Virginia, spellbound, is headed all her life, going there to be swallowed up, "exhausted swimmer,"[148] the body lovingly embraced by water. "There was an embrace in death."[149]

And now. . . .

And now, it is to Virginia the newborn that we must return, to Virginia Stephen, then to Virginia Woolf and their secret, and those of others.

In passing, we will learn . . . who Leonard married. And especially, who lived this life devoted to detecting life, reviving it, extracting it from its futility, capturing it in her pages, saved from lifelessness, fixed in its transience.

✳ ✳ ✳

Before accompanying Virginia on her journey, let us follow Leonard, who goes on without her to live to the age of eighty-eight. The years that would follow reflect upon the preceding ones. They make up part of Virginia's existence.

It took three weeks to find her body. Only Leonard would attend the cremation. The sublime cavatina of Beethoven's Thirteenth Quartet would not be played, though they had remarked one evening when they were listening to the music (Leonard kept a list of the records they listened to) how well it was suited to a cremation. "There is a moment in the middle of the cavatina when for a few bars the music, of incredible beauty, seems to hesitate with a gentle forward pulsing motion—if played at that moment it might seem to be gently propelling the dead into eternity of oblivion. Virginia agreed with me. . . . When I made arrangements for Virginia's funeral, I should have liked to arrange this." But he was unable to arrange it. "The long-drawn-out horror of the previous weeks had produced in me a kind of inert anaesthesia. It was as if I had been so battered and beaten." To his indignant surprise, Gluck's "Blessed Spirits" was played. After returning home that evening, Leonard listened to the cavatina.[150]

Alone, he buried her ashes at the foot of one of the two elms, their branches entangled, that they had named Leonard and Virginia. The tree would be uprooted one stormy night.

Leonard is alone. He changes nothing in his professional life. As early as the next day, he would go to see their lawyer. He refuses invitations. Vita describes for Harold her visit to Rodmell:

> The house was full of his [Leonard's] flowers, and all Virginia's things lying about as usual. . . . There was her needle-work on a chair and her coloured wools hanging over a sort of little towelhorse which she had made for them. Her thimble on the table. Her scribbling block with her writing on it. . . . I said, "Leonard, I do not like your being here alone like this." He turned those piercing blue eyes on me and said, "It is the only thing to do."[151]

He wrote this note found with his papers at his death:

> They said: "Come to tea and let us comfort you." But it's no good. One must be crucified on one's own private cross.

It is a strange fact that a terrible pain in the heart can be interrupted by a little pain in the fourth toe of the right foot.

I know that V. will not come across the garden from the lodge, & yet I look in that direction for her. I know that she is drowned & yet I listen for her to come in at the door. I know that it is the last page & yet I turn it over. There is no limit to one's stupidity and selfishness.[152]

But Leonard would not be the stoic, solitary widower of Rodmell, vestal for a sacerdotal wife, forever in the grip of his ruined marriage, as we might have imagined. Less than a year later, the austere Leonard falls madly in love. A passionate love affair that would last twenty-seven years, until his death.

No one would be surprised by it: Trekkie Parson is blonde and round, jovial, with a keen sense of the prosaic, the most mediocre of painters. She will not leave her husband, Ian Parson, a publisher like Leonard, with whom he would graciously share his wife, especially since he himself is having an affair that makes Trekkie jealous. Her relationship with Leonard would remain platonic; this time the alibi is age and his long abstinence, officially blamed on Virginia.

Trekkie soon replaces Virginia at Rodmell, without ever separating from Ian. A three-part arrangement: Trekkie Parson divides her time between Leonard and Ian, spending weekends and some vacations with her husband, weekdays and other vacations with Leonard. They often find themselves a threesome. The Parsons will become Leonard's tenants in his London flat; they buy a house in a village neighboring Rodmell.

The Parsons' interest? This bond with Woolf will let Ian, clearly aided by his wife, achieve one of his dreams: for a long time he has watched for the opportunity to acquire for Chatto & Windus (his own publishing house and one of the biggest in England) the Hogarth Press, the Woolfs' publishing house, much smaller in size, but the premier press of its day, among the most sophisticated and prestigious.

An impassioned, enthralling business for the couple and of major importance to Leonard; an immense triumph, carried out together with astounding, unforeseen success and creating a permanent bond between them. Leonard will take on more responsibility; editing will become his profession, his public identity, even more so than author, man of politics, or publisher; Virginia's will always be limited to writer.

When they bought (on sale) a printing press and installed it in their dining room in 1917, Leonard and Virginia hardly imagined that they had just founded one of England's most distinguished publishing houses. Their chief goals were to maintain Virginia's stability—she had just emerged from a serious crisis—with the help of a concrete occupation in her realm of interest, and to amuse themselves by printing and publishing a few texts written by them and their friends.

Hard to imagine them just starting out, immersing themselves in the work, trying to print two short stories, one of his, one of hers: "Three Jews" and "The Mark on the Wall." Thirty-two pages. One hundred fifty copies. And printing, sewing, gluing, bungling, binding, quarreling, preparing parcels, gluing labels, tying them up, and carting them to the post office.

An article in the *Times Literary Supplement*, and orders ensue:

> We came back . . . to find the hall table stacked, littered, with orders for Kew Gardens. They strewed the sofa, & we opened them intermittently through dinner, & quarreled, I'm sorry to say, because we were both excited. . . . All these orders—150 about, from shops & private people. . . . And 10 days ago I was stoically facing complete failure! The pleasure of success was considerably damaged, first by our quarrel, & second, by the necessity of getting some 90 copies ready.[153]

They tackled Katherine Mansfield's *Prelude* next, and soon bought a more modern press, as the first one printed only one page at a time. Soon they would seek out other printers, but for a long time they would continue to print certain works themselves in their dining room, binding them in the pantry.

Having become a renowned publishing house, the Hogarth Press, which began in Richmond, would always be part of their London residence. Printers, bookbinders, authors were received there. The room where Virginia wrote would serve as warehouse. "She had a large stripped wooden desk in it, surrounded by the piles of parcels of Hogarth books straight from the binders, which also overflowed into the corridor,"[154] remembers John Lehmann, who worked at Hogarth in 1930.

Even when the Hogarth Press was thriving and Virginia was famous, she would lend a hand in emergencies. When orders flooded in following the release of a new book, she would always work in the room with the employees, tying parcels, gluing labels. In a holiday atmosphere, joking,

eating biscuits, while "young authors, coming in to leave a precious manuscript and dreaming of encountering the famous author, would never
suspect that they were actually in her presence as the figure in the drab
overalls busied herself with scissors and string."[155]

She would read manuscripts up until the end, literary ones, attentively
and passionately. Leonard would read them all, including the essays. How
many writers worked as closely with books as she did? How many were
as familiar with the humble tasks of book making, which granted her
a physical knowledge of books? She often noted in her diary when her
hands trembled from carrying packages. Ink-stained hands that handled
typeface, fingered paper, tied bundles. She and Leonard shared the tasks of
selecting binding paper, finding cover illustrations, distributing the books.

The Woolfs always bore the entire financial risk for an enterprise
begun with no capital. Few writers, and even fewer at that time, understood the business and technology of the literary profession as Virginia
did. Her muscles, her body had experienced the actual weight of books,
parcels of them; countless volumes she and Leonard themselves supplied
to local bookstores on the automobile tours they took regularly as late as
1940. To a friend, Virginia asserted that the Hogarth Press was more work
than six little brats.

Leonard instantly, intrinsically, became an editor and proved to be an
unparalleled businessman, audacious and patient, an immediate authority in the publishing and literary worlds. As author and editor of his own
work, he would stand by those he published; like Virginia, he could be both
intimate and severe, and often very kind. The couple made no concessions
in their choice of books and writers, and often rejected manuscripts from
friends who were a part of their life.

Improvising at first, but soon proving to be an exceptional administrator, Woolf was in love with Hogarth and would take care to maintain it
on a human scale. Possessive, nervous, sometimes despotic, perhaps he let
loose a bit here, let down the mask and voiced the hysterical protests he
repressed elsewhere. John Lehmann, among others, bore the brunt of this.
A writer himself, Rosamond Lehmann's brother, he began working for the
Hogarth Press when he was twenty-four years old; he lasted only eighteen
months that first time, and he confided in me, still bitter:

> Nearly all the young men who came to work at the Hogarth Press—
> there had been four or five of them before me—found that excitability

very difficult. Leonard exhibited a kind of jealousy, as though the press was the child he had never had. That did not surface at first, but later, life became very difficult when the newcomer really began to understand Hogarth, take an interest in it, and want to make decisions himself.[156]

Virginia described his arrival to Clive Bell: "Young Mr Lehmann is now installed in the back room behind the W.C. at a small table with a plant which Leonard has given him on the window sill."[157]

Hogarth Press's main asset: a top-quality, often innovative catalogue. T. S. Eliot was to be found there from the first, among other young poets, like Stephen Spender; Katherine Mansfield, R. M. Rilke, E. M. Forster, Bertrand Russell, Gertrude Stein, Christopher Isherwood, Keynes, Hölderlin, Melanie Klein, Henry Green, and so on. And of course, Virginia Woolf and Leonard. But also all the works of Freud, translated into English by James Strachey, whose authorized critical apparatus would earn an international reputation.

It was that publishing house, that catalogue, which Ian Parson dreamed of acquiring. An old dream, dating back much further than 1938, the year John Lehmann returned to Hogarth, bought Virginia's shares, and became Leonard's partner (which did not change Virginia's role in the least). Alice Ritchie, one of the Woolfs' authors who also worked at the press, gossiped to her sister . . . Trekkie Parson: the Hogarth Press had been sold. Ian Parson reacts. Leonard denies it. Alice apologizes and writes to him: "The thing is that Ian has always had a day-dream of some sort of amalgamation between Chatto and the Hogarth Press. He often talked to me about it and when he heard, in the way of gossip, that the Press was sold he was in despair and begged me to ask you if indeed all hope for him was over."[158] That was the end of it.

At least until 1946, eight years later. Virginia has been dead five years. The threesome they comprise with Trekkie has brought the two men closer. Leonard has become and fancies himself the beau of Trekkie Parson, still attached to her husband, still officially Ian's wife, though she and Leonard are known as a couple who dance divinely together, entertain admirably, and like to drink. Leonard (whose wine cellar is well stocked) is, to their delight, most easily influenced.

Trekkie designs book covers for Hogarth, where she spends much time and manages to spark conflicts between Woolf and Lehmann, as well as between Lehmann and herself. "It was after Virginia's death that the real difficulties with Leonard began,"[159] John Lehmann confided in me in 1973, and still seemed bitter, twenty-seven years later, at having seen his life thrown off course. He had not read the letters in which Leonard Woolf responds to Trekkie's complaints and supports her against Lehmann regarding printing problems, telling her to let him know if John "bristles" and doesn't give in.

Woolf himself gives in. Ian buys the shares from John Lehmann, who, being too impulsive, finally makes a false move. The Hogarth Press is subsumed into Chatto & Windus, the larger publishing house, and is no longer exclusively Leonard's, even though, as full partner in the new company, he continues to direct it, with full editorial freedom guaranteed.

Mrs. Parson's entry into Leonard's life does not seem without advantages for Mr. Parson, whose dream has now become a reality. A coincidence? Alice Ritchie's letter raises questions about what transpired between Ian and Leonard, one absorbing the other's enterprise and fulfilling a lifelong wish. And Leonard, so stubborn, so tenacious, renouncing his possessiveness, his demand for exclusive rights to Hogarth, and declaring himself grateful to Ian Parson—he insists on this in the autobiography—for helping him get rid of John Lehmann, out of the kindness of his heart. . . .

Much later, when he steps down amiably because of his age, his letter of resignation will nevertheless express some bitterness, alluding to that promised but severely limited authority and editorial freedom.

No matter!

A new Leonard emerges on the scene, passionately in love, transfixed. Their correspondence has now been published: "Tiger, darling tiger,"[160] his "dear queen," was thirty-two years younger (although she hardly seems so in photographs). Imperturbable duo: he, always the more ardent and dependent, and willingly so; she, calm, epicurean, solidly grounded, ably controlling his life.

They would travel extensively together. Among their destinations: the United States, Israel, Canada, Greece and even . . . Ceylon. Returning with great ceremony, Leonard is received there as a hero. There where *The Village in the Jungle* is still a best-seller. He even took Trekkie to Hambantota. She would be fascinated by the birds there.

Their deep, shared passion for gardening, animals, flowers (which she painted prolifically) created a symbiosis between them. She sent him dismaying poems, which he admired. She truly loved to paint, but was (justly) considered an amateur, a good student of painting, except by Leonard who, unlike Ian Parson, saw in her a great artist and encouraged her. Her paintings are not exactly crude, only mediocre. She did produce a handsome, if academic, portrait of Leonard, and one drawing for which we can almost forgive her anything. An Annunciation in which the Angel appears in the open countryside to Leonard who, hands in his pockets, looks right through him and says: "I don't believe a word of it."[161] If the caption is Trekkie's, hats off to her!

The former circle, especially the Bloomsbury contingent, is still there, but they maintain their distance from the Parsons. Leonard retains his role among them, without Trekkie. As before the war, they still gather as the Memoir Club, where Keynes, Grant, the Bells, Forster, and others read, each in turn, from sometimes shocking, unadulterated memoirs in which the pathos is heightened by being shrouded in humor. Here, for example, Virginia read "Am I a Snob?" or "22 Hyde Park Gate" or "The Old Bloomsbury." Her portrait hangs on the wall now, beside Roger Fry's and Lytton Strachey's, all three dead. Leonard attends regularly, now immune to all subtle, possible, and improbable anti-Semitic barbs, either more or less implicit. He has escaped that mire, he has crossed that threshold. Since the war is over, has the time of discrimination and its arrogances passed? Sometimes it seems doubtful; traces of it remain.

One example: Christmas 1944. For the English, the war has basically ended; the Nazis are defeated. The truth is out about the genocide, the camps and their atrocities. Virginia is dead. So are so many others. In London, there is peace. Keynes and his wife, Lydia, are giving a costume ball. Vanessa, preparing for it, reports she has "been busy routing out our old theatrical properties—a mask for Clive, and other garments to make him look like a very obscene little girl. Duncan is making himself a wonderful wolf's mask. Q's [Quentin] Father C[hristmas] is a horrible old Jew who will terrify the children."[162] After Auschwitz, it is still the Jew who is terrifying!? And horrible? Apparently!

Three decades later, in the 1977 preface to Virginia's diary, Quentin Bell writes well-meaningly that, following the premature death of Leonard's father, "the Woolfs met this catastrophe with the supple fortitude of their race."[163]

Leonard Woolf actively manages the posthumous work of Virginia, publishing it successfully, including a volume of extracts from the diary, unpublishable in its entirety as long as those whom she spares nothing are still alive . . . that is, everyone. A note in one of her two farewell letters to Leonard asks him to burn all her papers. He sells them. Correspondences, letters sent or received, personal diaries, manuscripts in various stages of completion, photographs, and other documents. They are all in New York, part of the Berg Collection at the New York Public Library, where access to them must now be requested.

Leonard's papers will be offered to the University of Sussex by his heir and sole legatee, Trekkie Parson, on the condition that the university buys Monk's House, which she now owns.

In addition to a considerable sum of money, the inheritance includes the Rodmell property (house, grounds, and two cottages) and a London flat. Also, all the returns from Virginia's original modest fortune, the Hogarth Press, Virginia's work, Leonard's publications, and his compensation for directing the press.

With Ian's support, and backed by his lawyers, Trekkie proves intrepid in the face of the Woolf family, among them brothers and sisters, or their descendants, who have very little money. The Parsons will sell the London flat, evicting Cecil Woolf, Leonard's aged, impoverished brother, who is entitled to stay there and will put up a fight but will eventually back down, accepting a paltry compensation.

Ian Parson discovers an error committed by the lawyer: according to Trekkie (who was present at one of the dictations of the will before the lawyer), a bequest of five hundred pounds each was provided for two of Leonard's nieces and one of his nephews; whereas he indicated five thousand pounds on the written will. Trekkie refuses to relinquish that share, which she considers to be hers. The Woolfs take legal action against her. A scandal ensues. Headlines in the newspapers. The Parsons stand firm. They won't share a single cent of the booty, and it doesn't matter that they themselves are well off and many of the Woolfs are destitute. Two years of litigation before the Parsons agree to a settlement.

Trekkie? No doubt she loved, and especially appreciated Leonard over the course of almost three decades, at the end of which, it is true, she was seen much less at Monk's House. But Virginia Woolf's husband did not lack for female admirers glad to share his golden days . . . sometimes to the point of upsetting his "beloved Tiger."[164]

All the people in this book, whose names and traces remain, would have remained forever unknown, forgotten, if they had not been linked to Virginia Woolf, sometimes if they had not merely crossed her path. In his old age, Leonard himself would remark that the world wouldn't be the least changed if he had simply spent his life playing Ping-pong!

But what about Virginia? Let us discover her alone. . . .

Part 2

THE adolescent bicycling down the streets of London is a ghost, unless, flesh and blood, she is moving among fantasies. She lives between two worlds, each of which destabilizes the other. She struggles in these Victorian times, clings to details, to the everyday, takes note of it; she is afraid of horses, of the accidents they cause in the city thoroughfares, where she notices the dangers everywhere. Dressmakers terrify her, with their fittings, make her want to stab them with their own scissors (she is joking here, she is not mad). Books reassure her; she consumes them one after another, devours them. She . . .

She has lost her mother.

Her mother is a depraved dead woman. Elusive in her lifetime. Like everyone else, you say? Yes, but she is dead. It was two years ago; her daughter was thirteen years old. The other six children . . .

Her mother's words to her before she died: "Hold yourself straight, my little Goat."[1]

Her mother's death portends other deaths to come.

After the death that followed her mother's, the daughter remembers saying to herself: "But this is impossible; things aren't, can't be, like this."[2]

And we have seen that, at fifteen years old, she wrote: "How is one to live in such a world?"[3] (she is fifteen years old here, on this page). Her name is Virginia.

Her mother, who is dead, was named Julia. She was named Julia Jackson, Julia Duckworth, Julia Stephen, over the course of her birth, her marriages, time. Julia Jackson and Julia Stephen are dead. Julia Duckworth as well, and Stella Duckworth, her daughter from a first marriage, would soon be dead. Virginia's half-sister. Two years after their mother. She was twenty-eight years old.

"The world has raised its whip; where will it descend?" It would descend again and Virginia Woolf would describe Virginia Stephen: "my wings still creased, sitting there on the edge of my broken chrysalis."[4]

* * *

1895. With Julia, Virginia lost what she never had: her mother, elusive. When she was not dead, Julia Stephen was absent. If present, she was unavailable. "Can I remember ever being alone with her for more than a few minutes?"[5] her daughter would sigh. Dead or living, she slipped away, became the very essence of lack, the mark of absence. But how to intercept that absence (and with her death, the absence of that absence), how to seize hold of it? How to bring back to life what never was? How to safeguard it? How even to evoke it?

Virginia would struggle her entire life to define, to discern the absence that she had lost. To safeguard, recover, restore it. Forty-four years later, in 1939, World War II was approaching and Virginia was still searching for that perpetually lost mother. Virginia had already written in 1907: "How difficult it is to single her out as she really was; to imagine what she was thinking, to put a single sentence into her mouth! I dream; I make up pictures of a summer's afternoon." The following year, in 1940, under bombardment and a few months before her death: "What would one not give to recapture a single phrase even! or the tone of the clear round voice."[6]

Thirteen years earlier, *To the Lighthouse* had appeared, those pages haunted by Julia Stephen, alias Mrs. Ramsay, who is able to capture the excitement, incorporate it, offer it to her eight children, to friends invited to her enormous seaside summer home, all of whom depend upon the meaning she gives to them, as Mr. Ramsay depends on it, her tormented, begging husband. All of whom are drawn to her, the woman who asks herself, facing the long dinner table where the residents gather and while she fills their plates: "But what have I done with my life?"[7]

Mrs. Ramsay, whose weaknesses we can guess: her taste for power, her desire to seduce, her capacity to withdraw, her emotional rapaciousness, and the disarray beneath her many, delightful, slightly faltering perfections. Mrs. Ramsay, whose death is going to ravage a world nevertheless unchanged but whose survivors will suffer "the old horror": "to want and want and not to have."[8]

Her illusion: Virginia believed that through the Ramsays she had overcome that horror, exorcised the haunting, absent mother and father, and with them, their defection that "wrung the heart, and wrung it again and again."[9] But Mrs. Stephen escapes forever, even from Mrs. Ramsay. *To the Lighthouse* exorcised nothing. The memory remains incarcerated in the desperate waiting for what was (or what never was) in a world forever on hold, where things and beings become signs of what can only be called absence.

Here, a mother's absence seals shut her past and leaves no smiling image of her.

But being dead, it seems (it seems to me) that Julia does laugh sometimes, now settled in, and that accurate memories of her do not dare surface. The day that Virginia received the 1928 Femina-Vie Heureuse Prize for *To the Lighthouse*, for instance, Elizabeth Robins, formerly a great Ibsen actress, told her during the reception that her mother was not at all like the dying swan of the sublime photos taken by her aunt, Mrs. Cameron, the famous pioneering photographer, nor like Leslie Stephen's languorous memories, and "she [Julia] would suddenly say something so unexpected, from that Madonna face, one thought it *vicious*."[10]

The face of a madonna. So much beauty. Mrs. Cameron's photos, which seem dated today, testify to it. Julia Jackson, then Julia Duckworth, perfection itself. A little too smooth, according to Leonard Woolf, who considered the famous splendor of the Pattle family women, of whom Julia's mother was one, too feminine and not female enough. He preferred the Stephen side in Virginia and Vanessa, tougher, more masculine, which gave them character in addition to harmony, according to him.

Before her premature death, her premature aging, Julia (now) Stephen's face hardened, as if shattered, and she had an air of utter hopelessness and spite, even beyond the personal resentment that she seemed to embody in many of her earlier photos. She died at forty-nine years old and looked more like seventy. Such a discrepancy between the dazzling, youthful ingénue and the same woman in her mature years, suddenly aged, savage, disappointed, even vindictive. In the last photos, surrounded by her family, she seems not to be there and, more than ever, not to want to be there.

Julia Stephen's legend portrays her as exhausted, destroyed by the demands of Leslie Stephen, the domestic tyrant, sapped by his exploitation of her, by her life as a tragically sacrificing wife and mother. Whereas she was *self-sacrificing*, worn to a thread . . . but elsewhere, with others and despite the timid requests of the "tyrant," at a time when wives were supposedly restricted to the home.

Julia, who signed petitions against the suffragettes, was nonetheless often freed from her Victorian Angel in the House duties, from *her* house at least, to embody another cliché of the era, going about doing good in the community "as a sister of mercy,"[11] according to Leslie Stephen. She felt equally called to all suffering, the bedside of her sick parents, death watches over relatives, troubled friends in need of consolation, London slums, Cornwall paupers. She rushed from one to the other, sometimes traveling long distances for some days.

"When she had saved a life from the deep waters, that is, she sought at once for another person to rescue, whereas I went off to take a glass with the escaped,"[12] recalled Leslie, her husband.

Stella, the oldest, still a child, thus took charge of the house, the family, colds, meals, lessons, while Julia devoted herself to the passion that was her ruin and rushed off in all directions to care for the sick and afflicted, who were tactful enough to suffer bad health—even to die—a good distance away: from her husband and eight children, seven of which are hers.

Seven children. And what monopolized her, held her captive, simultaneously paralyzed and impassioned her—what, behind the "very quick; very definite; very upright" woman made her "the sad, the silent" absorbed woman—was the memory of her first three children's father, the unique, incomparable Herbert Duckworth, whose accidental death four years into their marriage seemed somehow to have killed Julia too. At twenty-four, she would spend hours prostrate on his grave, pregnant with their third child. She announced, "All life seemed a shipwreck," and she was tempted to let herself founder. A fascination with water, its tragic promises. Virginia saw her mother as "an exhausted swimmer, deeper and deeper in the water."[13]

So many images that would not leave her alone.

Julia Duckworth pulled herself together. She had lost her faith and "flung aside her religion."[14] In a state of vengeance. In a state of fury. Unexpressed resentment. Deliberate absence.

Rejecting those who had a claim on her, offering herself to those who expected nothing from her, because such devotion took on meaning as a vocation stemming from her grief, an edifying response to her broken life, a corollary to the tragedy of Herbert Duckworth, that is to say, a permanent tie to him. She would nevertheless live out the rest of her life fully and tenaciously . . . even as she turned away from it.

The care she so unsparingly lavished upon others is all the more striking for being unexpected; almost public, even showy, it conferred upon her an air of altruism, provided her her own domain. Gave her the right to be unavailable; never "more than a few minutes"[15] reserved for Virginia, who early on sensed Herbert's presence when her mother, often so distant, so sad and absorbed, seemed to be dreaming of him. And Virginia dreamed with her.

Julia's magic spells. And, not the least of them, reticence. Leslie Stephen claimed to have loved even her reticence when he went on about her, subjecting the dead woman's children to endless babble about their mother's love for him, a love she rarely demonstrated while alive, trying to persuade them, and himself, through his excessive theatrical grieving, which would lead him to reveal more intimate facts about their marriage than Julia would ever have tolerated.

Julia's ambiguities. Despite her deficiencies or because of them, they left Virginia with dazzling, delightful images. For example, the image of Julia finally nabbed by Virginia, descending the stairs with her, arm in arm, laughing, or letting her choose among her jewelry which to wear one evening. Julia, always on the stairs. Virginia asks her how Leslie courted her, and she doesn't answer. And the sound of silver bracelets, and the voice at night that sometimes suggested, before sleep, that she think of shining things, "rainbows and bells."[16]

And then Julia, the "omnibus expert," sitting in her "shabby cloak" near the driver, indignant that the bus company did not provide him straw to keep his feet warm. "Your feet must be cold." Julia accompanying Stella to dances, she herself surrounded by the suitors of the daughter she was chaperoning, whose successes, whose wooers "excited many instincts long dormant in her mother." She loved the young men confiding their secrets to her . . . and it was Stella, she complained, who "would insist upon going home, long before the night was over, for fear lest she should be tired." Stella, who worshipped her, always in her mother's shadow, "that passive, suffering affection," Virginia would write. A mother who did not like Stella and who called her "Old Cow," this girl almost as beautiful as she had once been, a little plainer perhaps, and who bore for her an "almost canine" devotion. Before their marriage, Leslie would try to call Julia's attention to her harshness toward her daughter, in vain. He would not insist.[17]

Julia's sly humor, sending Virginia to go "tease" Leslie, too attentive to a seductive American, Mrs. Grey, having her whisper in his shocked ear to stop flirting "with pretty ladies." And Julia's austere grace "as she came up the path by the lawn of St Ives; slight, shapely—she held herself very straight," remembers Virginia, who adds: "I was playing. I stopped, about to speak to her. But she half turned from us, and lowered her eyes. From that indescribably sad gesture I knew that Philips, the man who had been crushed on the line and whom she had been visiting, was dead. It's over, she seemed to say. I knew, and was awed by the thought of death. At the same time I felt that her gesture as a whole was lovely." The gesture indicating death.[18]

Virginia no longer distinguished Julia's beauty from these details, mixed emotions, contradictory sides. Beauty that she accepts "as the natural quality that a mother . . . had by virtue of being our mother. It was part of her calling."[19] And that was enough for childhood, for that time to unfold happily, dynamically, even jubilantly, under the maternal aegis, no matter how capricious the mother. Julia's swings were undoubtedly noticed and distressing, especially after their tragic interruption, which rendered every missed opportunity poignant, irreversible.

A before. An after. The big, dark house at Hyde Park Gate, in an elegant London neighborhood, seems at first like a nest where brothers and half-brothers, sisters and half-sisters comfortably nestle. Life was more serious and studious there than at Talland House, the summer home rocked by the waves, "one, two, one, two," a bright, sparkling spring surrounded by flowers, scented with every youthful joy under the Cornwall sun of St. Ives. Virginia the cricket champion writes: "Vanessa and I were both what was called tomboys; that is, we played cricket, scrambled over rocks, climbed trees." Every moment something fun; *The Hyde Park Gate News* kept by the family, its only readers: chronicles of everyday life, recorded especially by Thoby and Virginia, soon primarily Virginia, and her first thrill as author when Julia notices one of her entries and gives it to a friend to read: "It was like being a violin and being played upon."[20]

And then . . . the whip struck for the first time. "The greatest disaster that could happen."[21]

The lips, still warm, that one night pronounced: "Hold yourself straight, my little Goat." Addressing a child brought to see her mother alive for the last time; and at dawn, the cold face, of which touching cold metal would always remind her, the dead face that Virginia kissed before going to the window, saying to herself that she didn't feel anything except the desire to laugh because one of the nurses was pretending to cry, while she watched Dr. Seton head down the street and Stella caressed her mother's cheek and opened a button on her nightgown: "She always liked to have it like that." Passing her widowed father stumbling, distraught, from the death chamber. Virginia reaching out for him and being pushed away. The father wrapped hastily in big towels, given a few drops of brandy in milk. And the pallid Stella watching over them all, considered as slow as she was beautiful, but showing true genius when Virginia, distraught, confessed to her that she saw a man sitting beside the dead woman. Stella, a bit frightened herself, saying after a moment: "It's nice that she shouldn't be alone."[22]

And all that could no longer not have been.

But all that had been, where had it come from? How had this family come about? How had Vanessa, Thoby, Virginia, Adrian come to exist? How had Leslie Stephen married the eternally shipwrecked Julia and usurped Herbert Duckworth, the eternal prince charming?

And who was Leslie Stephen, minor philosopher, highly respected intellectual, surrounded by writer friends, among them Thomas Hardy, William Meredith, and Henry James? A former priest of the Anglican Church, he was one of the first English mountaineers, loved the Alps, and helped to found the famous Alpine Club.

And where did Virginia's mute fury toward him come from? Her desperate resentment and rage, as well as her equally desperate attachment? They surface in her diary and especially in *Moments of Being*, a posthumous work that includes, most importantly, two notebooks of memories recorded many years later by a Virginia forever ravaged by the eros of childhood and its libidinous currents; by urges and desires, frozen by grief, crushed by the living, yet emerging alive in these impatient pages from the past.

Two times, thirty years apart, Virginia revived and rehearsed the same history, the same scenes from her childhood and adolescence, and sounded the same complaint. Nothing had healed her. Not age, not the work, not her varied, intense, and often rich life, not even her hardships had diverted her from the original mysteries, parental figures, major suppressions. Time, work, their passions had only nurtured and intensified the original pain. Virginia Stephen, at twenty-five years old, in *Reminiscences*, and then Virginia Woolf, at fifty-seven years old, in *Sketch of the Past*, returned powerless, ecstatic, and horrified to the time of plenitude and its interruption, then to death and incest. To the crudeness and savagery of an existence that appeared to be utterly civilized.

At fifty-seven as at twenty-seven, she circles around and around the same events, without ever coming to the end of them. And at the center we find not Julia, but Leslie.

It is he who would haunt Virginia to the last, torn as she was by hate, love, but especially repression. It is he who would represent danger. A mention of him in her diary, even in passing—even a simple reference to mountains, especially the Alps, Leslie Stephen's domain—and there, a few lines or pages or days later, we find depression. Manifest. It at first seems like coincidence, but it isn't, it occurs systematically.

Her project, four months before her suicide: "I think of taking my mountain top—*that persistent vision*[23]—as a starting point"; a week before her death, she writes again to Lady Tweedsmuir: "All this afternoon I've been trying to arrange some of my father's old books." For months, she has been absorbed in Leslie's books, papers, letters, while around her unfolds that war whose end she will not witness.[24]

Thus, on June 20, 1940, John Lehmann met them for lunch and, deathly white, "his pale eyes paler than usual," announced that France had stopped fighting. "Whats to become of me?" writes Virginia that evening in her diary. And two days later, on June 19, she notes down the circumstances under which she is recording old memories: "Today the dictators dictate their terms to France." In what will posthumously become *Sketch of the Past*—an immersion into her troubled youth, troubled especially by Leslie Stephen—she writes of an organ grinder in the square, the heat, a man selling strawberries. Virginia goes on: "I sit in my room at 37 M[ecklenburgh S[quare] and turn to my father."[25]

Recalling how for a long time, until the publication of *To the Lighthouse*, she would catch herself moving her lips and silently laying into him, arguing, silently unleashing her rage toward him, revealing to herself what she did not say to him, what "was impossible to say aloud" and what she was finally trying to write here, at fifty-eight years old, but does not formulate, would never formulate, not even for her eyes alone, not even in thought: "How deep they drove themselves into me, the things it was impossible to say aloud."[26]

Like no one else, Virginia Woolf knew how to delineate, to capture and convey all those things still marked by what forbids them; but these things no one would hear, not even she who harbored them, knew them, did not say them; did not say them to herself, identify them, or free herself from them. Lurking in the shadows but felt, they would not leave her, linked to the livid hell that Hyde Park Gate became once Julia was dead and yet endlessly, obsessively invoked, harped on by Leslie. Who henceforth made this mother, undoubtedly elusive but lively and captivating while alive, into the dead object of his insatiable, unquenchable sexual desire.

Grief foundered at Hyde Park Gate, monopolized by the father's anguish alone, obsessed as he was by his wife, a fetish bordering on necrophilia, which he imposed upon Julia's children, forbidden to grieve with him around their shared memories and their shattered life, which together they could have mourned. Around a collective wound. Maimed children faced with the passionate instincts of a personally and physiologically frustrated man; children struggling with their urgent, insatiable plea for what, they knew, would never be again.

Emphatic to the point of obscene, Leslie dispossessed Julia's sons and daughters of their grief—those who were adults and already orphans, Herbert's children: George, Stella, and Gerald Duckworth, twenty-seven, twenty-six, and twenty-five years old; those from his own marriage: Vanessa, Thoby, Virginia, and Adrian Stephen, sixteen, fifteen, thirteen, and twelve years old. All were overwhelmed by Leslie's exhibitions of need for their mother, the missing object of his libido and not the beloved being, mourned by each of them, whose absence they all shared.

Leslie would make this loss the excuse for horrid scenes, sordid hours, an insidiously incestuous atmosphere. Misfortune was converted into the worst calamity.

"Quite naturally unhappy," Virginia and her siblings came to "almost welcome" "the sharp pang" that was "recognizable pain," even to take a kind of comfort in that inexorable but identified, anticipated distress, compared to the dubious atmosphere surrounding them that "hideous as it was, obscured both living and dead; and for long did unpardonable mischief by substituting for the shape of a true and most vivid mother, nothing better than an unlovable phantom."[27]

Damaged: both the memory and the mourning; with his shameless contortions of widowhood, Leslie Stephen discredited them.

In the last photographs of the couple, he and Julia both look extremely old and seem to compete for moroseness; both appear sullen and severe with their young band of children (whose sour-tempered grandparents they could be, exhausted by life). It's hard to imagine Leslie ever capable of infatuation. His frustration? It dated back a long time! The merciless shock, the wound of grief must have reawakened it, renewed the awareness of an older deprivation, habitually hidden until then and suddenly freed by a horrible jolt. Shaken loose was his long-buried sexual, sensual life, his paralyzed urges. What he lamented, through the wife he memorialized under all his talk, was also his inability to claim what he must have felt ready for again, open to again, although it was too late: a whole sexual arena, which seemed foreclosed to him.

His recourse? For the philosopher, writing is a weapon. He undertook the *Mausoleum Book* sixteen days after Julia's death, to her glory and to be read by her children. There he revives the time of feelings and puts Julia on display, anxious to convince them (and convince himself) that his "noble wife"[28] to him (as to Herbert Duckworth), even though he never got her to say it, he admits, loved him.

Wild passion is notably absent in his letters to his living wife, in which he describes not the state of his soul but rather that of his intestines.

If Julia laughed, embarrassed and a little shocked, at Virginia's questions on her courtship, the *Mausoleum* compensates—oh how it compensates—for that reserve and broadcasts with great emotion the intimacy of the couple and the couples they had each been part of during their successive marriages. Leslie's intimacy with his two "darlings," first with Minny, that is "my darling Minny," Thackeray's youngest daughter, with "her beautiful bronze hair, brilliantly white teeth and delicate complexion one minute with the soft tint of the china rose and then again white as a lily. . . . One day she would look like the young girl she really was and, on the next, twenty years older, so varying were her moods and expression . . . she was sincere almost to bluntness." Though elsewhere he calls her not very pretty,[29] sweet and gay, hardly brilliant: "She was a poem, though not a poetess."[30]

This sweet, gay poem, also in love with the Alps, would play with their baby Laura for a few summers in the Grindelwald meadows, never anticipating that their laughter, the looks exchanged between them, would be the last signs of kindness Laura would experience. Minny would die unsuspecting of her daughter's future difficulties, her abominable fate.

Laura, "Her Ladyship the Lady of the Lake," as the other children nicknamed her, "backward," in the words of her father, would be no more than an unseemly, disagreeable problem that had to be rectified. Scolded, punished, roughly handled, but most importantly, barely, grievously loved by Leslie alone, who was ravaged with pity, impatience, anger, and consternation, she would be permanently ruined in a time when nothing was known about such marginal cases, forced to fall into line regardless. Today she would be treated very differently. Ignorance, cruel as it was, thus incited cruelty; Laura would be lost among the three Duckworth children, more or less her contemporaries, and the four Stephens, born one after the other, whom she destabilized. As she did Julia.[31]

Virginia would flee her memory all her life. Nevertheless, indignant and terrified, she mentions that "besides the three Duckworths and the four Stephens there was also Thackeray's grand-daughter" (and not the daughter of her own father), "a vacant-eyed girl whose idiocy was becoming daily more obvious, who could hardly read, who would throw the scissors into the fire, who was tongue-tied and stammered and yet had to appear at table with the rest of us."[32]

Leslie, often wildly angry and distressed at his daughter's limitations, which he considered a "perversity,"[33] worked desperately to teach her to read and succeeded, but to whose benefit? Laura got to the end of *Aladdin* at eleven years old; at fourteen, she read *Robinson Crusoe* and at sixteen, *Alice in Wonderland.*

Pedagogical harassment, strictness, outbursts of rage followed by remorse were the extent of interactions with Laura. The distance and confusion grew. The anomaly was reinforced, the gap widened. A little kindness would no doubt have improved her life, allowed her a place in this already "blended" family, instead of a steady withdrawal from their life and her perceptions of it, unknown to them. Incongruous. At those rare times when someone reached out to her, like Minny's older sister, her Aunt Anny, Laura ran happily into their open arms, laughing with delight at their embrace. Those were the exceptions: Aunt Anny had her own life to lead; such "moments of being" were sporadic at best.

No longer quietly sequestered with her widowed father, Laura weighed on Hyde Park Gate, as Leslie's worries and remorse weighed on Julia, and this thankless cause, this heavy burden, excited her far less than others that drew her elsewhere. As she sent Virginia to distract Leslie from the beautiful Mrs. Gray, this time she undoubtedly drafted her son George Duckworth, a favorite with her husband. Leslie records this incident with feeling in his *Mausoleum Book*:

> Once when we were at St. Ives, my dear George, then a schoolboy, remonstrated with me, saying that his mother ought not to have such a task. I thanked him, I need not say, and fully agreed. I must add that in this matter I do not blame myself. I took considerable part in teaching or trying to teach Laura. I shall never forget the shock to me, when we were at Brighton after Mrs. Jackson's illness of 1879–80, I think. We had sent Laura to a "kindergarten" and the mistress told me that she would never learn to read. I resolved to try and succeeded in getting the poor child to read after a fashion, although I fear I too often lost my temper and was over-exacting. My darling Julia was, of course, vexed by my vexation and had her full share of trouble; but I do not think that my conduct in the matter caused her any needless trouble.[34]

But Laura?

After having been increasingly isolated and confined to one part of the house, she was sent away to special schools. Then, at nineteen, she was institutionalized, perhaps wrongly and certainly for life. She would live seventy-five years, abandoned in an asylum for nearly sixty of them, where her condition deteriorated completely.

After Stella and Leslie died, no one visited her, or only very infrequently, a distant relative perhaps, like a certain Dorothea Stephen who, during a visit with Virginia, spoke to her of Laura: "the same as ever, and never stops talking, and occasionally says, 'I told him to go away,' or 'Put it down, then,' quite sensibly; but the rest is unintelligible."[35]

The only time Virginia really includes her in her family is when, in "Old Bloomsbury," she mentions saying good-bye to Hyde Park Gate, where "not only had the furniture been dispersed. The family which had seemed equally wedged together had broken apart too," and she includes in that family a half-sister, "incarcerated with a doctor in an asylum." But that was a long time ago.[36]

Twelve years younger than Laura Stephen, Virginia Woolf died four years before her, and her every hour was lived simultaneously with those of that wasted life, discarded alive. A suppression perpetuated in the Woolfian opus, where she is practically omitted—we have just read one of the very rare passages mentioning her, a half dozen, including the following one—where Virginia willingly opts to leave her out of the biography of their father that Fred Maitland is preparing: "The history of Laura is really the most tragic thing in his [Leslie Stephen's] life I think; and one that one can hardly describe in the life."[37] Nevertheless, we will see how their brief cohabitation and her suppressed memory haunted Virginia. Her determination to forget it, to elude it, to erase all record of it may serve as proof of that.

She had witnessed Leslie's other daughter alienated, and thus rejected, despised, roughly handled, powerless. Locked up. Laura held Virginia spellbound, horror stricken and terrified. Laura's terrible difficulties with reading would drive Virginia to books as a child, to flaunting the incredible list of thick volumes she consumed. She knew that if you were called mad, you were at the mercy of a father, or a husband. And how not to think of the Great Lady of the Lake when Virginia ends up at the bottom of the River Ouse? Who was waiting for her there? Who would she go to rejoin?

Laura's would be a substantial legacy, growing from an initial investment that would have time to yield a profit. Leonard, widowed . . . would claim Virginia's share; to no avail. He was the one who remarked—on one of those rare occasions when Virginia mentioned this half-sister—that she was "the one we could have spared."[38]

Laura's mother's death: a disaster infinitely worse for her than Julia's death was for Julia's children. She was five years old when Minny was abruptly seized with convulsions one night and died the next day. It was Leslie's birthday (he would never celebrate it again). He was forty-three years old.

Now it was on the eve of this drama that Julia happened to appear in his life, when, as a young widow grieving for five years, she paid a neighborly visit to the Stephen couple, but found them to be so happy that she felt out of place, even sadder than usual, and she departed almost immediately. Only to return the next day to comfort Leslie, now the grief-stricken widower. Three years later, they were married. Twenty years later and Leslie relives this same drama, plunged into grief this time over Julia, who had become for him that "strange solemn music"[39] in which he had immersed himself. But also Julia Stephen, discretely elusive, impenetrable, and reticent, whom he now pursued posthumously, harassing her as he harassed their children.

The *Mausoleum Book* includes a litany on the intimacies of both marriages of both parents, Leslie the sole survivor among them. An exhibition of the conjugal feelings of the dead procreators, Herbert, Julia, Minny. Only Laura, in the asylum, will be spared word of the happiness her father provided his dear Minny. As for Herbert, he elicits some jealousy: "There is a touch of pain—I cannot deny it—in the clear consciousness . . . that my darling Julia owed her purest happiness to another man." Yet Leslie thanks his gallant posthumous rival for the "unqualified happiness," the "perfect happiness," he bestowed upon "my darling," who "made a complete surrender of herself in the fullest sense: she would have no reserves from her lover."[40]

Leslie paws through their personal lives, puts parental agonies and ecstasies on display. The *Mausoleum Book* is always proper and nevertheless oozes impropriety, especially since it was meant for children, fragile and grieving for their mother, a mother thus exposed, and for the Duckworths, exposed not by a father but by a second husband. Its sentimentality camouflages (or accentuates) the insinuated indecency. It flaunts a parental web permeated with tacit lusts, implicit omissions. Hyde Park Gate resounds with virtuous words, displays of remorse, sweet memories derived from the dead, aroused by her and behind which throb passions and desires that are very simply (and legitimately) sexual. But made mawkish, concealed under the dripping words of Victorian Anglicanism, they weigh even more heavily, equivocal, hybrid, in an atmosphere thick with cleverly circumvented prohibitions, furtively transgressed limits, with a licentiousness capable of transforming what would have been inevitable sexual deprivation, legitimate sexual urges, into depravity.

It is not Leslie's actions that are being questioned here, but the lugubrious, suspect atmosphere that he established, that he exuded, and his appetites masked under his lamentations; "in those days nothing was clear," writes Virginia. A lascivious, poisonous fog in which brothers and sisters struggled, that "choked us and blinded us," she recalls. An insidious permissiveness that would lead to incest but without coitus, as Lytton Strachey used to say. A groping, suspended kind of incest experienced openly and overtly and nevertheless unacknowledged.[41]

A long chapter in the life of Hyde Park Gate, which had become a trap. Stella's trap. The naturally and essentially submissive, devotedly self-sacrificing, malleable, and very beautiful Stella Duckworth, who could only accept Leslie Stephen as the sacred charge handed down from her mother. And who would henceforth provide him "any comfort, whatever its nature," according to Virginia. Who continues: "Whatever comfort she had to give. But what comfort could she give?" before noting "suddenly she was placed in the utmost intimacy" with this elderly man of letters, although, despite their long cohabitation, they hardly knew each other.[42]

He would descend upon this stepdaughter who so strangely resembled his "darling Julia" at the time of her beauty; he would depend upon her to such an extent that all she could absolutely depend upon was that dependence. Soon "she found that she had completely pledged herself to her stepfather; he expected entire self-surrender on her part," notes Virginia, who read the *Mausoleum Book* and knows the meaning Leslie gave to that expression.[43]

In *Moments of Being*, what is "impossible to say aloud,"[44] what is never said, surfaces: Virginia Woolf speaks *about* it, but without ever pronouncing *it*. For Virginia, nothing seemed to exist unless she wrote it down, she confided to Nicolson before writing it in her diary.

She gives explanations and finds excuses for what was merely suggested. Because Stella lacked self-confidence, "she gave indiscriminately, conscious that she had not the best of all to give." Being alone and unadvised, her stepfather considered it "his right." And Stella, who "could not give him intellectual companionship, . . . must give him the only thing she had." Virginia does not say what that was.[45]

But it is certainly what Virginia would have wanted both to reveal and to keep hidden in 1940, swept up in her memories: what alone was tangible: the suspicion. The suspense, the threat, the imprint of that which had not taken place.

Because there is nothing definite to say about that incest floating about Hyde Park Gate after Julia's death, in the form of fantasies. On Leslie's part, there were apparently only vague impulses, a duplicity paired with repression, and that repression oddly exhibited. What Virginia insinuates remains vague, but nevertheless seems relegated to the realm of the virtual: forbidden gestures would certainly be sidestepped, hardly hinted at; they would no doubt be avoided, like all overtly improper situations. Leslie Stephen was too attached to his illusions to shatter them so.

To his image and his convictions as well, to his own self-regard, his need to believe in his own innocence. But he and Stella knew what boundaries were crossed.

How far? The innuendos resound, equivocal, marked with shame, in the two documents that point to and clearly reflect what Leslie Stephen elsewhere managed to leave vague: two letters addressed to Stella Duckworth and eventually released by her. The first, from the very day she married Jack Waller Hills, a marriage that Leslie would have so liked to prevent; the second, three days later. Two years have passed since Julia's death.

An excerpt from the first letter. It is addressed to Stella Hills, married that same morning:

> My darling daughter. . . . The world seems to have turned topsy-turvy with me since this morning & I feel as I felt when I picked myself up after a fall—I cannot tell whether I am hurt or healed of a wound or simply dazzled. . . . The terrible sorrow I have gone through has taught me to know you as I never knew you before & to feel that you have— what could I say more expressive?—the same nature as my darling. I said to her that I not only loved but reverenced her & I never said a truer thing. Now one cannot exactly reverence a daughter but I have the feeling wh. corresponds to it—you may find a name for it—but I mean that my love of you is something more than mere affection, it includes complete confidence & trust. Well, I will say no more. It is only repeating what you know. Love me still & tell me sometimes that you love me. Good bye![46]

Under the guise of paternal duty and a passion devoted exclusively to Julia, Leslie hoped to be understood without risk, but here is a confession that, moreover, includes its retraction, as well as contrition, desire, a pathetic attempt to maintain the ambiguity of an equivocal—and now impossible—relationship. This is not a matter of a single, unusual outburst, but of a final effort to continue that morbid, covert game, played daily until now with his stepdaughter; a subterfuge aimed at maintaining it, which he knew to be in vain. With regard to his troubled relations with Stella, this is indeed his swan song.

Leslie was reminding the newly married wife of Jack Hills; he had already said such things to her, without saying what had to be kept quiet but that Stella understood, since she knew that she could not listen to her stepfather were he to express himself otherwise. Stella knew and he knew it, and she knew that he knew she was aware of the profaned memory of her mother, used to hide the meaning of tortuously convoluted behavior. They both knew what Leslie was trying to pull, and that it couldn't succeed. The others knew it as well. They were all ashamed—above all, of knowing.

Virginia's depression, her (feeble) suicide attempt after the death of her father, otherwise so dignified but faltering here, would stem from remorse at having once caught him unawares. For having suspected him, and even worse, detected the illicit behavior, the transgression, indeed the violation, and above all, for having guessed him to be secretly ashamed. And worst of all: discredited.

Virginia is quick to excuse her half-sister . . . of what she does not specify. But does she see Stella's role as so clear and simple? A certain rancor comes through, a certain irony. An unasked question is left hanging: how did the reserved, humble, inexpressive Stella position herself in relation to their mother? And to this stepfather? In this dark period, beneath her passiveness, beyond the pain of her abiding grief and the now definitive absence of her mother, was she taking revenge in some timid, confused, covert way (no longer the "Old Cow"), or seeking a deeper intimacy with the maternal idol? Or even just fulfilling a sacred mission, Julia's legacy . . . or all those things combined with, especially (or perhaps simply), a permanently masked and vanquished repulsion for her stepfather's theatrics, at once chaste and perverse? Stella, so pale and growing ever paler in her mourning dress, whom Virginia often caught in tears, though she would immediately hide them, her face turning suddenly serene. Stella, whom Virginia also caught ("often one would break in upon a scene of this kind") throwing her arms around a wailing Leslie.[47]

Stella Duckworth. Virginia Stephen. Perhaps Virginia harbored a feeling of being usurped by Stella, who always protected her, of being wronged by the daughter of Herbert, who had always kept this other father in his place until then, a father easy to love, unquestionably commended.

And who was now only a poor widower, an amorous old man, as incapable of disguising it as of accepting it: only capable of creating the libidinous space that would close with the two letters he sent to Stella after her marriage.

An excerpt from the second letter, written three days later, to say that he had nothing to say and that he no longer wanted to divulge his feelings:

one way or other, uttered myself rather too abundantly, if anything & must hold my tongue for a bit. . . . I shall probably be rather irregular, as I am afraid of not being a very cheerful correspondent. My love to———I cannot find a satisfactory name for him yet—was he ever called Waller? My dearest, I have tried to hold my tongue, as I said, though I fear that something may have peeped out. You will forgive it, I know; I wonder if I shall ever be able to write a cheerful letter. Your loving father, L.S.[48]

Nothing would "peep out" before that summer morning in London during the war when, with France defeated, Virginia turned toward a father not entirely capable of holding his tongue about what was "impossible to say aloud" regarding Stella, and for which "one of the consequences was that for some time life seemed to us in a chronic state of confusion."[49]

And when in 1940 she groped about in that difficult past and tried to record what could be said aloud, what she and Vanessa could still discuss regarding the terror, frustration, and rage caused by their father, her avoidance was still so strong that she altered the dates, shifting them forward so that Stella no longer played any part in what made Leslie suspect to his daughters. Virginia begins with their indignation over Stella's death; Stella Hills, dead three months after her marriage.

And the whip had struck for the second time.

Virginia writes that she and Vanessa found themselves alone, facing their father, "fully exposed without protection to the full blast of that strange character."[50] Aware that the terms "exposed" and "strange character" are loaded, she promises to explain them, but moves on to another topic without doing so.

The weight of the words remains. Like the weight of "illicit," which she uses to explain the violence of Leslie's weekly rages against Vanessa when she presents him with the house accounts, for which she is responsible following Stella's death. According to Virginia, these rages came from an "*illicit*"[51] need for sympathy, released by the woman, stimulated," which, when refused, "stirred in him instincts of which he was unconscious. Yet also ashamed."[52]

Here, a gap!

The violence, the seriousness of the reminiscences and the reactions prompted by Leslie do not square with their pretexts. Virginia locates the horror of those "unhappy years"[53] in a minor conflict and thus hides the seriousness of the trouble caused and experienced by a man successively in love with a mother and daughter. The daughter now dead, Virginia removes her from the scene and focuses on other situations and events, involving a different sister, as the source of her own fury, indignation, and obsessive rage.

In particular, one weekly domestic scene: each Wednesday, Vanessa, supposedly replacing the dead Stella who herself replaced the dead Julia, came to give her father the house accounts and unleashed his fury. But unlike Julia, who conspired with the cook to falsify those accounts, or Stella, who was no doubt terrified, "Nessa," as her family called her, would not tolerate those demonstrations that, Virginia emphasizes, echoed "other words of the same kind, addressed to the sister lately dead, to her mother even." Implacable, she remained impassive, unperturbed by her father's anger, which further exasperated Leslie, who erupted hysterically, proclaimed himself ruined, alone, misunderstood, and, red-faced, veins bulging, worked himself up into "an extraordinary dramatisation of self pity, horror, anger," beating his breast, roaring: "Have you no pity for me? There you stand like a block of stone," before signing the check with a flourish, with trembling hand, and collapsing, a prostrate spectacle, while Virginia gritted her teeth, powerless and mute, stifling her "unbounded comtempt."[54]

Chauvinist, Victorian, but most of all ridiculous, these rages of Leslie Stephen are straightforward, routine, and long familiar: those of an anxious man who fanatically imagines himself on the edge of ruin. Even in Minny's time, his conflicts with Anny Thackeray, who lived with the couple and kept the house accounts, often verged on high drama, as did their disagreement over Minny's estate after she died. When she watched over Leslie, stricken with cancer, for the two long years of his decline, Virginia would again write: "I hope as the weakness increases he will worry less about money."[55]

Trying ordeals, indeed, those Wednesdays, but stripped of troubling innuendos, there was nothing "illicit"[56] about them. They could arouse indignation, fear, outrage, but they do not correspond to the feelings of intense threat and convulsive panic Virginia records, the memory alone making her recoil, suffocated, ravaged by the horror, decades later—and less than six months before her death.

They are a kind of memory screen: they cover another memory tied to what is "impossible to say aloud."[57] Thus diverted, the masked distress can, through other memories, emit its cry, as the complaint that escapes from Virginia Woolf more than forty years later.

Leslie's pretentious displays of anger, suffered by his daughter over domestic problems, ward off the memory of his more shameful behavior toward his stepdaughter. And Virginia would be able to transfer to those scenes inflicted upon Vanessa all the rage and frustration aroused by Leslie's suspect behavior toward Stella, allowing her to remain silent, to insist, even to herself, that nothing happened, that Stella was not the object of "illicit" desires that created a "chronic state of confusion" never to be resolved.[58]

The spectacular hysterics to which Vanessa was subjected provide a screen for other quieter, intensely secret scenes bordering on illegal and vastly more disturbing, pernicious and furtive, of which Stella was the object. It is very much those scenes and that "strange" father whom we discover lurking beneath Leslie Stephen's displays of miserliness, playing the wounded patriarch, imploring the aid of his stepdaughter—"whatever its nature," that would haunt Virginia long afterward, unbidden.[59]

Let us watch her once again, searching for the right word to best express the turbulent scenes suffered by Vanessa. She crosses out the word "violent," which is appropriate, to substitute the term "illicit," which does not correspond, and describes the feelings aroused in her as she is writing, not by those Wednesday scenes but by the ones they screen out.[60]

"Illicit": what is forbidden by law, accomplished or attempted in an insidious way; what Leslie coveted, acknowledged to be impossible, experienced as taboo, a wild dream, but which he approached and aped to the point that the prohibition he tested threatened to appear in all its crudeness.

With that term, linked to his "dependence on women," and his need for them "to sympathise with him, to console him," Virginia Woolf introduces Stella Duckworth, in pages meant to exclude and cover only the seven years after her death.[61]

Thus what is silenced emerges in silence: the insidious threat of incest suffered by Stella when she was alive, which Virginia had guessed. It is that memory, unacknowledged, that produces "the horror, the recurring terror" felt by Virginia Stephen when Leslie vented his rage at Vanessa. "It was like being shut up in the same cage with a wild beast."[62]

It was not the father objecting violently to the kitchen accounts that alarmed Virginia, whose "next victim" she feared becoming, along with Vanessa, as they recalled how he had "tasked Stella's strength, embittered her few months of joy." No. They feared the man in love with a mother and her daughter, their half-sister, both of whom were now dead. That man forced to circumvent an "illicit" path in the lifetime of the timid, devoted Stella, and to become the humble, humiliated, deceitful creature who overshadowed the proud father of the past. The hypocritical roles that they all had to play at Hyde Park Gate. And the suspicions, the uncertainty, the silence and its cesspools: that code of silence Virginia Stephen would never break. Nor would Virginia Woolf.[63]

Here she is at fifty-eight years old; the war is on, Leonard has persuaded her to commit suicide with him if the Nazis invade England, and two days ago France was defeated. We know the scenario: an organ-grinder in a London square, a man selling strawberries, and Virginia, at her worktable, turns toward her father and sees herself again, fantasizes herself at fifteen, shut up in a cage with him: "He was the pacing, danger-ous, morose lion; a lion who was sulky and angry and injured; and suddenly ferocious, and then very humble, and then majestic; and then lying dusty and fly pestered in a corner of the cage." Here she is, hardly a year before her death, facing the memory of a defiled, undisciplined father, at once terrifying and discredited, stripped of prestige and threatening.[64]

A father immediately defined as extremely imprudent, who "had so ignored, or disguised his own feelings that he had no idea of what he was; . . . he was uncivilized in his extreme unawareness. He did not realise what he did."[65]

So many substrata, so many secrets throughout the years, so many mysteries and hidden elements. Nothing is certain; everything trembles, furtive, is hidden or hardly shows, hesitates around Virginia, and it is that trembling that she must capture, that reveals the disgrace suffered by a father and the unspeakable shame of having detected him. As if it were a matter of a shameless vision, even a violation perpetrated on a parent.

To a large extent, the most enduring difficulties arise from the coexis-tence of that corrupt father and the one so admired and respected, because Leslie Stephen remained intact, unscathed, pursuing his serious friend-ships, his life of writing and books; he forever remained the naïve, austere, honest intellectual, often full of wit, reverently surrounded by the thinkers of his day, even if he suspected himself of mediocrity.

Leslie was also that unequivocal father, passionate about his children, faithfully sharing their daily lives, walks, sports, thoughts: the one who for a long time drew and cut out paper animal chains for them; read out loud to them at night from Tennyson, Wordsworth, Scott, Meredith, and so on; made them debate freely, form judgments, indignant if they preferred a bland hero to some more captivating villain. He was truly "in league"[66] with childhood, with all his children. Up to a point: Laura was the exception.

Even with her humiliating memories, Virginia does not forget how she always admired, how she still admires "his honesty, his unworldliness, his lovableness, his perfect sincerity," as well as "his attractiveness . . . his simplicity, his integrity, his eccentricity. . . . He would say exactly what he thought, however inconvenient; and do what he liked." And that was true . . . as a rule.[67]

Most importantly, he always encouraged Vanessa and Virginia in their vocations: Vanessa in pursuing her painting classes, Virginia in immersing herself in his vast library, accompanying her in her reading, without censorship.

How to reconcile all that with Hyde Park Gate in mourning, dominated by this same father who, at Julia's death, had "replaced the beauty and merriment of the dead with ugliness"? How to reconcile the deception and betrayal with those "shocks of sharp pleasure" when Leslie happened to fix his "very small, very blue" eyes on her with this message: we are "in league," the two of us. That writer and her.[68]

Here begin Virginia's experiences as the future writer, by way of the child hungry for books, which she devoured one after another, guided by the father who supplied her: "I remember his pleasure, how he stopped writing and got up and was very gentle and pleased, when I came into the study with a book I had done; and asked him for another." There she found him, smoking his pipe, rocking in his rocking chair where he always sat to work. "Slowly he would unwrinkle his forehead and come to ground and realize with a very sweet smile that I stood there. Rising he would go to the shelves, put the book back, and ask me gently, kindly; 'What did you make of it?'" And his daughter left the study "feeling proud and stimulated, and full of love for this unworldly, very distinguished and lonely man, whom I had pleased by coming."[69]

The young Stephens rediscovered their father's unconventional free spirit when he showed them the way to pursue their previous life and render it even more meaningful by using their sorrow to intensify everything. "Beautiful he was at such moments; simple and eager as a child; and exquisitely alive to all affection; exquisitely tender . . . —but the moment passed."[70]

Nine years later, mourning Leslie, Virginia wrote to her comforter Violet Dickinson: "It was a most exquisite feeling to be with him, even to touch his hand—he was so quick, and that one finds in no one else."[71]

It was this conflict that tore her apart. Leslie was a composite, as each of us is, of so many portraits, facets, ghosts, so many various beings—or not. It is Virginia Woolf who asks, "Do we then know nobody? Only our versions of them, which as likely as not, are emanations of ourselves."[72]

Who was Leslie Stephen apart from his daughter's memories?

A daughter forever tortured by the ambivalence of her feelings for her father; by the repression that paralyzed her, prevented her from either blaming or reconciling with him.

After all, Leslie Stephen faltered just once, and without overstepping the bounds. He deviated momentarily before entering a solitary old age; the hope of escaping or at least delaying it had seized him, instinctively, hope of overcoming a wife's absence through the grace of Stella. A crisis. A crisis of aging and grief. But one that would compromise, if not Virginia's life, at least what lay hidden there: her memory, which would henceforth become a prison, marked by a fatal wound that would not heal.

Incest: Stephen did not physically practice it (his denunciatory letters to Stella seem to prove that), he only overtly fantasized it, verged on it with Stella Duckworth and hopefully her alone; in this sense, his daughters had nothing to fear from him. Nonetheless, the foul atmosphere of Hyde Park Gate, which had become a crypt, had penetrated its inhabitants, and it was an atmosphere of incest.

* * *

We will not go into the question posed by Virginia in the name of one of her novel's inhabitants: "Do I love my father sexually?" Quite a rational question, after all. But when Lytton Strachey brought her reports from the "British Sex Society's" discussion on incest between parents and children when they were both unconscious of it, Virginia's reaction was: "I think of becoming a member."[73]

While we are digressing, let us add, without comment, some strange signs involving a gesture with which we are already familiar.

We will remember Leslie Stephen, arms extended, staggering out of the room where Julia had just died. In some of the most beautiful pages of *To the Lighthouse*, some of the most beautiful Virginia Woolf wrote, she manages to write the impossible (but an "impossible" vanquished this time): a whole section of the work is devoted solely to the house deserted by the Ramsays ("the thing that exists when we aren't there"), throbbing with emptiness, out of time and entering the vibrant inertia of its abandonment, the rare echo of events. Someone dies at the Ramsays'. Each time, two cold lines punctuate the loss. And the first of those losses, like the others, appears in brackets: "[Mr. Ramsay, stumbling along a passage one dark morning, stretched his arms out, but Mrs. Ramsay having died rather suddenly the night before, his arms, though stretched out, remained empty.]"[74]

Elsewhere, in *The Years*, Colonel Pargiter also leaves a deathbed, but the one of a wife he does not love. He staggers out of the room, arms extended in front of him, passing his daughter Delia, who thinks: "You did that very well, Delia told him as he passed her. It was like a scene in a play."[75]

But when little Rose Pargiter, hardly more than a baby, sneaks out of the house and finds herself alone in the night, frightened, facing a man who "leered at her," he extends his arms "as if to stop her" and she runs, takes refuge in a shop; coming back, he is still there, grimacing, and this time, we read in *The Years*, "he did not stretch his hands out at her; they were unbuttoning his clothes."[76]

❧ ❧ ❧

End of parentheses. Let us leave the substrata, the underground places of the unspoken, their hell. Let us return to the adolescent still filled with trepidation, crossing the London streets on her bicycle, and who does not know, will never know, that she is overwhelmingly beautiful, and who is struggling to master everyday life, to move through it day after day, determined. Resigned to continue. Disciplined.

On the surface, the Stephens' life unfolds courageously, energetically, in another kind of hell—the hell of monotony, a routine that Virginia nevertheless needed, revolving around a network of stable, traditional occupations, a conventional course providing a structure that could alleviate their grief and its aggressions.

"Life goes on," we say, even if it doesn't exactly go on and the life of those repeating that refrain won't either, one day.

Down the unnerving streets of London, which she sees bristling with whinnying, kicking, rearing horses, with cars running into each other and over pedestrians, Virginia, trembling and tenacious, steers her bicycle. Through this city where she also knows familiar shops overflowing with notebooks, erasers, writing pens, gifts, consoling strawberry ices, irresistible buns, ineffable chocolates. She often walks in the parks here, especially Kensington Park, with her father or Vanessa, sometimes a brother or a half-brother, often with Stella. They go to the theater, they go skating, they visit the museums, the zoo, as a family or in pairs.

Virginia regularly sees Dr. Seton, who regularly advises rest, milk, medications—no lessons, but rather gardening in the Hyde Park Gate courtyard, where nothing ever grows. Concerts, visits, shopping are allowed; in short, a so-called normal life.

Virginia Stephen applies herself to living, vigilant, with conviction. Still a bit distraught. She records her way of submitting to life in a diary begun in 1897, the strange year with the promising start: Stella is engaged.

Let us listen to the version Quentin Bell offers or rather invents, a version that will stand as part of the quasi-official account of her life. This was a period of valor in the face of mourning, a time of latent hope and struggle that Virginia navigated in an almost dreamlike way, as through a strange fog. The mark of it would remain, offered by Bell as the main theme of her destiny; Virginia Woolf's legend would be built around it.

He decides upon a serious "breakdown" suffered by Virginia at her mother's death, "madness" that he admits leaves no trace and that no one remembers! It "must have" come over a young girl of thirteen, whose mother had just died suddenly.[77]

Here is what Quentin Bell gives (or rather doesn't give) as proof of these bizarre allegations, and here is the terrifying use he makes of them:

> The first "breakdown," or whatever we are to call it, *must have*[78] come very soon after her mother's death. And here we come to a great interval of nothingness, a kind of positive death which cannot be described and of which Virginia herself probably knew little—that is to say could recall little—and yet which is vitally important to her story. From now on she knew that she had been mad and might be mad again.[79]

Where did he get all that? It's a mystery. From what evidence, what document, what testimony? None. A description? Impossible, he admits. She herself says nothing of it? That's because she forgot it! But who remembered it? Silence. And nevertheless . . .

And nevertheless Bell declares "vitally important" the version he advances, totally arbitrarily, in this first biography of Virginia Woolf, which becomes her effigy. Invigorated by the certitudes he has just advanced, listen to what he dares to assert next: "To know that you have had cancer in your body and to know that it may return must be very horrible; but a cancer of the mind, a corruption of the spirit striking one at the age of thirteen, and for the rest of one's life always working away somewhere, always in suspense, a Dionysian [*sic*] sword above one's head—this must be almost unendurable." And in conclusion: "So unendurable that in the end, when the voices of insanity spoke to her in 1941, she took the only remedy that remained, the cure of death." And there you have it![80]

Q.E.D.

Leonard's version is established.

Nevertheless, a mystery remains: between the ages of thirteen and fifty-nine, her mind ravaged by cancer, her spirit thoroughly corrupted, Virginia Woolf really did write a few pages (one wonders how!), but the real question is: why the hell did she wait so long to do herself in?

Of course, it would have been abnormal for Virginia at thirteen not to go through extreme states following the disruptive death of her mother, but no trace of that remains. Agitation? Dejection? Denial? Shattered nerves? We can imagine them all, but there is not a single bit of evidence. Even if she had gone through some very bad periods, even if she had suffered delirium or hallucinations, they would not have warranted Quentin Bell's definitive diagnosis. A child's sadness over her mother's death, whatever her reaction's magnitude and manifestations, would not have been a matter in itself of "madness," especially in the sinister, simplistic, rigid sense that Quentin Bell uses the term. But more importantly, *nothing* attests to such behavior on Virginia Stephen's part after Julia's death. And still more importantly, Bell knows it!

Furthermore, Virginia herself, who never recoils from the idea of "madness," who would never have hesitated to mention and even to comment on such episodes if they had taken place, *never* refers to them *anywhere*, not even when she reconsiders (as she often does) this period of her past. And no one else alludes to them, not Leslie in his letters, not Vanessa later, no one close to her; not, through hearsay, a single acquaintance. Only Leonard, in his autobiography, speaks (obviously he doesn't *remember*) of a first serious crisis and a suicide attempt following Julia's death: at thirteen, Virginia supposedly threw herself out a low window without doing herself much harm. An actual event, but one that took place nine years later, at Violet Dickinson's house and after the death of . . . Leslie, whom Leonard confuses with Julia!

Quentin Bell presents his diagnosis like a definitive, established fact, drawn from proven, demonstrated information, even while he reports the absence of such information and offers only the diagnosis. Everything is invented, surmised.

And that is how myths are born.

* * *

Let us leave them and turn now to Virginia watching Stella Duckworth and Jack Hills approaching one summer evening near Haslemere. An anxious, almost mysterious evening. Jack has been pursuing Stella since Julia's time, Julia having defended him against her daughter's rejections. That honest young man, without great charisma, according to Julia, but with rare perseverance and very much in love, has finally won Stella over and opened her eyes to Leslie's hold on her. He plays what has become an invaluable role in her life.

It is 1896. Julia has been dead for a year. The Stephens and Duckworths are on vacation. Jack Hills has come by bicycle to dine with them. Stella takes him to see the garden. It is a "black and silver night," as experienced by an ardent Virginia. A moonlit night. From the garden, the young Stephens see the couple pass by, disappear, pass by again; for a moment they hear the rustling of a dress, a whisper, then nothing more. They imagine that Jack and Stella have gone back into the house, return to join them, but find Leslie alone, agitated, crossing and recrossing his legs, watching the clock, fidgeting. A strange tramp enters the grounds; he is hungry; Thoby chases him off (!) with much commotion and the others are a bit afraid, "for it was no ordinary night, and ominous things were happening." It is getting later, Leslie is pacing back and forth on the terrace; someone shouts: "Stella and Mr Hills are coming up the path together!" and Stella, usually so pale, arrives "blushing the loveliest rose colour," to say "she was engaged." Under her breath Virginia asks her: "'Did mother know?'" and Stella "murmured, 'Yes.'" [81]

Breakfast. Adrian, the youngest Stephen, is crying. He was Julia's favorite child, she called him "My Joy," and the others have always kept him a little at a distance. His father prefers Thoby. Adrian is all alone and Stella, his refuge, is going away. Leslie gently lectures him: they must all share the fiancée's happiness . . . although he complains to her a moment later that "the blow was irreparable." He will prolong the couple's wait, delay the wedding as long as possible. This engagement? Ten months of "clumsy, cruel, unnecessary trial" imposed by the moralist.[82]

Stella's life goes on, still burdened with the lives of others, with Virginia always at her side, whom she protects; just a few additional purchases for Jack, like the chocolate éclairs for his tea, a few more things to mend. Stella often visits him; he dines every evening at Hyde Park Gate.

In her diary, which never mentions her mourning or her mother, Virginia reports on the uniformity of the days, takes pains to enter the events, to feel what they mean, but as though at a distance. She seems to mimic what should be felt, or else to violently reject some detail, only to embrace it immediately afterward, resigned. She struggles to merge her own presence into the world's or to integrate the world's presence, which shrinks away, except when she is reading, insatiably addicted to the authors whose works she devours like a glutton, dissolving into them, enchanted. Alive. Approaching the edge of herself.

Nevertheless, Hyde Park Gate grows lighter, the future suddenly has a place there, the color seems to return as much to Stella's cheeks as to her eyes, now "bluer," to the "incandescence [that] was in Stella's whole body." "Something of moonlight" seems to emanate from her now. Filled with wonder, Virginia compares the love of these two young people to a ruby. Young people? Stella is twenty-eight, Jack, thirty-one.[83]

By way of the approaching marriage, Virginia enters into the—now welcome—banality of the elite, not quite aristocratic, society; rituals are performed, related to the moment at hand, the upcoming wedding: rituals of a formidably conventional environment, which the two Stephen sisters will escape.

Ceremony unfolds according to protocol. Gifts pour in; invitations, dressmakers, hairdressers. Even Leslie, muttering that any old clothes will do just fine, orders himself a new suit. Stella takes Adrian along to buy him one as well. Ecstasy over the opal and diamond necklace Gerald gives his betrothed sister, as prelude to his promised wedding present. Presents flood in from everywhere. A dismayed Virginia shares the role of maid of honor with Vanessa. The banns are read, as they had to be then, as part of a religious service. And the family, solidly agnostic, searches everywhere for a few prayer books. During the ceremony, they don't know when to kneel, and Virginia refuses to do so.

The hundreds of presents must be displayed, the flowers arranged, the nerves calmed. Tense, uneasy, often strangely quiet, Virginia and Vanessa promise each other to remain calm and collected.

In the absence of her father, the handsome Herbert, and to the indignation of Gerald and especially of George, the eldest, whose prerogative it is, Leslie does not think for a moment of not leading Stella to the altar himself. And he is right. For better or, more recently, for worse, hasn't he been the *pater familias* of this blended family for almost twenty years?

Virginia goes through those hours as though in a fog; recording them in her diary seems to her to verify the reality to which she submits, mechanically or sometimes with conviction, most often resigned. She threads her life through the days and begins to feel a growing interest in them, punctuated with bursts of pleasure or anger, but muted, whereas the blind obedience expected of young girls at that time remains a constant. Through those days, the diary begins to vibrate nevertheless, often with what she does not write but that trembles, however vague, below the surface.

The house is no longer so much under the yoke of the past. Hyde Park Gate looks toward the future, busying itself with the classic preparations for a conventional Victorian wedding. Leslie is surprised at no longer being able to delay the union: "I could do perfectly well without Jack—Why should not she?"[84] he writes to an old friend, Charles Norton. Unimpeachable logic!

But the day comes. The moment arrives.

Leslie appears with Stella on his arm, "very white and beautiful"; what he is feeling then, no one will ever know. She moves forward, she walks "in her sleep—her eyes fixed straight in front of her." And what she is feeling—but this is true for every event in her life—will also remain unknown. It all seems to be a strange dream, a vision. "It was half a dream, or a nightmare. Stella was almost dreaming, I think; but probably hers was a happy one." The evening before, she had lost an opal ring that Jack had given her.[85]

The newlyweds depart for Italy. "Mr and Mrs Hills!"[86] exclaims Virginia.

The next day George Duckworth takes Gerald and the young Stephens to place the wedding flowers on their mother's grave in the Hydegate cemetery.

The first mention of Julia in her daughter's diary.

The newlyweds must return from Italy two weeks later, but Stella takes things in hand: to Leslie's outrage and despair, she refuses to live with Jack at 22 Hyde Park Gate. They will live . . . at 24.

Not for long.

* * *

Not many lives were tortured and fretted and made numb with non-being as ours were then. That in shorthand, was the legacy of those two great unnecessary blunders; those two lashes of the random unheeding, unthinking flail that brutally and pointlessly killed the two people who should have made those years normal and natural, if not "happy."[87]

Virginia had behind her an entire body of work, fifty-eight years of life; she had six more months to live, and here we find her again, in 1940, in the midst of war, sounding this cry, repeating the same unanswerable question, from which she cannot get free.

Forty-three years earlier, Stella had returned from her honeymoon ill. It was thought to be an intestinal flu. A nurse stayed with her. The nightmare began again, "everyone getting miserable. Everything as dismal as it well can be."[88] The whip was going to strike once more. Everyone feared or sensed it.

Stella was in pain. Dr. Seton made some "frightening" remarks. More nurses were called. The sign of grave illness: straw spread in the street to lessen the noise of the car wheels and horses' hooves. "No getting rid of the thought." No mention of Julia's death, which loomed. Virginia took refuge in her beloved "Macaulay, which is the only calm and un-anxious thing in this most agitating time."[89]

The next day, Stella improved, was no longer in pain. The doctor declared her out of danger. Until the end, Seton said he was "pleased," "delighted," "perfectly happy," "still more satisfied," "most cheerful," and "very cheerful." He would recommend eating ices for the peritonitis, avoiding cherries and chocolate. Stella was pregnant, he said.[90]

Three months of fluctuations, of relapses and remissions: "Now that old cow is most ridiculously well & cheerful—hopping about out of bed etc," ventured Virginia; once Stella came for lunch at 22 Hyde Park Gate and she and Virginia sat together in the park for a while, chatting as in the old days. "Mr. Henry James" met them; they ran into Leslie; the two men headed off together into the gardens. Stella could soon return to the London streets with Virginia; then the nurses returned, the doctor three times a day, the pain, the panic, the improvement; calm settled in from time to time, uneasiness remained.[91]

Whether Stella was doing well or poorly, Virginia's distress never left her, though she hid it, and her terror of the city and its traffic knew no bounds: "Hyde St even more diabolical than usual—the horses in a most wicked & rampant condition." Accidents occurred one after another, which she kept watch for obsessively. The same month: "I managed to discover a man in the course of being squashed by an omnibus, but, as we were in the midst of Piccadilly Circus, the details of the accident could not be seen"; three days later she "had the pleasure of seeing a cart horse fall down." There were nothing but mad horses escaping into the crowds, car collisions, an overturned hansom, a crushed cyclist—the surprise of being right about the danger of crossing the streets on foot and finding oneself at home, safe and sound. The daily carriage outings with Stella, convalescing from a bad bout, and Virginia daily gritting her teeth, in a panic.[92]

Chaos on the streets, the chaos of those weeks. The pretense of leading a normal life, even a little festive: visits with friends, mad laughter, tears of hysterical laughter, concerts, boating, and ice cream orgies; at dinner, Gerald told funny stories,[93] "indecent" ones, actually; other evenings, the guests listened with delight as Leslie recited Tennyson's *Maud* or Macaulay's *The Armada*. Nessa, wearing a gown by the famous Mrs. Young, made a magnificent entrance into society—and Stella in seventh heaven, playing the proud mother's role, though from her bedroom. She takes three steps into the street, goes out in the park in a wheelchair, then relapses and remains bedridden, then improves and can be up in her dressing gown, improves some more, returns to an almost normal, slow-paced life, goes through a crisis, is in pain—perhaps from having eaten three cherries, pronounces Dr. Seton, who fails to understand the problem. Sometimes he claims to have prevented or impeded the development of peritonitis.

No one acting. Everyone waiting.

Volumes flowed through Virginia's hands: Pepys in four volumes and all of dear Macaulay; Carlyle's *Cromwell* in a matter of weeks, three volumes; the letters of William Cowper; a work by Leslie Stephen: *Life of Henry Fawcett*; Lady Burton's memoir, two volumes; George Eliot's *Adam Bede*; Charlotte Brontë's *Shirley*; a *History of Rome* by Arnold, followed by one of England by Froude . . . twelve volumes! Books were "the greatest help and comfort." Virginia raced through each work more quickly than the last, impatient to choose another recommended by an impressed, almost worried father—"Ginia is devouring books, almost faster than I like."[94]

Stella was struggling, but who knew against what? Is it absurd to write this? Julia seemed to be lurking. As for Jack, he was sad, no question. Stella still played (she had to play) the role of protectress, responsible party. Leslie kept his distance, rediscovered his rightful place; he seems to have been indifferent to Stella's illness. At her death, everyone would notice his detachment, Jack with indignation. The reaction of jealousy appeased? Dare we say of old passion avenged? Or perhaps, more than resigned: satiated?

Virginia, however, spent her time at Stella's house, would not leave her alone. We can sense her panic, silent, petrified. Her terror. In the midst of a suffocating heat wave. One cousin thought it "so bad for Stella to have Ginia always with her." Another day, Virginia grumbles about "that old shop keeper Mrs Hills," Jack's mother, who turned her out of her daughter-in-law's house after five minutes.[95]

But Virginia came back, she returned every day; she clung, she hung on. The nightmare vaguely continued, without tragic moments, without remitting. The flail threatened. Ups and downs succeeded one another, and that disparity itself made the days around Stella all seem alike. Virginia does not say it, but knows them to be almost over.

The whip would strike for the second time, and it was the memory of the first time that was on everyone's mind for weeks, especially Virginia's.

Beginning July 10, the diary is abandoned, until July 27. Stella died on July 19. From memory, the adolescent filled in the gaps. And gradually the portrait of the dying Stella emerges . . . at Virginia's bedside.

His daughters would accuse Leslie of having worn out first Julia and then Stella, of having broken them, killed them under the weight of his demands and managerial tasks . . . surrounded by seven servants. We know that the truth with regard to Stella, or rather the trouble, had nothing to do with overwork.

But for this whole agonizing time, it was Virginia who, racked with terror and repressed distress, plagued her half-sister, occupied the whole field, encroached upon Jack, required care, demanded the attention, solicitude, and last moments of the patient whose doctors and passive entourage let her die.

Everything was going wrong. Jack was suffering from an abscessed leg. Gerald had fallen ill. Stella arranged for their care. On July 11, it was Virginia's turn to feel sick with rheumatism, and to seek out Stella who, stretched out on a sofa, was taking tea with Jack close by in a "big chair." Virginia sat at their feet, and Jack soon left the room. "We talked together," Virginia writes contentedly. The next day, she managed to impose upon them for the entire day: Stella would not let her leave, the rheumatism was too painful. Thanks to which, she took Jack's place in the "big chair."[96]

She was simply regressing, like a weak, plaintive, defeated child. And dependent, demanding. Desperate.

July 14: at Stella's house, she declares herself worse, with a mild fever, and achieves her goal: Dr. Seton sends her to bed . . . at the Hills', in Jack's dressing room, across from their bedroom. And Stella sits with her for a long time. The next day, after refusing to see her in the morning, Stella spends the afternoon with her, brings her tea . . . before going to prepare tea for Leslie, next door at 22! At the end of the day, Virginia suffers from "the fidgets," nervous agitation, and Stella rubs her forehead until she calms down . . . till eleven o'clock at night.

The next morning: "She came in to me before breakfast in her dressing gown to see how I was. She only stayed a moment, but then she was quite well. She left me, & I never saw her again."[97]

Stella takes a turn for the worse and is in pain. No one tells Virginia, to whom Stella often calls through the open doors to ask how she is doing. July 17: Virginia is sent home by a doctor, in the arms of George, wrapped in Stella's fur coat, and as they passes her room, Stella calls good-bye to her. July 18: an operation is scheduled for that evening. July 19 at 3 a.m.: George and Nessa come to announce to Virginia that Stella Hills is dead.

No one in the family attends the burial. Five days later, Jack takes Virginia and Nessa to the tomb, beside Julia's, "near you as you go in."[98] We have nothing to add.

* * *

Leslie would be next on the list of the dead. Seven years later, intestinal cancer. Virginia would care for him day after day, for two years. She would often be eager for the end to come, and with his death, the waiting was over. Guaranteed remorse! That would haunt her for the rest of her life.

Vanessa continued to detest their father and kept her distance.

Since we have already confronted the question of incest between Leslie Stephen and his stepdaughter, Stella Duckworth, hardly detected until now, it is time to consider the Duckworth brothers, George and Gerald, whose incestuous misdeeds are much better known. They are both considered, George in particular (the two sisters saw to that), to have ruined Virginia's life.

Virginia would hardly mention the horrible manual exploration of her "private parts"[99] by Gerald, when he was seventeen and she was five years old, and her sharp awareness of the shame and the seriousness of the offense. But at fifty-nine years old, she would tremble with shame again, three months before her death, at the memory of that violation, which she had almost left unrecorded.

George, on the other hand, would become the target for the two sisters, delighted to divulge his infamy throughout Bloomsbury. Virginia would devote a bitter, hilarious session of the Memoir Club to him. Together Vanessa and Virginia took great pleasure in ridiculing him when their paths crossed (less and less often) as he aged, gracelessly, according to them, increasingly trapped in his conventional shell and his self-importance, whereas they would free themselves from whatever or whomever resembled him.

George's misdeeds? Unconscious hypocrisy regarding limits. Familiarity, affectionate gestures deviating toward more amorous ones, leading to sensual bordering on sexual relations. He made demonstrative public displays, infuriating Vanessa by "whispering encouragement, lavishing embraces which were not entirely concealed from the eyes of strangers."[100]

Their senior by fourteen and twelve years, he used his prestige, his charm, and Julia's memory (who would have encouraged him to fulfill his role as brother and "launch" the two young women into society) to persuade them in turn to accompany him to those London dinners and elegant dances he adored. He dragged Vanessa to them and when she had had enough, he took Virginia. Trophies. Each exceptionally beautiful, but Virginia more timid, still shy and reticent. In the end, she decided they were failures, as she wrote to Emma Vaughan of the 1901 London Season: "Really, we can't shine in Society. I don't know how it's done. We aint popular—we sit in corners and look like mutes who are longing for a funeral."[101]

The eldest Duckworth must have often been dismayed, as, for instance, when Virginia, gripped with remorse, finally decided to "shine" and chose to address the Victorian elite on Plato over the course of a grand dinner. The agonized George would remind her on the way home of what young women were customarily allowed to say: nothing.

But here it is, described twenty years later for the Memoir Club, the younger sister coming home from a dance with this older brother so universally admired for his brotherly protection of the two motherless girls. Here he is entering Virginia's bedroom, where Virginia is already in bed: "'Don't be frightened,' George whispered, 'And don't turn on the light, oh beloved. Beloved—,' and he flung himself on my bed and took me in his arms."[102]

"Yes, the old ladies of Kensington and Belgravia never knew that George Duckworth was not only father and mother, brother and sister to those poor Stephen girls; he was their lover also,"[103] Virginia declares at the end of the meeting, with a sense of her secret effect. But we may doubt that things went so far as her accusation implies.

Or else, why would Vanessa, at twenty years old, travel and stay with George in Paris, and delight in his discoveries, the painters' studios, the museums she visits? Virginia writes to her "dear old Bar," one of George's (or Georgie's) nicknames, that "Nessa's letters are frantic with excitement." When Vanessa returns, her sister thanks him again: she "seems quite intoxicated with all the things she has done and seen . . . she says she felt like a child, and enjoyed everything like a child. . . . I had no idea that she would enjoy it all so much. You must have managed everything with the utmost skill and care and I am most grateful to you." To the point that we will find Vanessa traveling with George again two years later for three weeks, to Rome this time, and then to Florence.[104]

Even when the young Stephens were still children, George dreamed up all sorts of small festivities like ice cream feasts, boating, walks in

London, riding lessons. In another vein, we have seen him taking them to the cemetery.

He loved to be generous. If the Stephens were comfortable, the Duckworths were very well off, and under the same roof they maintained different lifestyles. George was prodigious with gifts. For Vanessa, for example: an Arabian horse; an opal necklace; amethysts; gowns from famous dressmakers, in particular, a certain Mrs. Young; fans; jewelry for her hair; travel . . . and so on! The manuscript of *A Sketch of the Past* contains a crossed-out sentence: "He paid for clothes; he bought enamel brooches; to the public he represented the good brother; doing his duty by motherless girls." And if the young girls rebelled, George appealed to his female admirers, who defended him indignantly: "How could we resist his wishes? Was not George Duckworth wonderful? And anyhow what else did we want?"[105]

And as for George?

George, who claimed (Jack Hills quotes him) to be a virgin until his marriage, at thirty-six years old, to Lady Margaret Herbert (look! his father's first name).

A note: Virginia would describe her moment of sensual delight as a young girl slipping out of her ball gown, letting it slide the length of her naked body upon returning home one evening. And that memory resembles the scene in which she undresses after the dance the night that George bursts into her room.

But about this George who so resembles his father, the marvelous Herbert, about whom Virginia, like her mother, seems to have once dreamed. In the *Mausoleum Book*, Leslie draws a (generous) portrait of his posthumous rival and addresses Herbert's son: "I vividly remember his smile, for I often see it on the face of his son George. I might have spared any attempt at description by saying to you, my dear George, and to your brothers and sisters, that you are strikingly like your father." (But Leslie cannot resist adding: "I think that he was a little heavier of build and slower of mind.")[106]

Whatever the facts may be, George left a harmful, not to say disastrous (but especially ridiculous) mark in the memories of Virginia corroborated by Vanessa. And that is what matters here, but it does not render completely repellent (unlike his brother Gerald) this Duckworth of very average intelligence, the most conventional mind, who was no doubt himself lost in the uneasy maelstrom of his strangely blended family and his own griefs, the weight of which he had not the means to measure. He seems to have hoped to become his family's benefactor, consoling and restoring his own, as Julia, his mother, had loved doing elsewhere, among others. And like her, he hoped to be recognized in this gratifying role. But his bursts of enthusiasm went awry and came to exceed the good ends he had in mind, when he confused erotic desire with family ties and, thus absolved, gave way to his impulses. His desires.

A situation not entirely unfamiliar to Virginia, no doubt. Which explains the remorse that sharpens the uneasiness.

Virginia conveys (and transmits) this uneasiness to Janet Case, her Greek teacher, who has become a friend. This scene takes place in 1911, as related to Vanessa. Janet and her old student have been talking for hours, and Virginia discovers that Janet, elderly, unmarried, "has a calm interest in copulation," a term that Virginia adores using. Whereupon they take up

> the revelation of all Georges malefactions. To my surprise, she has always had an intense dislike of him; and used to say "Whew—you nasty creature," when he came in and began fondling me over my Greek. When I got to the bedroom scenes, she dropped her lace, and gasped like a benevolent gudgeon. By bedtime she said she was feeling quite sick, and did go to the W.C., which, needless to say, had no water in it.[107]

George? Virginia never tired of denouncing him, as she did eleven years later to Elena Richmond, "that gigantic mass of purity," whose husband ran the *Times Literary Supplement* and who admitted to her: "I am going to be perfectly frank about your brother—your half brother—and say that I have never liked him. Nor has Bruce [Richmond, Elena's husband]." Henceforth the Richmonds would have a thousand reasons to like him even less. And Virginia, delighted, to Vanessa: "Dont you think this is a noble work for our old age—to let the light in upon the Duckworths—and I daresay George will be driven to shoot himself one day when he's shooting rabbits."[108]

The Duckworths . . . *Duck*, and that word or that creature punctuated Virginia's life in a significant way. Two examples among many others: at seventeen, she works on a story with revealing content, published posthumously as "A Terrible Tragedy in the Duck Pond"; and she vomits for the first time in her life when Leonard forces her to "eat an entire cold duck."[109]

The "Terrible Tragedy" recounts at great length, in a parodic and pontificating style, the triple drowning of Adrian and Virginia Stephen and a friend in the pond covered with a "carpet of duckweed," "the green shroud alas of three young lives": "The angry waters of the duck pond rose in their wrath to swallow their prey—& the green caverns of the depths opened—& closed. . . . Alone, untended, unsoothed, with no spectator but the silver moon, with no eye to weep, no hand to caress, three young souls were whelmed by the waters of the duck Pond." Then follows a "Note of Correction & Addition to the above by one of the Drowned": "The corpses, however, emerged from their watery grave, & the corpse who writes this note can testify that her first impulse when she reached the shore was to sink upon its muddy bosom."[110]

There is humor here, but also a fatal submersion, no doubt long imagined, in that angry water, the domain of *ducks* and covered by duckweed: "I sank & sank & sank, the water creeping into ears mouth & nose, till I felt it close over my head. This, methinks, is drowning, I said to myself. It seemed an age passed under water." And it is the struggle between the desire to live or die, and finally, salvation, but "hair & body covered with innumerable bits of duckweed." One of the first signs (not the first) of an obsession with water, a fascination for drowning. One of the first steps toward the River Ouse. Here, the pond of the Duck(worth)s.[111]

The Duckworths and Stephens would part ways after Leslie's death, encountering one another less and less. Still, Gerald would be Virginia's first editor, and George would lend the Woolfs his luxurious country house during one of Virginia's convalescences. A strange choice for Leonard, aware of the past.

Despite that past, or because it existed and was also shared by their mother and Stella, as well as Thoby, and their father, a faint complicity would remain between George and the two sisters, based on shared memories and griefs. One day in 1930, when Virginia was working on a caricature of the aging George, now Sir George, more pompous and self-satisfied than ever, she concluded pensively, "Still some sentiment begins to form misty between us. He speaks of 'Mother'. I daresay finds in me some shadowy likeness—well—& then he is not now in a position to do me harm. His conventions amuse me. . . . He preserves a grain or two of what is me—my unknown past; my self; so that if George died, I should feel something of myself buried."[112]

When he died, four years later, the Woolfs were vacationing in Kerry and read the announcement in the *Times* only later, and Virginia asked Nessa: "Did you go to the funeral? I've just with great labour composed a letter to Margaret [his widow]. Now suppose this had happened 30 years ago, it would have seemed odd to take it so calmly. . . . I hope to goodness somebody went to the service—I wish I had been able to." Three days earlier in the diary, she described the childhood that was disappearing with him, "the batting, the laughter, the treats, the presents, taking us for bus rides to see famous churches, giving us tea at City Inns, & so on—"[113]

Afterward, she would not hesitate to vilify him as before, but for the moment he was once again the George she had described when, at twenty-seven, she had decided to record Vanessa's childhood for her newborn nephew Julian Bell: "He had been once, when we were children, a hero to us; strong and handsome and just; he taught us to hold our bats straight and to tell the truth, and we blushed with delight if he praised."[114]

She describes him as "a stupid, good natured young man, of profuse, voluble affections," but whose characteristics had nothing simple about them, "modified, confused, distorted, exalted, set swimming in a sea of racing emotions until you were completely at a loss to know where you stood . . . [he] proved more and more incapable of containing them . . . profoundly believing in the purity of his love, he behaved little better than a brute." He alternately elicited confidence and suspicion, spent vacations with the family, took his stepfather on walks, listened to and worried about Vanessa's problems, arranged "little plans for our amusement."[115]

Nonetheless, in the eyes of their half-sisters, George and Gerald would share the role of the more or less unconscious perverts who ravaged Virginia's life.

A question: what about Laura? What about the child, then the young girl, completely defenseless, a half-sister as well, introduced at eight years old—the same age as Gerald—into the Duckworths' world? What about Laura Stephen at Hyde Park Gate, the Great Lady of the Lake, Leslie's "backward" daughter, the completely vulnerable Laura, at the mercy of all eventualities?

Is there some reason for recalling here the single, recurrent intelligible sentence of the institutionalized Laura: "I told him to go away"?[116] Not in reference to George, the more sophisticated one, attracted by the beauty of his almost sisters turned young women, and who seems to have made his incestuous advances in a sentimental mood, no doubt less extreme, perhaps less repulsed than Virginia proclaimed. But what of Gerald, capable at seventeen of obscenely fondling a little girl of five: Virginia?

Whereas Virginia makes George her primary target. But did he really ruin her life?

She went on at such length about all his deeds and misdeeds, spoke so much of them, told them so often, commented on them, she avenged herself so thoroughly, mocked him, denounced him, endlessly accused him, ridiculed him with Vanessa, vilified him in public and "aloud,"[117] so that what had happened must have been largely exorcised; it had not been repressed, in any case, and those memories, whatever their degree of accuracy, were not ruined over time; were not deceitfully undermined.

These too seem rather to have served as memory screens, for what it was "impossible to say aloud"[118] and what was not clearly conveyed: the ambiguities, the thick atmosphere of Hyde Park Gate, its libidinous secrets, its sexual and virtual, mawkish gibberish between generations, and especially the discovered shame of a father. Of a father in all his states. And then the death of Stella, for which no one could be accused, without turning to the supernatural. And nevertheless Julia and her hold, haunting them beyond the grave, and nevertheless Leslie. . . .

So many thoughts, so many words that remained forbidden, so many emotions closed to analysis, even to enunciation: "impossible" to give voice to. Even the voice of one who knows how to talk so well!

To talk. But to speak? Speaking is another matter.

Which could explain the still mysterious last line of the last page of the last book Virginia wrote. The announcement, which she will not survive, of an imminent transgression, of a liberation about to occur: the announcement of a voice finally about emerge, but in tandem and in the night and within a silence that it will not interrupt:

"Then the curtain rose. They spoke."[119]

Part 3

1904. Leslie Stephen is dead. Virginia has watched over him for more than two years. Vanessa, having firmly and definitively rejected her father, has kept her distance. Hyde Park Gate is over. The Stephens and the Duckworths look for new addresses, they go their separate ways. The Stephens consider Bloomsbury, an unusual neighborhood.

Henceforth, Virginia Woolf cuts a path through Virginia Stephen. One will soon come into being so that the other, shortly before dying, can write: "I feel in my fingers the weight of every word."[1]

Some of these words surfaced over the course of the crisis that followed her father's death and that can be called madness . . . but not in the restrictive way Bell uses the term. Not to confirm the clichés.

With Leslie dead, Virginia broke down. Guilt. Emptiness. Remorse. The already heavy years of loneliness. The futility of a life not yet begun. Of a deadening routine. Of energy that still hadn't found its outlet.

"My madness has saved me,"[2] she would write, but that was not exactly true: rather, she saved it by attaining a reality that language was inadequate to express, which would make her fragile, keep her on the edge, and undo her three times. At twenty-two, beyond this new grief, the writer she was preparing to become, the person she already was, for whom the given everyday reality was not enough, threw her off balance.

Attentive, anxious, solely responsible, she could tend a solid, too solid father, dying of intestinal cancer. Near him, with him. He remained calm as she followed the ups and downs of the illness, the operations and their aftermath. He was patient and stoic, and she could provide for him.

With Leslie, it was the long good-bye that never ends: "There is nothing so abominable as saying goodbye in this world." She admits her impatience for this slow, gentle, implacable end to come to an end: "I sometimes wish everything would happen directly, and be done with." But it would go on; Leslie had unusual, "wonderful strength—terrible strength." At Christmas, two months before the end, Virginia writes: "If only it could be quicker!" and for once she complains: "I know that death is what he wants, but oh Lord, it is hard." And at Leslie's death: "We have all been so happy together and there never was anybody so loveable."[3]

Virginia's warm, comforting nature, later often masked, surfaced here for her father. A love as deep as it was ambivalent, endlessly resisted, disturbing. She would never stop struggling against him. Consider this strange exclamation, twenty-four years later: "Father's birthday. He would have been 96, yes, today; & could have been 96, like other people one has known; but mercifully was not. His life would have entirely ended mine. What would have happened? No writing, no books;—inconceivable."[4] Strange? Yes, because Leslie never stood in the way of the books or the writing, quite the opposite. Whereas dead, he became for her a springboard to death. We will see how his memory, when she dwelled on it, would become a catalyst for depression.

Guilt at having suspected this father, invaded his privacy, witnessed his downfall, his unworthiness, his moment of shame; not so much having hated him and known him to be hateful.

Nevertheless, with Leslie dead, the dark, coercive era of Hyde Park Gate comes to an end. The bright, sharp, exciting era of Bloomsbury is imminent: a time of emancipation and, in a few years, growth. But they still seem far away: Virginia's brilliant friends, her reign among them, her sparkling presence, which would not prevent the doubts, the inner panic, the obstacles. Also far off: the incredibly organized restlessness, the varied professional life, the taste of worldly success, the haven at Rodmell with its gardens and, in London, the circle of so many lives surrounding hers. The occupation with writing, the books that follow one after another, her blossoming that will do nothing to avert her suffering.

The eight years until her marriage, then until the publication of her first book, were certainly more free, but bitter, weighed down with loneliness. Closed out of the universities forbidden to women but available to Thoby and Adrian, she had already found studying alone to be a kind of solitary confinement.

She would reproach that male-dominated society for having kept her out of schools that welcomed her brothers; she would be right, so very right. But in her particular case, didn't the freedom of a more solitary, personal, truly more emancipated—even sovereign—course, however lonely and thankless, lead her to become the writer we know?

Nevertheless we understand when she sighs: "I dont get anybody to argue with me now, and feel the want. I have to delve from books, painfully and all alone, what you get every evening sitting over your fire and smoking your pipe with Strachey etc. No wonder my knowledge is but scant. Theres nothing like talk as an educator I'm sure."[5] She is addressing Thoby here.

She did not know that the whip would strike again . . . taking Thoby this time. He would never know his sister's work.

In the meantime, freed from all parental shackles, the young Stephens would scandalize their circle (soon to be left behind) by settling in the Bloomsbury district, considered disreputable. Or worse: inelegant. Bloomsbury, which would suddenly come to life, thanks to Thoby and his Cambridge friends.

But first, a serious setback: Virginia's breakdown. As Vanessa finds, organizes, and decorates their new residence, 46 Gordon Square, her sister, at the end of her strength, loses her grip, crushed by the successive deaths, the troubling corpses and troubled lives. By the morbid distortions of grieving. Since the age of thirteen—for the past nine years—she has stoically witnessed her losses, because one isn't supposed to cry or get upset, but press forward impassively, never yielding to affliction. "Life goes on": that is the cool, composed British response, so foreign to Leslie Stephen. All her life, Virginia would display energy, a will to endure, to live, to survive, and above all, not to be isolated, to participate with others, to be part of the group. . . . And to carry on alone.

But this time, Virginia yields to *her* life, as she experiences it, to which she returns and with which she is in accord. She reacts to *her* life by letting her tragic excesses vanquish her, rather than forever yielding to the demands of social etiquette. She stops resisting *her* life, even if it is hopeless to the point of insanity; she lets it run its course, allows it to think, to speak for her.

And, because it is already so late, too late, because the delay has been too long and too filled with emotions too long repressed, with too much pain too long censored, she can only respond by overstepping the "norm." She is twenty-two years old and goes through the mirror. A forced entry is opened for her into other regions, different logics, languages uttered another way. A kind of freedom, but suspect, perilous.

She yields (or rebels) three months after Leslie's death, following a trip, initiated by Gerald, that the Stephens and the Duckworths take to Venice, where Virginia discovers "a place to die in beautifully: but to live [in] I never felt more depressed"; "Geralds figure never did make part of the Venetian foreground I have in my mind!" Upon their return, in the Hyde Park Gate room that she must soon vacate, she hears horrible voices and furious, infernal, intolerable regions open, which engulf Virginia, but whose harrowing sadness, whose reality she absorbs and will restore intact, rehabilitate, or nearly, through Septimus Warren Smith in *Mrs. Dalloway*.[6]

Septimus, who goes through what Virginia Stephen went through, hears what she heard, which Virginia Woolf reproduces, exposes through his voice: the pathos of having to experience simultaneously two orders of truth that contradict each other and that mutually impose upon and condemn each other, that superimpose or annihilate each other, freed of all logic, space dilated, life in the raw; the words scathing, endowed with pain and especially with forbidden exactitude.

Septimus Warren Smith's suffering, directly transcribed by one in the grip of it, testifies to the respect that is owed to them both, and indicates the crime that threatens them both, and that will destroy him.

Septimus, impaled on the fact of believing he feels nothing when too much feeling ravages him.

The cries of suffering because one has not suffered.

Feeling nothing is what Virginia felt so strongly before the dead Julia, when, led to her bedside, a desire to laugh had seized her and she had said to herself, as she has "often done at moments of crisis since, 'I feel nothing whatever.'"[7] On the anniversary of that death, forty-two years later, she again recites that incapacity to feel anything. The very thing that makes her and Septimus blazing torches of emotion.

In 1940, when she returns to the image of the whip with regard to Stella's death in what would become *Moments of Being*, does Virginia Woolf recall having already written and published that same sentence in 1927 in *Mrs. Dalloway*? "The world has raised its whip; where will it descend?"[8] She is referring to Septimus Warren Smith and his wife, Rezia, the little Italian milliner, in exile, so alone and lost in London, whose author, Mrs. Woolf, so wrenchingly understood. But had Virginia ever left Septimus, and had he ever left her?

Had he already been born when Virginia, taking refuge at her friend Violet Dickinson's home after Leslie's death, attended by three nurses, heard the birds in the garden speaking Greek and King Edward speaking obscenities below her window, among the azaleas?

The birds were because of Thoby, who was passionate about them and studied them, drew them. A long time later at Manorbier, Thoby now dead, Virginia: "I have been thinking of Thoby all the time here; I suppose it is the birds."[9] And if they spoke Greek, that was because of Thoby too, who had introduced the Greek language and literature to his sister, who would discuss it with her for hours.

With the birds, all of nature, the whole environment, speaks, giving orders to Septimus Warren Smith. Let us hear what Virginia heard and what Septimus suffers sitting in Regent's Park, where, without Rezia, talking to himself, he asks to whom truth, the meaning of the world is entrusted: "'To whom?' he asked aloud. 'To the Prime Minister,' the voices which rustled above his head replied. The supreme secret must be told to the Cabinet; first, that trees are alive; next, there is no crime; next, love, universal love, he muttered, gasping, trembling."[10]

No crime; love; he repeated, fumbling for his card and pencil, when a Skye terrier snuffed his trousers and he started in an agony of fear. It was turning into a man! He could not watch it happen! It was horrible, terrible to see a dog become a man! At once the dog trotted away. . . . The trees waved, brandished. Welcome, the world seemed to say. Men must not cut down trees. There is a God. (He noted such revelations on the backs of envelopes.) Change the world. No one kills from hatred. Make it known (he wrote it down). He waited. He listened. A sparrow perched on the railing opposite chirped Septimus, Septimus, four or five times over and went on, drawing its notes out, to sing freshly and piercingly in Greek words how there is no crime and, joined by another sparrow, they sang in voices prolonged and piercing in Greek words, from trees in the meadow of life beyond a river where the dead walk, how there is no death.[11]

The hallucination is less of a torment than guarded contact with another reality, with his earlier fate that, uncompromising, pursues itself, destroys itself; with Rezia's pain; and also always with life's delights and memory's anguish, memories of World War I resisted in vain, and of Evans, his officer, with whom he was in love without knowing it and who is dead, killed right in front of him in the trenches, although Septimus felt nothing, has felt nothing since. "There was no excuse; nothing whatever the matter, except the sin for which human nature had condemned him to death; that he did not feel. He had not cared when Evans was killed; that was worst; but all the other crimes raised their heads."[12]

And, as Septimus begins to sing in Regent's Park, he hears Evans answer him and sing in turn "among the orchids," as he hears Rezia say to him: "But I am so unhappy Septimus," since a little earlier he announced to her: "'Now we will kill ourselves,'" while he is "standing by the river . . . with a look which she had seen in his eyes when a train went by, or an omnibus—a look as if something fascinated him."[13]

Virginia Woolf's artistry lies in having the couple cross paths with Peter Walsh, Clarissa's old lover returned from India, who will encounter them again, but who, melancholy at seeing them arguing, says to himself: "being young."[14]

And it is Clarissa who, uneasy within her tranquility, thinks for no reason: "What horror!" with regard to her disappointed life, while a nameless horror surrounds Septimus and Rezia Warren Smith, who soon will know how "once you fall. . . ."[15]

Virginia goes through her crisis period at Violet Dickinson's long before Septimus's name is ever written, but like Septimus, she throws herself out a window—though her window is located close to the ground, so she comes to no great harm.

Violet, to whom Virginia turns for refuge, would play that role in their correspondence, already spanning several years. "My food is affection!" Virginia implores her. Violet, much older than Virginia, unmarried, was immensely tall and phenomenally aristocratic; she was a snob, socially prominent, very conventional, but quite intelligent and won over by the younger woman, having sensed Virginia's talent and merit early on.

Vanessa to Virginia, who was then twenty-two: "I went to see Violet this afternoon. . . . She thought you would undoubtably be a great writer one day. . . . Is that enough for you? She really thinks you are a genius."[16]

It is as a lost child that Virginia confides in Violet, but it is also as a future writer when, at twenty, she gives her the synopsis of a play she plans to write (with Jack Hills!) which already parallels the actual work:

> Im going to have a man and a woman—show them growing up—never meeting—not knowing each other—but all the time you'll feel them come nearer and nearer. This will be the real exciting part (as you see)—but when they almost meet—only a door between—you see how they just miss—and go off at a tangent, and never come anywhere near again. There'll be oceans of talk and emotions without end. Im sure all this interests you so much![17]

She nestles close to her friend, nestles mentally through her letters, but physically as well. Physically attracted? Violet is surely attracted to her, and Virginia: "It is astonishing what depths—hot volcano depths—your finger has stirred in Sparroy—hitherto entirely quiescent."[18]

"Sparroy" (derived from "sparrow") is the painfully regressive nickname Virginia gives herself, desperately seeking someone in whom to confide, no longer evasive, finding (instead of losing) someone, for once. Hence the abundant sentimental chatter of Sparroy, the sparrow. But also of a wallaby, when it is not a kangaroo: "Would you like to feel the Wallaby snout on your bosom?" "Who thinks of him now, or licks under his fur?" Or, "I wish you were a Kangaroo and had a pouch for small Kangaroos to creep to," and other affectations.[19]

But Violet Dickinson is a bastion of support. After spending two months with her, Virginia emerges still shaken, so that she can't place the voices she no longer hears and writes to Violet: "You will be glad to hear that your Sparroy feels herself a recovered bird. . . . All the voices I used to hear telling me to do all kinds of wild things have gone—and Nessa says they were always only my imagination."[20]

Yes, it could be called madness. But what will it be called? That is the question.

Two more very calm, very boring months in Cambridge with a very pious, intellectual Quaker aunt (Leslie's sister). The crisis has passed, end of parenthesis.

Then, suddenly, freedom. Hyde Park Gate is already consigned to memory. The curtain opens for Virginia and Vanessa at 46 Gordon Square, in that improper neighborhood of Bloomsbury, the symbol of their emancipation. On their way to becoming Virginia Woolf and Vanessa Bell.

The edge of the woods is in sight. Salvation. Surrounded by Adrian and Thoby, the two sisters emerge autonomous; they have found other outlets in a time when, for young women like them, the only path available was marriage. Here we have a painter, a writer, two women with open futures; two sisters bound since childhood in a "very close conspiracy."[21] A way presents itself, unthinkable until now for the daughters of an antisuffragette Julia Stephen. They can be considered saved, liberated, not from life, not from suffering, nor even from frustration, but from an insipid and deadening future.

A friend of Violet introduces Virginia to the *Guardian*, and she becomes one of its literary critics. Almost immediately she starts writing for *The Academy*, *The National Review*, and most importantly, weekly, for *The Times Literary Supplement*, the holy of holies! She also volunteers at Morley College, teaching history and literature to impoverished girls. The days take shape.

But above all, youth forges ahead at Gordon Square. Gaiety. Thoby invites home his friends, those Virginia envies him.

Like Vanessa, Virginia is exceptionally beautiful, a beauty resembling her sister's, moving and singular, but which she always seems to forget or not to recognize, and that plays no role in her new dealings with young men who share her passion for art and thought. At first she remains shy and reticent among the young Cambridge men Thoby brings home (that's when Leonard comes to dinner at "the Goth's" before leaving for Ceylon).

Soon they would gather every Thursday evening at the Stephens', and gradually Virginia Stephen begins to resemble the brilliant, formidable Virginia who becomes Virginia Woolf. She is still rarely heard but already listened to on those lively and serious, almost ascetic evenings: cocoa and whisky, buns and biscuits are served. There is talk and talk and more talk. And quiet moments too. Above all, there are no taboos anymore . . . at least not in conversation. There is the famous: "Semen?"[22] uttered by Lytton Strachey, pointing at a spot on Vanessa's dress. And everyone in hysterics, even decades later. Good-bye Edward! Good-bye Victoria!

Life lies ahead, all of it. But the whip is going to strike.

1906, a journey. Adrian and Thoby are traveling on horseback across Albania and Greece, where Virginia and Vanessa are meeting them, accompanied by Violet. Thoby returns to London; the others follow as far as Constantinople, where Vanessa falls ill. They return to England on the Orient Express. In London, Thoby is confined to bed. Vanessa, still sick, takes to her bed as well. At her home, Violet also falls seriously ill.

The beginning of a new nightmare that the stoic, competent Virginia faces alone.

Surrounded by nurses, Thoby is in dire straits; the doctors' visits begin again, as useless as with Stella. Until the end, the doctors say they are "satisfied"; according to them, the young man's horrible pains don't come from cherries, as in Stella's case, but from an "irritation caused by" eating too many grapes with seeds! The "irritation" becomes a perforation.[23]

Three weeks of torment for Virginia at her sister's side (who suffers from appendicitis, according to the doctors) and at the bedside of her brother—before Thoby dies from typhoid fever the doctors have misdiagnosed as malaria. He is twenty-six years old.

Thoby!

His presence, henceforth based on his absence, would never leave Virginia. His memory would serve as catalyst for *The Waves*, and twenty-five years later:

> I must record, heaven be praised, the end of The Waves. I wrote the words O Death fifteen minutes ago, having reeled across the last ten pages with some moments of such intensity & intoxication that I seemed only to stumble after my own voice, or almost, after some sort of speaker (as when I was mad). I was almost afraid, remembering the voices that used to fly ahead. Anyhow it is done; & I have been sitting these 15 minutes in a state of glory, & calm, & some tears, thinking of Thoby & if I could write Julian Thoby Stephen 1881–1906 on the first page. I suppose not.[24]

Thoby, the fourth loss—and what losses—suffered by Virginia since the age of thirteen; she is now twenty-four. And this time, after having already experienced the depths of despair, having already hit bottom, she seems to have acquired a rare mastery, allowing her to accomplish a touching feat: she continues to provide Violet (seriously stricken with typhoid herself) with news of Thoby as if he were alive.

For a month, twenty long letters full of news. Detailed, varied, plausible accounts that she invents each day regarding her dead brother, combining her skills as a writer (who would not publish a book for another seven years) with her innate gifts for friendship and tenderness, often masked henceforth by irony, even fierceness, which didn't prevent her from otherwise demonstrating compassion and fidelity toward her beloved victims.

Twenty letters to relate Thoby's struggle to regain his strength, his fluctuating temperature, his quarrels with the nurses, his long-awaited, slow convalescence. He is allowed to have chicken broth, then minced chicken, then chocolate. He is drawing birds.

Sometimes, a stifled cry: "My Violet, if only the British public would not celebrate their makers praise—or if only their maker would provide adequate voices, and Broadwood pianos. O God! how I suffer." Sometimes the news of Thoby turns macabre: "Dear old Thoby is still on his back," "Thoby slept better. He still isn't allowed to move." "He is not to eat anything solid yet, and he is not to sit up . . . he cant write much, and he dont get letters"; on the other hand, he receives "a great many flowers," though destined for his tomb.[25]

Maybe by prolonging it in this way, she was better able to endure the horror of his death; somewhere in the world, on paper, for the time of the writing and in the mind of Violet, Thoby was still a living subject.

We must not forget Virginia's immense powers of dissembling. Just a few months before Leslie's imminent death: "We are really the cheerfullest family in Kensington." Later: "I am the happiest woman in England," she will often insist . . . often to persuade herself of it.[26]

Violet would discover the truth a month later, in an article on the Leslie Stephen biography by Frederic Maitland, which mentions that it was published "almost on the very day of the untimely death of Sir Leslie Stephen's eldest son, Mr Thoby Stephen." And it is Virginia who consoles Violet: "You must think that Nessa is *radiantly happy*."[27]

Because she is. Beaming, a rose in her hair, overflowing with joy, engaged to Clive Bell two days after Thoby's death. When she passes her sister's room, Virginia hears the laughter of the engaged couple. The "very close conspiracy"[28] is no longer between the two sisters. Virginia feels excluded. Deserted!

Another exclusion: Clive and Vanessa want to continue to live at 46 Gordon Square once they are married. Virginia and Adrian must find another place, less grand, to live. She feels "elderly and prosaic." To Violet, who believes ardently in God, she remarks that "he has a heavy hand."[29]

Thoby is dead, Vanessa growing distant. Yes, many desertions.

Nessa's cruelty? Virginia says nothing about it. Or almost nothing. She does not waver, she moves on. As she always does. The last step will be into the River Ouse.

When the engagement becomes official, Virginia's friend Madge Vaughan asks her what she thinks of it. Virginia doesn't know how to answer: she doesn't "think very much yet" and says only that Clive seems "clever, and cultivated—more taste, I think, than genius; but he has a gift for making other people shine, and he is very affectionate." But to Violet: "When I think of father and Thoby and then see that funny little creature twitching his pink skin and jerking out his little spasm of laughter I wonder what odd freak there is in Nessa's eyesight. . . . But I dont say this, and I wont say it, except to you." "It will really be some time before I can separate him from her." From one letter to the next, she changes, stumbles. Nessa is "tawny and jubilant and lusty as a young God. I never saw her look better." She is delighted, but "I did not see Nessa alone, but I realise that that is all over, and I shall never see her alone any more; and Clive is a new part of her, which I must learn to accept." Her way of accepting Clive would come as a surprise.[30]

The wedding took place in February, less than three months after Thoby's death. Let us remember Leonard in Ceylon, reacting with incredulity, jealous of Clive. To Madge, Virginia admitted her confusion after the ceremony: "It is very strange to watch—or rather not to watch—It does seem all a dream still. . . . Adrian and I try to get a house, and I hope I have found one now in Fitzroy Square—but they always fall through at the last. . . . Thoby used to say that you were the most beautiful person he had ever seen. . . . It is very hard not to have him here—I cant get reconciled—but we have to go on. Adrian is well—but I cant be a brother to him!"[31]

"Poor little boy," she had already called her younger brother when Leslie died. Adrian was now twenty-one, but would always be the twelve-year-old deposed by Julia's death. "He was a deprived child," Virginia would admit. He would never be happy, and she would grow away from him, fleeing the memories of their unrewarding cohabitation and Adrian's sarcasm, the brother always on the defensive, the sister so vulnerable and easily dominated. Later, their encounters brought back to her "the old despair; the crouching servile feeling which is my lowest & worst; . . . &

the old futile comparisons between his respect for Nessa & his disrespect for me." Despite a few intermittent efforts, she would never like Adrian's wife, Karin, whom Leonard would detest, just as he wouldn't warm to their two daughters, whom Virginia would have loved to love.[32]

Adrian's scars? They were old ones: he was Julia's "joy," her pet, and so excluded by the others, before being fixed for good in his isolation after their mother's death. A child thrown off course, forever at bay and solitary, supported only by Stella, who disappeared. Leslie, who championed Thoby, shows little interest in his youngest son. The charismatic older brother occupies the whole space, everyone's heart.

Long after Adrian's death, his daughter Ann was certainly conveying her father's bitterness but also the old, implicit general impression, when she said with regard to Thoby's early demise that "the wrong man died."[33]

Adrian Stephen would become James Ramsay, the little boy in *To the Lighthouse* who cannot wait to go there, who is always dreaming of it. Here Virginia finds a way to commiserate with Adrian. She enters into the impotent rage of James, who has also lost his mother, and who, throughout the brief, overwhelming crossing to the lighthouse, is haunted by the desire to put a knife through his father's heart . . . while the widowed Mr. Ramsay drones: "We perish, each alone," or "I beneath a rougher sea."[34]

First trace of the forbidden beacon: an issue of *Hyde Park Gate News*, September 9, 1892; Adrian is nine years old: "Saturday morning Master Hilary Hunt and Master Basil Smith came up to Talland House and asked Master Thoby and Miss Virginia to accompany them to the light-house as Freeman the boatman said that there was a perfect tide and wind for going there. Master Adrian Stephen was much disappointed at not being allowed to go."[35]

Whatever his age or circumstances, Adrian's blue eyes would be noted for being large, opened, astonished. He would remain the twelve-year-old child, receptive and disappointed, who, thanks to his mother, for whom he was everything, was always waiting for everything, and who found himself isolated, facing nothing, upon her death. Even in his sister's memoirs or his father's *Mausoleum Book*, he is almost absent. He would remain thoughtful, bitter, suspicious, measured, intelligent, slow, passive, athletic, completely depressed or completely vibrant depending on his breakdowns, captivated by so many things, and increasingly enclosed within an ever threatened indifference.

He would lead an independent, fascinating, dreary life; he would have a passionate lover, the inescapable Duncan Grant, with the inevitable Maynard Keynes always at his side; next, a fascinating wife, intellectual, dynamic, friend of philosophers, deaf, graceless, with whom life would be exciting, chaotic, and sad. His profession, serious and absorbing, would distance him even further from the Bloomsbury circle, who already did not accept him: he and Karin became very eminent psychoanalysts; she the author of sensitive, profound essays published by the Hogarth Press. They lived a secluded life, even as they threw parties attended and enjoyed by all of Bloomsbury. A leftist, Adrian was more or less absentmindedly anti-Semitic like many of his crowd, but he would fight against anti-Semitism at the end of World War II.

An event: during the period when he and Virginia shared various residences in London, the superb, renowned *Dreadnought* farce, organized by Adrian. The visit of the Abyssinian emperor with his attendants was announced on the Royal English Marines ship, the *Dreadnought*. Admiral May and Commander Fisher (a cousin of the Stephens), the officers, and the entire crew (in new white gloves purchased for the occasion) solemnly received the imperial party. The visitors cut fine figures in Oriental dress; they had their own interpreter and spoke a funny language . . . invented by them, vaguely resembling Swahili, with the recurrent expression "bunga-bunga." It was Adrian, Virginia (wearing a beard), Duncan Grant, and a few friends in disguise, faces darkened with shoe polish, who majestically accepted the tributes and speeches; they refused the gun salute and accepted apologies: a score for the Abyssinian national anthem was sought in vain and the Zanzibar national anthem was played as a substitute. The escapade ended well and in time: Duncan's moustache was beginning to come unglued. . . .

One of the imposters revealed the joke to the press. Scandal, newspaper headlines, questions at Parliament. There was a great fuss. Commander Fisher couldn't contain his rage; according to Virginia, boys followed Admiral May in the streets shouting "bunga-bunga." Adrian had scored a success.

One detail: although until the age of fourteen, he remained very short in a tall family that nicknamed him "the dwarf," Adrian suddenly went through a growth spurt, achieving inordinate, exceptional, immense height. And he was handsome, as were all the Stephens.

One word more: after their sister's suicide, Adrian, mobilized as a medical officer, wrote to Vanessa:

> I had actually seen in some Sunday paper about Virginia's body, but thank you for telling me. . . .[36] The whole thing is very unreal to me. . . . It is like a distant dream. For a good many years I had not heard . . . much of her and of course had never been nearly as close to her as you have always been so that anyhow it could not effect me like you. Since about 1914 in fact I have seen her rather seldom and have never been quite sure that she wanted to see me when we did meet. On the other hand in many ways the life before 1914 seems more real than life since then. Hyde Park Gate and St Ives are extraordinarily vivid and so are the days which, I suppose, ought to be called "Early Bloomsbury." It does seem odd that, as you say, we are the only people left to remember our childhood.[37]

A final note: shortly after Adrian's death, Karin committed suicide.

Virginia moved to Fitzroy Square, still in Bloomsbury, with her younger brother; Adrian would escort her to dances, concerts, costume parties, which she enjoyed; they would travel together, sometimes with Clive and Vanessa, to Paris, Florence, Milan, Bayreuth, Portugal, and the English countryside.

Despite an active, conventional social life, or perhaps because of it, Virginia, now deserted, would struggle against a heavy, undermining boredom, a dull solitude. Torments that heighten what foments in her, which they feed: an unchanneled rage to write. "I begin to feel the desire of the pen in my blood." "When I see a pen and ink, I cant help taking to it, as some people do to gin." She vows she will become "the writer of such English as shall one day burn the pages." When Madge Vaughan affirms that she considers her a genius (as Violet already has said), Virginia thinks the idea plausible and comments on it seriously, concluding: "I cant help writing—so there's an end of it."[38]

She pursues her occupation of literary criticism, but it is primarily her solitude, bitter as she finds it, that allows her to devote herself entirely to the sensual pleasures that would make her into the writer she already is. For example, she writes to Violet, "I could be wed—pure simple notes—smooth from all passion and frailty." She continues: "Now do you know that sound has shape and colour and texture as well?" She is already in the mind of the books, in the fullness of that thinking, and in the pungency of the circumstances that often surround the one who thinks.[39]

Nevertheless the lack of other, more ordinary sensual pleasures, any love life for example, weighs on her. "I have been talking to young men for the last fortnight—Lamb and Sidney-Turner, but they remain so disinterested that I see how I shall spend my days a virgin, an Aunt, an authoress." She imagines Nessa's progeny: "Who was cousin Mia? Dont you like Uncle George? Why has Aunt Goat never married? I think you very beautiful Mama!" And this worry, trivial as it may seem, opens into gulfs of agonizing emptiness; she is overcome with "dreadful weariness . . . that we should still be the same people, in the same bodies; wandering not quite alive, nor yet suffered to die, in this pale light." She is twenty-five years old.[40]

Long walks over the course of solitary days in the country or by the sea, and the difficult, underground labor of a work about to be born, throbbing in her veins but there alone, which she herself does not yet know but which needs, demands to emerge and, by its nonexistence, heightens an atmosphere of isolation, desertion, a certain futility. A profound state of disarray.

The void as a wall.

Which her great perversity, or more bluntly, her bitchiness, will get her through. Or rather, will distract her from.

Without the slightest scruple, the least pity (and moreover without really alleviating her depression), she is going to spoil her sister's marriage, thus calculating her own power, feeling real desire and some pleasure in provoking the very masculine Clive, winning him over with a cunning, a talent, a method that would allow her to monopolize her brother-in-law openly before a paralyzed Nessa. Whom she never stops and would never stop loving. Whom she could never leave emotionally. And who, thus paralyzed, would have a delayed but enduring reaction to this suffering, this offense, lasting throughout their lives, punctually, instinctively, until the last fatal stroke, borne by Virginia.

Virginia, whom she loves, who holds an essential place in her life and who will often charm her, but whom she will keep at a greater distance than is apparent, even though her sister will often be aware of it. In the Charleston circle, the tone will be the one inherited by Quentin Bell. Virginia's superiority, arrogance, fierceness will be denied, as will her frantic demands for affection, and she will appear humble before the emotional and sexual life she attributes to Nessa, whose maternity she reveres. She likes to think of herself as her sister's child, asks her why she gave birth to her, and is anxious to be a willing partner from the start, symbolically, with the children who follow Julian. "We both very much wanted a daughter this time," she writes to a friend with regard to Angelica. And to Vanessa: "You've given me Julian and Quentin and Angelica."[41]

But the first birth, Julian's, will hardly move her. Babies have not yet entered into her desire or imagination. She doesn't know yet that they will be denied her. As for Vanessa, she is monopolized, obsessed by her first-born. Clive complains of never seeing her anymore, of no longer sleeping with her, now that she is interested only in the baby . . . whom he is afraid even to hold. While Virginia proclaims herself inept as a nurse.

Together brother- and sister-in-law flee the cries of the newborn, of whom they say they are jealous. Together they go on long walks, which remained completely innocuous, unlike Virginia's letters to Clive or even those addressed to her sister. Because it is through her attachment to Nessa—which she likes to describe as a love affair and which never wanes—it is through courting her sister through Clive, or courting Clive through her sister, that Virginia manages to achieve her goal: paralyzing Vanessa, beaten in advance, disarmed, strangely silenced. Bound hand and foot, as Virginia was a year earlier, facing her sister's marriage and desertion. The illusion that nothing has changed in their relationship is part of the game, and at first glance, nothing seems to blemish, much less spoil their bond.

But will Virginia ever know the extent, the depth of the wound Vanessa hides, letting nothing show, including, from now on, any heartbreak? Vanessa will remain forever closed, impenetrable on this point, locked down. Throughout her future life, she will let herself only be seen as a fulfilled woman, resolutely natural, happily provocative, a lavish mother, a satisfied lover, and fundamentally a painter.

Does Virginia suspect the seriousness of this new divide, which Vanessa will manage instinctively and which will often shape Virginia Woolf's destiny?

Virginia alters the trajectory of Vanessa the young wife, sensual and jubilant beside Clive: "It is like being always thirsty & always hav[ing] some delicious clear water to drink." The trajectory of a young woman overflowing with exhilaration, eager for sensual pleasure and fulfilled, confident in life, and who moreover *will always seem that way*, to the point that Virginia will rejoice in their mature years: "I always measure myself against her, & find her much the largest, most humane of the two of us, think of her now with an admiration that has no envy in it: with some trace of the old childish feeling that we were in league together against the world; & how proud I am of her triumphant winning of all our battles: as she [battles?] her way so nonchalantly modestly, almost anonymously past the goal, with her children round her."[42]

That is one aspect of Vanessa, the aspect she wished to present, but if she seems always to float in peace, sensual delight, and idyllic romance with Duncan Grant, she lives forever in terror of being left and . . . accepts living by his side in chastity.

She might have envied Virginia for Leonard's unconditional presence, the unquestioned durability of their marriage. That peaceful zone. But it is Virginia, forever deceived by the role of sensual, fulfilled woman Vanessa played, who envies her sister: "I was rather depressed when you saw me—What it comes to is this: you say 'I do think you lead a dull respectable absurd life—lots of money, no children, everything so settled: and conventional. Look at me now—only sixpence a year—lovers—Paris—life—love—art—excitement—God! I must be off!'[43] This leaves me in tears."

Virginia has no cause for such tears, even if she is joking. Henceforth Vanessa lives as chastely as Virginia, but desiring, scorned by, and accepting, claiming for life in order to keep close to her for life the irresistible, delightful, volatile Duncan Grant. Who will never leave her.

Real tears, on the other hand, weighed heavily on the two sisters' lives: tears secretly shed by Vanessa, betrayed from the start of her marriage. Eighteen years later, promising to tell the recently widowed Gwen Raverat the whole story of her life, Virginia mentions only "my affair with Clive and Nessa I was thinking of when I said I envied you and Jacques at Fitzroy square" that wounded her forever and "turned more of a knife in me than anything else has ever done."[44]

Her niece, Vanessa's daughter, Angelica Garnett, holds that this time left "a permanent scar. Years later, seeing them together, in spite of their habitual ironic affection and without any idea of the cause, I could see in their behaviour a wariness on the part of Vanessa, and on Virginia's side a desperate plea for forgiveness." So much so that, faithful to the Stephen tradition, they never confronted each other on that point, never said anything about it, "aloud" at least.[45]

And it's true, Virginia will implicitly, endlessly seek pardon from her sister. Throughout their constant, delightful exchanges, their elegant familiarity, the irresistible grace with which each of them shows up for the other, full of enthusiasm, closeness, never letting themselves go, as if always wanting to dance for the other. Often daily, their letters pass between their Rodmell and Charleston houses, a short bicycle ride apart, irresistibly funny or deeply moving; simultaneously mocking, immediate, sincere, and warm; savage toward their circle; carefully written as if they each had to win back the other, though they had just left each other, or would lunch together the next day. But only Virginia tells all.

Vanessa would remain her lodestar, refuge, landmark, and always in a playful way, her triumphant rival. But for Nessa, there was nothing playful, much less triumphant about suffering a sister's rivalry in the early years of her marriage, resulting in isolation, one disaster after another, and a futile search for a husband. "No one has asked me to marry them,"[46] complains Virginia to Violet. But Virginia Stephen is primarily caught up in what is developing within her, what she lets shape her: what creates the writer about to become Virginia Woolf.

From this tangle, from Virginia's emotional misery, arises a formidable foe, surprisingly well-armed, who charges at her sister. Caught off guard, Vanessa hasn't a chance and serves as intermediary for Virginia, who writes to Clive: "Kiss her, most passionately, in all my private places—neck—, and arm, and eyeball, and tell her—what new thing is there to tell her? how fond I am of her husband?"[47]

To this husband, she will soon write: "The main point of all this is that we are very fond of each other; and I expect we shall make out a compromise in time. I suppose we shall see more clearly what is what." She will have her goal in sight: "Why do you torment me with half uttered and ambiguous sentences? my presence is 'vivid and strange and bewildering.' I read your letter again and again, and wonder whether you have found me out. . . . I was certainly of opinion, though we did not kiss—(I was willing and offered once—but let that be)—I think we 'achieved the heights' as you put it. But did you realise how profoundly I was moved, and at the same time, restricted, by the sight of your daily life." And singing her habitual praises to Vanessa: "Ah—such beauty—grandeur—and freedom—as of panthers treading in their wilds—I never saw in any other pair. When Nessa is bumbling about the world, and making each thorn blossom, what room is there for me?" Clive's response: "I wished for nothing in the world but to kiss you. I wished it so much that I grew shy and could not see what you were feeling."[48]

No, Vanessa hasn't a chance, she is in checkmate. Withdrawn, fierce, silently she paints with Julian at her side. So powerful in appearance, a fighter, from now on she will always withdraw in such circumstances. She barely alludes to it: "Dont forget to keep my husbands letters for me to see or are they too private?" From her own torments Virginia seems to have learned the art of tormenting better. She is ruthless. When Nessa wants out of the game, wants to lay all the cards on the table . . . Virginia immediately writes to Clive, feigning humor: "Your wife gave me such a talking to the other day; she will deny it, but dont believe her. She said I never gave, but always took. In this case, as she must own, I have been forced to take."[49]

Her many letters to Vanessa are very often intended for Clive, written for him. She explains to her sister: "Ah! there's no doubt I love you better than anyone in the world! . . . I dont in the least mind your showing Clive my letters; because I dont make much difference between you." And when she writes to Vanessa: "Shall you kiss me tomorrow? Yes, Yes, Yes. Ah, I cannot bear being without you. I was thinking today of my greatest happiness, a walk along a cliff by the sea, and you at the end of it," yes, when she writes these words, whom is she addressing?[50]

But it is to Clive that she apologizes when one of their rendezvous at her house is interrupted: "Next time (which I dont dare to suggest) I will make the proper arrangements, but I'm certain that I shall never have the courage to turn people out when they're on the stairs—not if I'm in my lovers arms!"[51]

The lover's arms that moved Virginia, that elicited from her both desire and pleasure. A woman's feelings for a man. Did she compare those experiences with Leonard's attitude (and aptitude), his avoidances? To Ethel Smyth, she would confess: "When 2 or 3 times in all, I felt physically for a man, then he was so obtuse, gallant, foxhunting and dull that I—diverse as I am—could only wheel round and gallop the other way."[52] Such was Clive's reputation in the Bloomsbury circle, as the two sisters later lampooned him, but the Clive that had attracted Virginia had aroused her desire, and she had not run in the other direction.

Clive, also aroused, nevertheless rekindles an old affair with Mrs. Raven-Hill, a "very experienced" woman in their circle.

Clive and Virginia's exchanges play another, more serious role, however: Clive becomes Virginia's first reader, the confidant for her writerly hopes. She recognizes in him dreams he already knows he is incapable of converting into works, but he is equal to them. Though he no longer dreams, or rarely. She addresses herself to him, awaits a hearing, a reading from him. To him she has already claimed: "I shall re-form the novel and capture multitudes of things at present fugitive, enclose the whole, and shape infinite strange shapes."[53]

She began to write *Melymbrosia*, an early version of a novel that, after seven years of work, would become *The Voyage Out*. It is this early manuscript that she nervously entrusts to Clive: "They [her words] accumulate behind one in such masses—dreadful, if they are nothing but muddy water."[54] Water, always and once again. . . .

Objective, often very critical, Clive immediately understands the importance of these words. A strange man, Clive. Perhaps, out of the whole Bloomsbury group, the one who will live with the most fervor and style. Nevertheless a shallow man, tawdry sometimes, born into wealth in the English countryside; his tastes are regarded as rural, unrefined, and his Cambridge friends consider him the most trivial among them, a socialite, nouveau riche, and superficial (judging, once again, from Leonard's reactions in Ceylon). In fact, he is among the most instinctively elegant men, with a facility and passion for art—he is an art historian—which he reveres with discernment and modesty. No narcissist, he is thus more sure of himself than of others. Behind the frivolous air of amateur aesthete, ladies' man, hedonist, he is perhaps the most sensitive, possessing the most conviction. The most faithful. The most resigned to being only himself, but able to take advantage of it.

Reading Virginia and advising her, seeing these pages emerge still shaky or too stiff, recognizing in his sister-in-law a writer of original and still unknown power, he stops in his tracks, considers his own life, his own place in his own life, and concludes: "*Tout va bien, le pain manque!*" And then this heartfelt cry, confided to Virginia: "I sometimes . . . could almost cry for the beauty of the world; that is because I am not great, I can't lay hold on it; I just go fingering the smooth outside, for ever pushing it out of my grasp. . . . I am condemned all my life, I think, to enjoy through an interpreter; but then as the interpreter is art one must not complain too much." He sees with perfect clarity.[55]

A surprising Clive Bell, like the one who offers Virginia magnificent advice, proof of a deep intuition about her aims, which he discerns better than she does: "We have often talked about the atmosphere that you want to give; that atmosphere can only be insinuated, it cannot be set down in so many words. In the old form it was insinuated throughout, in the new it is more definite, more obvious, &, to use a horrid expression—'less felt'—by the reader I mean."[56]

And again: "To give more 'humanity' to your work, you sacrificed the 'inhuman,'—the super-natural—the magic which I thought as beautiful as anything that has been written these hundred years; in so far as the book is purely Virginia, Virginia's view of the world is perfectly artistic, but isn't there some danger that she may forget that an artist, like God, should create without coming to conclusions." He analyzes Virginia's manuscript in detail, with severity, but marvels: "It seemed to me that you gave your words a force that one expects to find only in the best poetry."[57]

"Ah, how you encourage me!"[58] cries Virginia.

Ten years later, the trio's relationship, stripped of all amorous feelings, had long since calmed down. Vanessa left Clive for Roger Fry, then left Fry for the ever adored Duncan Grant. But they all remained close friends, often gathering in London and almost every weekend at Charleston, where Clive also spent extended stays accompanied by his successive mistresses. He and Vanessa always remained officially married; he approved of Nessa's pregnancy by Duncan, and until Angelica Bell was sixteen years old, she believed him to be her father, an attached and inattentive father, as he was for his two sons, Quentin and Julian.

Virginia had become Virginia Woolf, and Clive, nicknamed "the parrot"[59] by the two sisters, became the target of their private jokes, though they remained very attentive and curious about him; his successes with women may have sometimes vexed them a bit, especially Virginia, who still felt vaguely proprietary.

Ten years later, Clive writes to Virginia of his admiration for "The Mark on the Wall," which has just been published, and wonders if it is wise for him to send this laudatory letter at the risk of making himself ridiculous. Virginia answers him:

I've always thought it very fine—the way you run risks. . . . You know you always told me I was notorious for vanity, and its still a fine plant, though growing old. But please dont put it all down to vanity. I do like you to praise me, not only because of your gift for knowing whats what, but for you would call sentimental reasons too—as for instance that you were the first person who ever thought I'd write well.[60]

In 1956, Virginia long dead, Clive writes to Leonard regarding his sister-in-law's letters, which would not be published until 1975:

> I have a notion that the earlier and less "gossipy" letters—the letters in which Virginia talks about her writing and her difficulties as an artist—are the most interesting. I will confess that I very much hope you will print a letter dated "Tuesday, Hogarth House," and beginning with "I've always thought it very fine etc." Vanity? Not exactly perhaps. But there is a sentence—"you were the first person who ever thought I'd write well," which seems to me the finest feather I shall ever be able to stick in my cap.[61]

Virginia's sister also read *Melymbrosia*. The havoc its author wreaked on her married life did not prevent Nessa from exclaiming: "How envied I shall be of the whole world some day when it learns on what terms I was with that great genius."[62] She's hardly joking.

Virginia would always turn to her, dependent upon the one she shamelessly offends and wrongs: "Beloved, To my great melancholy, I have had no letter from you today. . . . If I were to hint at all the miseries which steal out when you don't lull them to sleep, I should only be chidden."[63] Nessa responds tenderly.

They are bound by so much past joy, emptiness, grief, by what they call a "very close conspiracy":[64] the two of them so long united against the world in general, and Hyde Park Gate in particular. Neither of them could bear that memory without sharing its weight with the other one. What each of them would lose in losing her sister's love, ambiguous as it may be, is immeasurable. The past that undermines them and comprises them would grow even heavier, weighed down for each of them by what they could not share. The past would waver, becoming murkier or disappearing from memory, one more loss to suffer—one more absence to bear, and more devastating than any recollection, no matter how heavy or morbid. Each of the two sisters maintains the other in the weave of her history.

Many entries in Virginia's diary resemble this one:

> Mercifully, Nessa is back. My earth is watered again. I go back to words of one syllable: feel come over me the feathery change: rather true that: as if my physical body put on some soft, comfortable skin. She is a

necessity to me—as I am not to her. I run to her as the wallaby runs to the old kangaroo. She is also very cheerful, solid, happy. . . . And how masterfully she controls her dozen lives.[65]

The letters they exchange over those two or three years of betrayals, snubs, and wounds inflicted by Virginia remain so intimate that, Vanessa remarks, anyone else reading them would take them for passionate love letters.

But Virginia lacks a husband, and Vanessa reassures her: "I know that we are near the end of another stage and you soon will be married. Can't you imagine us in 20 years' time, you and I the two celebrated ladies, with our families about us, yours very odd and small and you with a growing reputation for your works, I with nothing but my capacities as a hostess and my husband's value to live upon? Your husband will probably be dead, I think, for you won't have boiled his milk with enough care, but you will be quite happy and enjoy sparring with your clever and cranky daughter. I'm afraid she'll be more beautiful than mine, who I know will take after the Bells."[66] She resolves during her next pregnancy to avoid the Bell family and concentrate on Mrs. Cameron's photos of the sublime Julia.

Virginia's marriage in Vanessa's eyes? A major stake, the best means of detaching her from Clive; it is with all the greater zeal that she follows the tribulations of her sister, hard pressed for suitors—an abiding mystery. And Virginia is twenty-eight years old.

Vanessa's ideal brother-in-law: Lytton. But, she admits, he would have to fall in love with Adrian! Failing that, she worries about Hilton Young's wavering, "like an elephant in a china shop," who would not be suitable for Virginia. For lack of a better option, she resigns herself: "Has Hilton Young written and come and proposed yet? At this moment you may be refusing him. . . ." Alas, no. And Virginia: "No answer from H[ilton] Y[oung], I am begin to feel nervous," and three days later, again: "Nothing from H.Y." It's not a question of love, but rather a matter of escaping the much maligned status of "spinster." (Julia had been a frantic "matchmaker," resulting in disastrous couples; she considered marriage the only way a woman could achieve meaning and social standing.) Clive doesn't count here, he is only a bitter digression, a compensation, a temporary substitute, and Virginia dreams of "all the lovers (who wont love me) in the world."[67]

Strange symptoms surface. At Manorbier where she is staying in Wales, she slips and talks about the cliffs where she walks, claiming she doesn't want to fall; she recounts murders that have taken place in the area, climbs a hill imagining herself as Christ at Calvary and finds it so funny that she begins to laugh, comforted. In a very strange letter to Emma Vaughan, she makes incoherent erotic remarks about the old cousins turned lecherous, who seem to hold some kind of weird witches' sabbaths until one of them cries, after nightfall: "I'm only a little bag of bones—And the bed is so big!" Finally Virginia makes fun of the Vaughans with the farmer who rents her a room and they laugh "till the spiders waltzed in the corners, and were strangled in their own webs."[68]

She is at the breaking point, and there's still the neurotic exchange with Clive, the powerful, treacherous bond with Vanessa. No one else loves her, and she mourns Thoby: "It is just two years since he died, and I feel immensely old, and as though the best in us had gone. But what use is it to write? It is such an odd life without him."[69]

The work will take over, even in this limbo. And spitefulness. Vanessa's difficulties become public, under the pretext of a role-playing game through letters, no doubt invented by the malicious Lytton: some friends, Lady Ottoline Morrell and her husband, Philip, Hilton Young, Walter Lamb and Clive, Virginia and Lytton, among others, play imaginary characters whose letters will supposedly form a novel. Vanessa plays Clarissa. And here is Eleanor Hardyng (Virginia) responding to Mr. Hatherly (Lytton): "So you've noticed it then? How clever you are, and how unkind! For don't you think that these 'extraordinary conclusions' you like so much may be rather uncomfortable . . . for Clarissa? We were not happy—no—and yet I know its dangerous to imagine people in love with one . . . I don't admit for a moment that you have any real ground for your 'extraordinary conclusions,' and I suppose I should do better to say no more about them. You always tempt me to run on, and justify myself and explain myself, with your hints and subtleties and suggestive catlike ways."[70] Bloomsbury must be abuzz with gossip.

All the more so because Vanessa (Clarissa), through this other name, dares to let her distress surface and complains to Eleanor what she keeps silent about to Virginia:

Dearest Eleanor . . . I never get you at first hand now; it is always through James [Clive] that I have to find out how you are behaving

& his accounts cannot be taken too literally. You seemed to have seen a great deal of him lately . . . it is late at night & James [Clive] has deserted me. He said he was going to see Roger [Hilton Young] & might look in on you on the way. So I shall perhaps hear of you from him—as usual.[71]

But the bond between Virginia and Clive is weakening. Virginia is persuaded to accompany her sister and brother-in-law to Florence. Her opportunity for a tantalizing letter:

Why should I excite you? Why should you be glad to hear that I and my bundle of tempers come with you to Italy? Ah, how pleasant a world, where such facts do exist! how exquisite that you should recognise them. When I have melted down the whole of my illusions, one or two things remain, bright as gold, or diamond. One is—well, that you care for me, and that we are likely to spend many years in the same neighbourhood.[72]

Virginia's "bundle of tempers" wins out nevertheless. The trip, Florence friends, the city itself, its atmosphere depress her. Clive—avenging himself for not going beyond flirting with her?—acts the loving husband toward his wife. Arguments ensue. Virginia feels excluded, jealous, and decides to return to London. Vanessa's opportunity to reestablish the "Clarissa" version and to sigh sweetly to a friend: "It was rather melancholy to see her start off on that long journey alone leaving us together here! Of course I am sometimes impressed by the pathos of her position & I have been more so here than usual. I think she would like very much to marry & certainly she would like much better to marry Lytton than anyone else. It is difficult living with Adrian who does not appreciate her & to live with him till the end of their days is a melancholy prospect. I hope some new person may appear in the course of the next year or two for I have come to think that in spite of all the drawbacks she had better marry. Still I don't know what she would do with children!"[73] Already!

Yes, everything seems to have cooled off, evolved. Except the attachment, troubled as it is, between Virginia and Vanessa. Who falls in love with Roger Fry, desperately in love . . . which revives Clive's interest in his wife, cooling his interest in Virginia. That's the end of the trio. Leonard will soon return from Ceylon.

The few years she shares with Roger would be the most fulfilled time of Vanessa's life. Thirteen years her senior, Roger was completely hers. A man of rare energy, an engaged scholar, a rather academic painter himself but a critic for the prestigious avant-garde; the first exhibition of postimpressionist painters that he organized in London introduces Van Gogh and Cézanne to England ("There are 6 apples in the Cézanne picture. What can 6 apples *not* be?" muses Virginia) as well as Matisse and Picasso, among others. He becomes the enthusiastic mentor and lover of a self-assured, flourishing Vanessa: "Oh Roger, how horribly I want you. . . . You seem to know so exactly what I want, physically and mentally. How do you do it? Being with you is like being on a river and being with most people is like driving a jibbing horse along a bumpy road." And she uses the same metaphor as she did with Clive: "Oh Roger, it was delicious today in spite of sordid surroundings, like a little water when one was very thirsty."[74]

With all his good taste and talent for living, Clive accepts the situation, very agreeably. When Vanessa writes to him or to Roger, each man adds a cheerful postscript to the letter. She is relaxed, all anxiety has left her, all resentment, and her letters to her husband, often cold until then, become tender: she courts him, it is she who flirts now, wanting to keep him around, close by, wanting there to be no rupture, but a friendship, a lasting affection and, for her, for their children, some kind of priority. Detached from him, she now makes the demands she refrained from, trying to secure him within a lifestyle that, in the end, suits her husband very well and corresponds marvelously to the Bloomsbury style, where affection always outlives intimacy. Where one remains close, faithful beyond all the torments suffered. At present she risks: "Do you really miss your Dolph, my legitimate male? . . . Shall you all be glad to see me next week . . . ?" She insists: "Are you fond of me?", a letter at the end of which Roger describes to Clive the latest of Vanessa's endearing blunders, for which she has a talent.[75]

It will take her a few years to grow weary not of Roger Fry, who is indispensable to her (despite his anguish, he remained her confidant), but of the demanding love he bears for her. And most importantly, Duncan Grant, such a regular until then, enters the stage as a new character. Adrian leaves Duncan, and Nessa tries to console him over the rupture with her brother. Thus blossoms Nessa's undying passion for him, though her sexual life almost immediately and permanently comes to an end, since Duncan will put a stop to any intercourse of this kind with her. Without ever projecting it, without Virginia ever guessing it, Vanessa Bell thus becomes another symbol for the lament: "to want and want and not to have."[76]

The limits of proud Vanessa's combativeness, despite her former rebellion against her father, her obstinacy in preserving everything, hiding her wounds and yielding when vanquished, surface in the face of Clive and Virginia's betrayal, as does her tendency to suffer without breaking or losing anything. Her silent withdrawals, her resignation will become the secret keys to her existence, without ever diminishing her aura. That part of her nature will remain unknown to her circle, even (and especially) to Virginia. A mute pride will make her conceal all humiliation. Secret, unknown to others, she will appear to be following a perfectly obvious itinerary.

Sensual being that she is, she will submit, suffer the torture of begging, of being denied sexual intercourse, and by the most desirable and desired of men. Desiring him physically, desiring him in vain, she will no longer consider anyone else. But at the cost of a thousand humiliations, and often anguished, always anxious, she will manage to retain Duncan's (mutually) delightful presence for life.

Their life will be linked to Charleston, the home she created, luminous, full of work, sensual richness, fertile disorder, and proclaimed freedom. But Nessa's existence will be based on frustration, a castration she masochistically asks for, almost demanding to be scorned, deferent, anxious (and loved), and ready to do anything to avoid losing Duncan, which will never happen.

Everyone sees her as dominant, vital, sexual, and liberated, professional, surrounded by men she loves and has loved and who remain, even with one another, dear close friends. No one will leave her, except through death.

Clive, as we have seen, remains her husband and becomes the official father of Angelica, Duncan's daughter: the proprieties given a passing nod! They will gather regularly in London and Clive joins her at Charleston, where he sometimes resides, for a long time accompanied by Mary Hutchinson, receiving regular visitors, the Woolfs, Adrian, Maynard Keynes (much later with his wife, the Russian ballerina Lydia Lopokova), or Dora Carrington, Lytton and other Stracheys, many mutual friends, often the same ones as at Rodmell, which is perhaps less grand and worldly, but more relaxed. And then Roger Fry, heartbroken, but later with Helen Anrep, his new companion. Julian, Quentin, and Angelica will be at the center of all events. And Duncan, who participates with such ease and grace in all the activities and who dances, disguises himself, disputes, enchants, loves them all, those whose lover he has been as well, among them Lytton, Maynard, and Adrian.

All their lives, Nessa and Duncan paint together, each of them absorbed in their bold investigations; Duncan already famous in England, Vanessa quite well known, admiring him, considering him superior— wrongly. Encouraged and nurtured by Leslie, she has been devoted to her future as a painter since childhood. All her life she will work, think about, dedicate herself to her vocation. She and Duncan were among the very first English painters to accept both the figurative image and abstraction, little concerned about the boundaries between them. Though different from one another, their works belong to the same family. Boldly constructed, Vanessa's canvases express the inexorable solitude of a nude woman, of grouped figures, objects, abstract compositions, fixed each time in an insurmountable isolation to which she holds the key. A calm, distant, inflexible violence, often very captivating, and which belongs to her.

Negligently beautiful, heavier than Virginia, less quick and nervous, more practical, Vanessa, often provocative, saucy, even coarse, always maternal, will live surrounded by her own, by calm, gaiety, trivial uproars, deep friendships.

And all her life, she will struggle in secret, humble and terrified, deprived of the sexuality that is intrinsic to her. Willing at every moment, ready to bear anything, even to provoke anything so that Duncan Grant will not go to live elsewhere with one of his lovers. Lovers whom she often tries to keep under her own roof.

After having obtained his necessary consent, it is with David (Bunny) Garnett that she first shares Duncan. A trio, once again! But real, immediate; they live together. Later, pregnant by Duncan at her request, she fears Bunny's reaction (which will be favorable) and not Clive's, who encouraged her and will become the official father.

World War I is approaching. David Garnett is twenty-six years old. He is then writing his first work, *Turgenev*, which would appear in 1917. Five years later, then completed detached from the trio, he would become famous with a novel: *Lady Into Fox*.

He prefers women, has already flirted with Lytton, Maynard, and others; heterosexuality is more natural to him. With Duncan? He is his lover, they love each other.

With World War I under way, and both of them conscientious objectors, they are able, thanks to Vanessa's maneuverings, to work for the state in the orchards near Charleston, but also in Wissett and in Suffolk, and it is there, in a house without electricity or telephone, that Vanessa gives birth to Angelica.

Angelica. Born the first Christmas of peacetime, in 1918. After her birth, or even since her conception, demanded by Nessa, no further sexual ties between her parents; Duncan decreed it. Henceforth her mother will have no more sexual ties with anyone, and she is thirty-nine years old.

Two sisters, two of the most liberated women of their time, unbelievably beautiful, are united in exile, deprivation, the denial of their bodies, decided by two men. To all appearances, at least.

At Lytton Strachey's death, Duncan and Vanessa will fall into each other's arms and will hold each other in a long embrace, sobbing together. The only time, their daughter will remark, when she ever saw them so physically close!

Until she was sixteen years old, Angelica believed she was Clive Bell's daughter, whose name she bore. Before an alarmed Virginia, she happened one day to refer to her real father, with whom she lived and whom she loved very much, as "Mr. Grant."

She was unaware of all the circumstances that surrounded her arrival into the world, to the point of marrying . . . Bunny, without knowing that he was her father's lover, with whom her mother shared Duncan at the time of her birth, when all three lived together as a threesome.

Above all, she didn't know that upon discovering her, a newborn in her cradle, Bunny had written to Lytton, "I think of marrying it; when she is twenty I shall be 46—will it be scandalous?"[77]

He does marry her.

In the interim, he marries Rachel Marshall and becomes a father.

But beyond Angelica's beauty and youth, what attracts him is the link to the past, to the trio he, Nessa, and Duncan formed at Wissett and Charleston, which haunts him still. Something remained unresolved for him, entangled; some bewitchment, some bitterness.

Horrified, Duncan and Vanessa tried to prevent the marriage, but without daring to reveal the past to their daughter. Bunny, who had never stopped seeing them, was once again part of their intimacy. What revenge, what somnambulant reprisals was Angelica the object of? Hoodwinked, what stake did she represent?

Angelica Garnett would have four daughters by Bunny.

She would be a painter and sculptor, and . . . wounded.

Duncan and Bunny? Their love affair twenty years earlier? It lasted five stormy years, interrupted by scenes of jealousy and despair on one side or the other. Nessa was not the cause, but rather outside rivals (or rival). It was Vanessa who would calm and console the two men—which often became her role between Duncan and his partners, and served her well in maintaining her place at Duncan's side.

Between Bunny and Nessa, a latent war: Bunny, attracted, desires her in bed; she rebuffs him; he resents her.

Duncan feels guilty to the point of writing to Bunny: "I am ashamed she should be so fond of me and you are fonder of me than I deserve and I must just abjectly love both of you."[78]

But he adjusts, plays one against the other. In his personal diary, regarding a not yet pregnant Vanessa: "I copulated on Saturday with her with great satisfaction to myself physically. It is a convenient way the females of letting off one's spunk and comfortable. Also the pleasure it gives is reassuring. You don't get this dumb misunderstanding body of a person who isn't a bugger. That's one for you Bunny!"[79] Duncan isn't always so serious. . . .

For Virginia, Bunny's presence at Charleston seems completely natural. "My visit to Charleston was spent mostly in sitting in the drawing [room] & talking to N. [Vanessa] . . . Duncan wandered in & out; sometimes digging a vegetable bed, sometimes painting a watercolor of bedroom china, pinned to a door. In the evening there was the lumpish Bunny, inclined to be surly; & N. inclined to take him up sharply." Or that enchanting evening spent with them, despite "the rather obtuse barrier of poor Bunny." Unwell, he finally goes to bed, "without sympathy from Nessa, who had often put him to bed, she said, for no perceivable cause."[80]

She says this in Virginia's presence. But within the trio, Vanessa remains dependent on Garnett, afraid that he will leave with Duncan; to keep him around, she admits that he is indispensable to her, as are her companion's future lovers. Here she is imploring, entangled in a disagreement with Bunny and apologizing for herself in apologizing to Duncan:

> One other perhaps gloomy subject I must write to you about because
> I've been thinking and thinking about it—this difficulty with

Bunny. . . . All I want to tell you is that I think that I behaved very badly and stupidly. I will write and tell him so . . . having thought about it all, I do understand why I think I felt as I did. It wasn't that he was on my nerves or that I was jealous of him. I think I can simply forget about it all and there's no reason for all this bother. I can behave ordinarily and as usual when we meet and I see that if it hadn't been for other bothers I could have done so before. Please don't mind my telling you about it. . . . My bear, don't be severe with me for writing you a gloomy letter.* (*Not that I expect you to be). You know I'm really cheerful as a rule.[81]

But Duncan is not so complex and notes, for example, in his diary:

Last night Bunny and Nessa had a terrific conversation over my body after supper, about my jealousy and the treatment of it. . . . But at the end I only felt increased affection and respect for Nessa. . . . She spoke about me so much as I should have myself had I dared to defend myself, that I left everything in her hands. . . . We all discussed later whether our high opinion of a rival made us more or less jealous. Nessa thought the higher the opinion the greater the jealousy with which I later agreed. She produced Virginia of whom she has been more jealous than anyone at a time when she admired her more than any woman she knew.[82]

Thus Vanessa reveals what she silently endured in Clive's time, and to what extent she is able to stifle, to internalize, her suffering. She also indicates, perhaps, the source of her masochistic obsession, how she needs obstacles, torments, rivalry to obtain the satisfaction of not obtaining, of preserving and maintaining the presence of a permanent rejection, a persistent denial of her desire. And from then on, she is obstinately and endlessly focused on this desire—that is, on the presence of Duncan Grant, maintained in the fullness of his companionship and the severity of his rejection.

Roger Fry, entirely available, never stood a chance.

And it is Duncan, diverted, so gentle, used to being courted, loved, and possessing a loving nature himself, quick to be amused, to take pleasure in everything, fickle, but above all centered on his art—it is Duncan, accustomed to dejection, to problems of love and morality, and desired by everyone, who becomes in fact . . . Vanessa's prey. Anxiously he asks himself:

> I am so uncertain of my real feeling to V that I am utterly unable to feign more than I feel when called upon to feel much, with the consequence that I seem to feel less than I do. I suppose the only thing lacking in my feelings to her is passion. What of that there might be seems crushed out of me, by a bewildering suffering expectation of it (hardly conscious) by her. I think I feel that if I showed any, it would be met by such an avalanche that I should be crushed. All I feel I can do in this case is to build slowly for her a completely strong affection on which she can lean her weary self.[83]

What attachment, or acquiescence, because nothing obliged him to love Vanessa.

Twelve years later, they are almost exactly at the same point. Only Bunny is gone, replaced many times over. This time, Duncan is dangerously in love with George Bergen; he believes he's on the brink of leaving Vanessa, who believes it as well. Nothing could be less true. Vanessa will always know how to stop him. Stoic, flexible, she is expert at submitting, stubbornly suffering and living in torment, docile and deserted . . . guilty. She is the one who writes to Duncan: "Please don't ever be unhappy about me. . . . Sometimes at night—when I used to give you such bad times—I get tired and feel melancholy. I think now the only thing I really mind at the moment is the complete uncertainty, not knowing in the least how long you will be away, nor what can happen afterwards." "But the fact that I don't know if he's the kind of person who ever can live quietly near you and see us both and work and be happy with you makes it much harder for me."[84] And it is Duncan who comes back. With George.

Is this the same Vanessa who shook with rage before the flouted Leslie? The Vanessa who, when the young Stephens all hid one evening from the calls of a widowed, aging, solitary father, was the only one to break the long silence after he asked them if they had intentionally tried not to hear him, to fling at him a "yes!"? Now she lives by one principle: "It seems better not to feel more than one can help."[85] And she does not succeed.

But the Charleston song continues, strangely enduring. The song of a triumphant Vanessa, surrounded by her children, her husband, her lovers. Virginia admires her, adores her . . . and there is jealousy once again, a jealousy that Vanessa could not do without. Sometimes, but so rarely, she can no longer keep from unburdening herself, and Virginia, stupefied: "I have now written myself out of a writing mood; & cannot attack melancholy, save only to note that it was much diminished by hearing Nessa say she was often melancholy and often envied me—a statement I thought incredible. I have split myself among too many stools she said (we were sitting in her bedroom before dinner). Other peoples [*sic*] melancholy certainly cheers one." But when she remarks, no doubt by chance and joking: "You and Duncan always seem to me, though some appearances are against it, marmoreally chaste,"[86] Nessa, disconcerted, crushed, can only manage to answer: "It is terrible to be thought chaste and dowdy when one would so much like to be neither."[87]

She can rest assured: badly dressed or not, for Virginia, she will always pass for the most beautiful, the most free of women, the most filled with happiness and plenitude, living in rich sensual pleasures, bordering on luxury, satiated.

When the Woolfs returned after their less-than-stimulating honeymoon, Nessa, then still content with Roger, took small revenge in happily writing Clive: "As I was in the middle of dinner in came the Woolves. . . . They seemed very happy, but are evidently both a little exercised in their minds on the subject of the Goat's [Virginia's] coldness. . . . Apparently she still gets no pleasure at all from the act, which I think is curious. They were very anxious to know when I first had an orgasm. I couldn't remember. Do you? But no doubt I sympathised with such things if I didn't have them from the time I was 2."[88] So much for you, Virginia, to quote Duncan Grant. . . .

In truth, they are both very similar to Mrs. Dalloway, relegated by her husband to sleep alone, and who "could not dispel a virginity preserved through childbirth which clung to her like a sheet." This Clarissa Dalloway who entered her room "like a nun withdrawing . . . narrower and narrower would her bed be. The candle was half burnt down. . . ." "It was all over for her. The sheet was stretched and the bed narrow. She had gone up into the tower alone and left them blackberrying in the sun. The door had shut."[89]

✳ ✳ ✳

Here we return once more to the Woolfs, newly married and having just returned to London, each of them ready to fashion *their* life. A miraculous feat, because a life that leads to a work representing an existence rooted in the age can only belong to the order of miracles, whatever the obstacles and torments that lead it to tragedy.

Long stretches of serenity, underlying conflicts, throughout years undercut by spite, resentment, deep contention: they will learn how to create their own choreography. To dance their pas de deux in mutual territory.

Even while leading a contingent life of infinite emotions and excitement, Virginia will always manage to return to the limbo of perception. To watch for, to invoke, to confront what is going to dawn in its first essence, to emerge fragile and forbidden, all by itself, and which Leonard, on the sidelines, will not impede. Which is, in itself, enormous!

Here are Leonard and Virginia on the brink of an alliance and here, springing from the ashes of Virginia Stephen, is Virginia Woolf. Ready to make her life exist, to bring her work to life.

Here they are beyond the serious disturbances already mentioned: the two crises at the very beginning of their marriage that might be called attacks of madness. But certainly not in the sense of a "cancer of the mind" or a "corruption of the spirit," an incurable ill, nor a cause for repudiation and exclusion as defined by Quentin Bell.[90]

"Madness"? Often a dangerous simplification, a name given to the disasters encountered on the demanding journey of a man (or a woman) in search of her identities, in a manipulated world where she must, to her peril, approach the truest language.

In addition, in Virginia's case, the simplest, most mundane, clearly definable causes, which will go unrecognized despite their obviousness: for instance, the despotic brutality with which she has just been denied children. Under the pretext of mental instability, which will, in fact, precipitate it. The arrogant, abrupt prohibition imposed by Leonard left a powerless, somehow mutilated Virginia cornered. And she felt guilty.

Too uncertain, self-doubting, shaken by the past, she could only accept the verdict that disqualified her. Which was not the result of a ban imposed by medical experts, as Leonard claimed and as she believed, but was decided by him, counter to the opinion of the attending doctor and strangely supported by practitioners who immediately accepted his version, responded to it as if asked to, and, let us repeat, without ever having seen, heard, examined, or even met Virginia.

Added to the sexual fiasco of their marriage, it is Virginia's whole female, sexual being that is denied, inversely violated, outraged, and it is her immense longing for tenderness that is ravaged.

Which seems very much like another loss, a mourning this time for something essential that has never been and will never be.

Her anguish? The same as so many women have felt, prompting in them the same kind of breakdown. Heightened by all the heavy losses of the recent past, all the ordeals suffered.

In the final analysis, the instinctive pathological nature of her reaction, her violence, protected her. Remember her conviction: "Madness saved me"? By which she meant, from acquiescence, from resignation to dullness. But here madness saves her by letting her rage, very rationally shrieking her fury, her hatred for her husband, her rejection of an "equal world," her sorrow at being ill used and perhaps having always been, under the guise of kindness. Having resigned herself so many times. Having so often resisted devastation.

"I am alone in a hostile world, the human face is hideous,"[91] she makes Rhoda say.

As for Virginia, she will weep, refuse to speak, slam the door on Leonard; she will insult and injure him, reject all food, be violent toward the nurses; she will either remain mute and prostrate or talk nonstop for days on end. Leonard:

> in this stage she talked almost without stopping for two or three days, paying no attention to anyone in the room or anything said to her. For about a day what she said was coherent; the sentences meant something, though it was nearly all wildly insane. Then gradually it became completely incoherent, a mere jumble of dissociated words. After another day the stream of words diminished and finally she fell into a coma. . . . When she came out of the coma, she was exhausted, but much calmer; then very slowly she began to recover.[92]

That "stream of words" must have been among the most significant and eloquent ever uttered (think of Antonin Artaud's glossolalia). Perhaps it was there she could express herself in absolute secrecy, under the veil of incoherence—incoherent only as compared to normal rhetoric and no doubt full of meaning. That logorrhea? Perhaps it was what she had to make heard, analyzable, what she externalized, brought forth and poured out, without freeing herself from it. And what gave her permission to be reintegrated among the others. Here where Leonard would never be completely reintegrated. Making his wife's "madness" is indispensable to him.

With this crisis, the last one, it is decided of course that Leonard will take Virginia in hand, but . . . for as much as he would like to: "Though you can tell a person like Virginia not to go for a walk or to a party, you cannot tell her not to think, work, or write."[93] Alas!

Let's be fair: he didn't prevent her from thinking, working, or writing. On the contrary. The work is there. And perhaps the Woolf therapy method did some good? Because, even if he always spoke of Virginia's madness as having punctuated their whole existence, having haunted her until the end, after those two crises, corresponding to their marriage and coming so close together, Virginia never experienced *a single other one.*

Braced, even vigorous, dynamic, she suffered states of depression, despair, went through "horrors"[94] she dreaded; she suffered from headaches, passed out two or three times; she experienced recurring health problems, but nothing analogous to "madness." But the tension of having accepted such suffering or ecstasy, of having submitted to it, defenseless, stripped naked, in order to pursue her quest, her work, tested her nerves to the limit. She experienced life through all the fibers of her being. As she was. And she was fragile.

Every single day Leonard would record—in the Tamil or Singhalese language and alphabet!—Virginia Woolf's appetite, menstrual periods, sleep, weight, mood, her slightest symptoms or what he considered symptoms. He rules over her, leaves no stone unturned, and directs his wife's daily existence beginning with the diagnoses that result from these intrusions, and that were as good as verdicts.

Because she is in his hands, and she knows it. He has the power to institutionalize her, as Leslie (and Julia) had done to Laura. Henceforth, her freedom depends upon him, upon the husband to whom she gave herself.

In truth . . . she is in no danger. He is already very attached to her: they each believe in the other's value in areas essential to them. And after all . . . he is the one who depends on her. What would he become without Virginia Stephen in that sphere where his wife's place is obvious and his is not yet, if he were not linked to her? Being an Apostle, a friend from Cambridge days, might allow him to remain in contact with those intellectual couples, but not to enter their circle, outside of which he suffocates. Except for finances, nothing would stand in the way of his returning to Ceylon or similar vicissitudes. And what would people say if Virginia entered "the occupation of madness,"[95] as Van Gogh put it? And if Leonard had her put away? She must absolutely stay with him and watch over his ascendancy.

He had already avoided having her "certified"[96] in 1913, during a first crisis that followed almost immediately after she was forbidden children. That first time, she had not suffered from hallucinations or delirium, as in 1915. It had been a matter of unbearable anxiety, violent melancholy, prostration followed by a serious suicide attempt that, in England, would have justified automatic institutionalization, even legal proceedings. Leonard is urged to visit some asylums. But, horrified by what he discovers there, he sees that his wife is surrounded by nurses until she gets well.

One can imagine his confusion, his terror at what falls to him. With hesitant authorization from the doctors, he takes Virginia away from London, but settles upon an inn in Holford . . . where their honeymoon had begun. His choice could not be worse, and Leonard is unaware of it.

Holford for him? "It was primitive but extraordinarily pleasant." Virginia had a tendency toward anorexia then. Not her husband: "Nothing could be better than the bread, butter, cream, and eggs and bacon of the Somersetshire breakfast with which you began your morning. The beef, mutton, and lamb were always magnificent and perfectly cooked; enormous hams, cured by themselves and hanging from the rafters in the kitchen, were so perfect. . . ." And so on.[97]

But Virginia takes no interest and refuses to eat, founders, goes from bad to worse. He takes her back to London, fearing the whole trip that she will throw herself off the train. Nevertheless she agrees to see Dr. Head, one of the doctors with whom he had met privately regarding "no children," but whom "she could not possibly have known that *I* had consulted,"[98] Leonard reassures himself. Which doesn't prevent him from accusing his wife of fantasizing conspiracies. . . .

Head explains to Virginia that she is sick, as with a cold or typhoid fever, and that she must take care of herself, spend a few weeks in a nursing home. She seems to accept. They return to Brunswick Square. And Leonard suddenly remembers not informing Dr. Savage, Virginia's attending physician, of their infidelity. He hurries to do so, leaving Virginia with a friend and . . . a box of medications containing veronal within her reach. Would you believe what happens? Leonard is alerted at Dr. Savage's: Virginia, unconscious, is hardly, irregularly breathing. Geoffrey Keynes, a young surgeon and Maynard's brother, happens to be at the house. He rushes Virginia, at death's door, to the hospital and saves her.

Sixty years later, Leonard, remembering, considers himself responsible:

> I had always kept my case containing the veronal locked. In the tur-
> moil of arriving and settling in at Brunswick Square and then going
> to Head, I must have forgotten to lock it. . . . She must have found
> that it was unlocked and have taken the veronal. I suppose, as a truth-
> ful autobiographer, I ought to record two psychological bad marks
> against myself in connection with this catastrophe. Though I was the
> cause of it, I did not at the time and have not since felt the misery and
> remorse that many people would think I ought to feel. . . . I seem to be
> without a sense of sin and to be unable to feel remorse for something
> which has been done and cannot be undone—I seem to be mentally
> and morally unable to cry over spilt milk. In this particular case I felt
> that it was almost impossible sooner or later not to make a mistake
> of the kind.[99]

More importantly, sooner or later it was "almost impossible" to prevent oneself from doing so.

Difficult. But difficult for him as well, such trials at the very beginning of this marriage; a terrifying situation for which he was not prepared, that he doesn't know how to manage, even if he bears much more responsibility for it than he admits.

It is to Dalindridge, a luxurious property lent to them by George Duckworth and swarming with staff, countless chambermaids, housekeepers, and gardeners, that Leonard decides to take his wife to convalesce. An unfortunate choice, once again. For whether it was Vanessa or Dr. Savage who had spoken to him of it, Leonard knew the role of this half-brother, for whom he felt . . . only deferential admiration!

His description of the master of Dalindridge, Sir George Duckworth:

> a man of the world or at any rate what I think a man of the world
> in excelsis should be. As a young man he was, it was said, an Adonis
> [dear Rupert Brooke!] worshipped by all the great and non-great
> ladies. He was still terribly good looking at the age of 45. A very
> good cricketer, Eton and Trinity College, Cambridge; he knew
> everyone who mattered; was a friend and private secretary of Austen

Chamberlain . . . an extremely kind man and, I think, very fond of Vanessa and Virginia.[100]

George was undoubtedly elegant and good looking. Kind? Perhaps. And he had *certainly* been fond of his half-sisters. But dangerously and excessively so. At least that was a certainty for them, which weighed on and seriously affected their lives, and which they went to great lengths to make known. Unbelievable to find Leonard not referring to it here, ignoring it to the point of not even mentioning it, even contradicting Virginia's view, which was hardly insignificant and which, God knows, she did not hide.

Woolf had been deeply impressed by George since his first visits with his fiancée's family. Another description: "Virginia's half-brother, Sir George Duckworth. Eton, Trinity College, Cambridge, married to Lady Margaret Herbert, very handsome, immensely kind and charming, and—it has to be admitted—a snob."[101] Snob? All the more validating! Nothing if not demonstrative, George must have proved to be very cordial and even affectionate.

Whereas Leonard describes himself as having a terrible complex about his social background. The Stephens and the Duckworths were for him of

a social class and way of life into which hitherto I had only dipped from time to time as an outsider, when, for instance, I stayed as a young man with the Stracheys. I was an outsider to this class, because, although I and my father before me belonged to the professional middle class, we had only recently struggled up into it from the stratum of Jewish shopkeepers. We had no roots in it. . . . The Stephens and the Stracheys, the Ritchies, Thackerays, and Duckworths had an intricate tangle of ancient roots and tendrils stretching far and wide through the upper middle classes, the county families, and the aristocracy. Socially they assumed things unconsciously which I could never assume either unconsciously or consciously. They lived in a peculiar atmosphere of influence, manners, respectability, and it was so natural to them that they were unaware of it as mammals are unaware of the air and fish of the water in which they live. Now that I was going to marry Virginia and went round to see her relations, I began to see this stratum of society from the inside. I said in *Sowing* that I know that I am ambivalent to aristocratic societies, disliking and despising them and at the same time envying them their insolent urbanity. In a milder form there was the same ambivalence in my attitude to the society which I found in Dalindridge Place and St. George's Square. I disliked its respectability and assumptions while envying and fearing its assurance and manners.[102]

These social differences, he adds, had since been swept away by the two world wars.

If they first lived outside of London, in Richmond, it was to allow Virginia tranquility and to limit the social life that he considered disruptive for her, and that, more importantly, he found intimidating at the time and never to his liking. "I have always felt psychologically insecure. I am afraid of making a fool of myself, of my first day at school, of going out to dinner, or of a week-end at Garsington with the Morrells. What shall I say to Mr. Jones, or to Lady Ottoline Morell [*sic*], or Aldous Huxley? My hand trembles at the thought of it, and so do my soul, heart, and stomach. Of course, I have learnt to conceal everything except the trembling hand: one of the consolations of growing old is that one learns to talk to Mr. Jones and Lady Ottoline Morrell."[103] A hint here of the Leonard Woolf of Ceylon and of *The Wise Virgins*, elsewhere so well concealed under the mask he constructed for himself, which became his true face.

A beautiful face, moreover, intent, sculpted by living as well as thinking. When Gisèle Freund photographed them together in 1938, he and Virginia resembled each other like brother and sister, illustrating Virginia's definition of their marriage: "Are you in your stall, brother?"[104] She is beautiful as well, more moving than in photographs of her at twenty; her look is poignant, tired of being forever fresh, expectant, searching for what is not given and taking delight in it.

By that time, they have each constructed a life all their own and have learned how to live together. No longer is there a question of social hierarchy, as at the beginning of their marriage.

A beginning in which Virginia's fragility allows Leonard to dominate and even turn the tables. Newly married, broken down, Virginia thus allows him a mastery that alleviates his complexes and distracts their circle from their class differences, then such a powerful force in England. Their roles counterbalance each other. He is considered marginal as a Jew? She will be considered marginal as a mad woman.

And she is the one who must, or believes she must, implore him to let her return to ordinary life a few months after their marriage, when she is confined to a rest home before her two crises which, despite everything, occur. Thus she has become the illegitimate one, the "strange" one, the outcast.

We hear her frightened, anxious to cajole Leonard, courting him, playing a regressive role akin to the one of "Sparroy," but this time with the urgency of convincing her husband that she loves him. Sparroy has disappeared, but they have become his Mongoose to her Mandrill (a species of baboon!). Exhausted, Mandrill tries to elicit enthusiasm difficult to access; breathlessly she declares herself, trying to demonstrate to Mongoose that she does not detest him, since she must make him listen to her.

A few examples. "I've not been very good I'm afraid—but I do think it will be better when we're together. Here its all so unreal." "I do believe in you absolutely, and never for a second do I think you've told me a lie—Goodbye, darling mongoose—I do want you and I believe in spite of my vile imaginations the other day that I love you and that you love me." "I have been disgraceful—to you, I mean." "To begin with, I am to say from nurse, that I have been very good. . . . Dearest Mongoose, I wish you would believe how much I am grateful and repentant."[105]

Finally leaving the nursing home, we find Sparroy again, converted into Mandrill, but closer to Virginia and more sure of herself:

> Immundus Mongoosius Felicissimus, I could write this letter in beautiful silver Latin, but then the scurvy little heap of dusty fir could not read it. Would it make you very conceited if I told you that I love you more than I have ever done since I took you into service, and find you beautiful and indispensable? . . . Goodbye Mongoose, and be a devoted animal and never leave the great variegated creature. She wishes to inform you delicately that her flanks and rump are now in finest plumage, and invites you to an exhibition. Kisses on your dear little pate.[106]

Intimate, erotic games, complicit exchanges adapted to their tastes, which will continue: in 1928, Virginia, departing regretfully (with Vita) for four days in France, is all the more nervous upon returning because Leonard, a subtle psychologist, has hardly written to her. After reassuring him on Vita's role "always running about with hot water bottles," she prepares her reconquest. "Poor Mandrill does adore your every hair of your little body and hereby puts in a claim for an hour of antelope kissing the moment she gets back." "We adore dadanko do-do—we want to talk with him; and kiss the poos. Have they really begun to play violin, daddie? Are you fonder of them than of the marmoteski?—Now stop mots; go under the table. I cant hear myself speak for their chatter. How they sobbed when there was no letter from Dinkey to Avallon! Shall you be glad to see us all again?"[107]

Unexpected dialect, far removed from the pages of Virginia—and of Leonard! Games, complicities that a posthumous intrusion allows us to witness and that often seem grotesque to outside eyes.

We know that they lived out a long conversation together; but in writing, this self-conscious prose, this defensive regression in a stilted register seems to serve as a shell. An artificial, leaden register—playful, of course, but it keeps them at a distance from each other, prisoners of redundant roles, rehearsed speeches, repeated childishnesses, the skins of animals that disguise their actual presence and mask a great timidity. They do not address each other person to person.

How different from the natural warmth in the streams of pages that flow not only from Virginia to Vanessa, "My dearest," "My dear Dolphin," but to Lytton, Clive, Maynard, or Quentin and of course to Vita, to so many others as well, Ethel Smyth in particular. What a gift for communication in them, what ease, what suppleness and what spirit, what laughter, sometimes what confessions or tears, and what casualness . . . how present Virginia is!

Yes, but it is at Leonard's side, leaning on him, having become his wife and once restored from her double breakdown, that Virginia will flee, will fly away from her identity in the end, delivered to a certain degree from the past, if not from its memory. It will manifest itself only later in its new version, so sad and uneasy, dangerous, and that version will be fatal to her.

At present, that past will serve the work. It will be part of the pleasure—and the torment—of producing it.

Her first novel, *The Voyage Out*, appeared, published by Gerald Duckworth, turned editor; still ill, she was not immediately aware of its publication. Its reception? Favorable, sometimes enthusiastic. Virginia Woolf ranked immediately as a writer the literary circles considered major, or soon to be so. She is present, just as she is, and thus she will remain, with her music, her writing, her obsessive fears, her place and her pursuit acknowledged, recognized.

The Voyage Out? From the first pages, water, death, madness unleashed within the framework of a refined life, a controlled gentility. Immediately, savagery breaks through civilization's makeshift calm and denounces the fundamental brutality of life, its deprivations, its essential threats, all the more terrifying in that they manage to spring up despite all the guarantees of safety and well-being promised to the privileged classes by post-Victorian British society, so able, unrelenting, practiced in sealing the cracks against all peril. A reckless, abrupt opening—without much connection to the rest of the novel. It is the threshold of a work; the voice of a writer immediately exposing the voices that will cross it.

And what is it?

It's night and the murky waters of the Thames ripple under a bridge. On the bridge, an impoverished crowd, making an elegant couple, unusual here, nervous. The woman is crying, leaning over the parapet; a tear falls and mixes with the dark fluidity of the river. The man tries to calm the woman. She tells him that he understands nothing. The poverty all around oppresses them. Their confrontation with the masses, the poor. And a fine rain begins to fall over London.

"Lord, how gloomy it is!"[108] Mr. Ambrose groans, and "the poor, and the rain" render "her mind . . . like a wound." These are not the novel's actual characters that Virginia has introduced: the scene is still all her own, personal, the place of mental fury, a familiar disaster that she must initially project, establish, presenting the Ambroses there before the other protagonists enter.

In this deep, gloomy night, one shelter: the elegant freighter where Mrs. Ambrose will embark alone; a cruise in the company of its owner, a rich cousin. Nothing more reassuring. Inside, the human oasis. A soft cage. Flowers, lights from the Thames. An old servant. A meal. . . . Amiable guests.

But what do we hear? The text becomes frenzied without becoming meaningless. Fragments of sentences drifting from a learned conversation. They refer to people and events unknown to the reader, which never come up again in the novel. This is not the beginning of a plot or structure but an exchange of voices punctuated by exchange of signals, of ships lost in the fog. They speak of a devastated world. Blasts that obsess Virginia.

A random glance at those first pages: "On a dark night one would fall down these stairs head foremost . . . and be killed. . . ." "There was a book, wasn't there? . . ." "There *was* a book, but there never *will* be a book. . . ." "There never will be a book, because some one else has written it for him."[109]

And also: "He's dead. . . ." "Drink—drugs. . . ." "There was a theory about the planets, wasn't there? . . ." "A screw loose somewhere. . . ." "The accumulations of a lifetime wasted."[110]

Outside, the night, the sea, "the great white monsters of the lower waters" and "the white, hairless, blind monsters lying curled on the ridges of sand at the bottom of the sea." The sea "grew dimmer and dimmer until the sand at the bottom was only a pale blur. One could scarcely see the black ribs of wrecked ships."[111]

We discover Rachel, the main character, for whom the others appear like "aimless masses of matter, floating hither and thither, without aim except to impede her."[112] The voyage has begun.

Virginia's men and women from England find themselves on another continent, in Argentina, very exotic for them at the time. With diverse backgrounds, they come to vacation in villas, ordinary luxury hotels, nestled in luxurious vegetation. They do not know the laws of this new world and so maintain their own rules: those of propriety, which protect them from the panic of living, deprive them of the pleasure of existing. The water that pounds the luxurious shores and crosses the South American continent is still tied to that of the Thames; it is only an extension of it.

A love affair develops finally, almost regretfully, in the last third of the book. What her fiancé Terence asks from Rachel and what he listens to feverishly in the voluptuous, tropical climate is the account of her life as a young girl in Richmond, among her shriveled old aunts and facing the eternal roast in a hideously decorated room: "Aunt Clara carves the neck of lamb. . . . There's a very ugly yellow china stand in front of me."[113] Terence drinks in Rachel's words, the secrets of a drab life, which he records and which evoke what matters to him, what worries and enthralls him: banality.

They scarcely touch each other, remaining distant in an artificial happiness, and Terence watches her dreaming of being "flung into the sea, to be washed hither and thither, and driven about the roots of the world." In ecstasy, he sees her in the hotel knocking into chairs, staggering about "as if she were indeed striking through the waters . . . she seemed to be cleaving a passage for herself, and dealing triumphantly with the obstacles which would hinder their passage through life." He pins her to the ground. "'I'm a mermaid! I can swim,' she cried, 'so the game's up.'"[114]

Virginia's game. So many years yet, so many pages before it comes to an end in the River Ouse. . . .

If Rachel dies in bed, carried off by fever, it is with the sensation of falling

> into a deep pool of sticky water, which eventually closed over her head. She saw nothing and heard nothing but a faint booming sound, which was the sound of the sea rolling over her head. While all her tormenters thought that she was dead, she was not dead, but curled up at the bottom of the sea.[115]

A first work in which a great deal is said.

Part 4

VIRGINIA Woolf is well known, and thus she is protected. Soon, between her and those close to her, between her and Leonard, between her and herself, there will be a rampart consisting of her anonymous readership, her literary circle, and, most intimately, the Bloomsbury group. They will keep her steady with regard to her legitimacy. Her public persona. That of a recognized author, who will become famous. They will free her, in appearance at least, from the uncertain Virginia Stephen, confined until now within the family circle (nest or cesspool?), the pool of memories from which she will always draw.

Beneath the armor of Virginia Woolf, Virginia Stephen will forever tremble, vulnerable, anxious. But Virginia Woolf is going to take off. She is in the public eye, prominent, encouraged. Better than accepted: required.

"And there, I gave you a new book!" she rejoiced one evening, walking the streets of London.

The first offering, *The Voyage Out*, drawn from the roots of her desire, her fears, her being; from seven years of work. The next one will stem from her fear of being judged a victim of insanity: she will want to present it as proof to the contrary, resulting in the "platitude" she recognizes it to be. It will be mediocre, and well received: *Night and Day*, in which she conceals the author she really is, hides Virginia Woolf . . . even while over the course of writing it she wholly becomes that author.

> After being ill and suffering every form and variety of nightmare and extravagant intensity of perception—for I used to make up poems, stories, profound and to me inspired phrases all day long as I lay in bed, and thus sketched, I think, all that I now, by the light of reason, try to put into prose (I thought of the Lighthouse then, and Kew and others, not in substance, but in idea)—after all this, when I came to, I was so tremblingly afraid of my own insanity that I wrote Night and Day mainly to prove to my own satisfaction that I could keep entirely off that dangerous ground.[1]

Six novels later, she confesses to Ethel Smyth that she wrote that "bad book" still in bed after the second breakdown, when she was allowed to work half an hour each day. As small treats, she then allowed herself a few short, unrestricted texts now and then, a kind of compensation. A reward: "I shall never forget the day I wrote The Mark on the Wall—all in a flash, as if flying, after being kept stone breaking for months."[2]

And suddenly, she had known. She knew. She had recognized her "method of approach." The future books appeared. She knew how she would find the form each time to shape her experiences. That moment she was completely at one with herself: soon, "Jacob's Room, Mrs Dalloway etc—How I trembled with excitement."[3] But . . .

"Then Leonard came in, and I drank my milk, and concealed my excitement, and wrote I suppose another page of that interminable Night and Day (which some say is my best book)."[4] The book that avoided danger and let her discover what she would avoid from then on: all concern for danger.

We are in the arcana, in the veins of the work. Of its genesis. A secret stratum.

Leonard and the milk will no longer do anything but come in, go out—a man nursing a woman he has denied children! Nothing will interrupt Virginia at work anymore. At work, she is untouchable.

It is often with ironic indulgence that she lets Leonard pursue his obsessions. She lets her frustrations out on Richard Dalloway: "'An hour's complete rest after luncheon,' he said. And he went. How like him!

He would go on saying 'An hour's complete rest after luncheon' to the end of time, because a doctor had ordered it once." She denounces those doctors (and Leonard too) through Dr. Bradshaw, "insisting that these prophetic Christs and Christesses, who prophesied the end of the world, or the advent of God, should drink milk in bed, as Sir William ordered; Sir William with his thirty years' experience of these kinds of cases, and his infallible instinct, this is madness, this sense."[5]

Still anxious to prove her stability, Virginia would sometimes make a great display of logical reasoning in her literary criticism, making her pieces dull and scholarly.

Elsewhere, she accepted every risk. The risk of approaching her work unarmed, confronting it naked, without certainty, stripped of what stands in the way of anguish: those protections, those . . . parapets; the construction around the general, hegemonic discourse, which has already catalogued, organized, compartmentalized, and restricted perception.

The cerebral is organic, it adjoins emotion; Virginia knows instinctively, and she seizes thought raw, before the established meaning has corrupted it. The precise sound of the sentence thus reaches her and leads her to the pulp of what she covets. She will compose each novel according to methods not burdened by theorizing, new for each one, but without ostentation. Nothing deliberated, no plan: a plunge. A desire. And merged there, the body, a time of life, a musical technique extended toward this desire, in order to achieve it, fulfill it, discover what it harbors, develop it, and pour it into an invisible, skillful, and always unforeseen architecture. A work that, produced well out of bounds, could lead Virginia Woolf to the threshold of stability and make its author seem a stranger to reason.

Leonard, open to his wife's work, is not a worry on this point. Even if he considers madness inherent to genius and likes to think Virginia is continually threatened by insanity, he stands solidly behind each of her books,[6] fully welcomes them, and defends them as editor as well. Each work will be given its due; each will be law within its own domain.

For many readers, that will be the case. But what if her rampart, her readership, if . . . suddenly the rampart collapsed? What if her literary circle, her Bloomsbury friends, and above all, the critics undermined her readers' intuition and each group undermined the others' intuition, if they suddenly (or gradually) came to destroy Virginia precisely through the protective work?

That fear makes her tremble. She will always tremble before judgments pronounced on her work, which she will take as official verdicts, validating or invalidating her sanity. Her work defends her from any sentence imposed by her private circle, but if that work itself threatened her? Those pages that exposed her utterly, to the point beyond which she could not go, too far, along paths alarming to those terrified by audacity, especially not displayed. Those who would then be in a position to terrify her, Virginia.

And here, once again, Leonard poses no threat; passionately he enters those territories where, as a young man, he had hoped to go and that remain open. No vague impulse of envy or jealousy; his editorial passion, his political life, his own works provide an expansive field of existence that fulfills him. As a couple, they share a profound understanding with regard to Virginia's books. But she also sees how an outside judgment could support and reinforce her husband's power, the symbolic threat he represents in her eyes. And above all, she sees herself under suspended sentence from a higher court, a sentence that threatens those who can declare, like Antonin Artaud: "I am a body that suffers the world and disgorges reality."[7]

Quentin Bell was right when he said to me: "An unfavorable review was, for her, a condemnation to madness. She is seen as too sensitive to criticism, but the circumstances were difficult."[8]

Yes. Thus Virginia's terror: "They will say it's a tired book; a last effort . . ." "the long drawn twaddle of a prim prudish bourgeois mind," "A physical feeling as if I were drumming slightly in the veins: very cold: impotent: & terrified. As if I were exposed on a high ledge in full light. Very lonely. L. out to lunch. Nessa has Quentin & dont want me. . . . Very apprehensive. As if something cold & horrible—a roar of laughter at my expense were about to happen. And I am powerless to ward it off: I have no protection. . . . I looked at my eyes in the glass once & saw them positively terrified." "I'm going to be beaten, I'm going to be laughed at, I'm going to be held up to scorn & ridicule."[9]

She is the primary source of that exploding laughter. Without malevolence toward her dear targets, without compromising her fidelity, her actual tenderness toward them . . . but not without spitefulness, she knows the art of inflicting wounds—as she herself has long been a wounded target.

But for now Virginia knows how to combine life's pleasures with those wounds. She and Leonard have established a place for themselves, where they can live together, act, exist jointly within a maze of activities, harmonious surroundings, abundant friends, without renouncing their respective paths.

Leonard is that companion Virginia Stephen so painfully lacked—that husband she anxiously awaited. If he creates other frustrations, anxieties, shackles, his constant presence, his fidelity frees her from much angst . . . even at the price of becoming the obsession of this obsessive man who imposes a maniacal hold on her, and who, deep down, does not want any more from her than she wants from him.

Relying upon their balanced imbalance, upon a real attraction both limited and powerful, bound by professional solidarity and the seductive ease of habit, both will be able to exploit their prodigious dynamism, well served by an ambient peace, notwithstanding "the horrors," the distress Virginia often experiences, although it now becomes propitious, absorbed into the work.

Happiness and the throes of writing encompass Virginia's life. A kind of euphoria sets in, since she has written what she'd hoped for. Fortified by the preceding books, their important triumphs, she sets off each time for new territory.

Around her, the Bloomsbury circle, this already old family in which she navigates with ease, in which the destiny of each member continually unfolds before the others' eyes, all of them implicated and ever barraged with opinions and gossip, never spared sarcasm or support.

The others. They are indispensable to her, circumscribing her space, as reference points, providing desired warmth. But she is the one who adapts to them, needing to be recognized as part of them, to be accepted. She is not really on their wavelength, nor anything or anyone else's, but from them she draws the strength to forbear, to bear up. The strength to stay grounded at the surface of things, always vibrant, sometimes desolate. Here she finds the strength not to hide and never to flee into the sublime: even while aiming for the real, never to leave the ground of "reality."

Bloomsbury, friendship, the well-being of friendship, quarrels, presences! As for her excursions into the purely aristocratic, elegant, worldly spheres, what an escape, what a respite! For a time, they keep the pathos away and let the fibers of her work rest, even as they nurture it, despite the pathos she perceives in these excursions' futility.

Whirlwinds. Anchorage.

In truth, no one in the Bloomsbury group is tied to her. There are affections, long intimacies, endless conflicts, shared hardships, as well as

Thoby's memory, that bind them. And it is Virginia, for the most part, who weaves and maintains the bonds of what has become her natural environment, where she can seek comfort.

A circle no more clearly circumscribed than the list of those who compose it. Intellectual art lovers; avant-garde scholars; writers; painters; critics; one major economist, Maynard Keynes. Above all, friends. No writer there is a match for Virginia Woolf. Only one other work is at all groundbreaking, that of Keynes.

They are all gifted, often no more than that, and clever, curious within a range of disciplines. Many will be forgotten; for some, their fame will be limited to England. But the group has a major influence, introducing painting, ballet, music to England, a breath of fresh air from Europe. They swept aside, swept past the Victorian era. Above all, Bloomsbury set an example of incomparable personal freedom, undoubtedly unmatched since.

For all of them, their genius lay in their freedom, their independence, their influence over their time and their style of living; their natural suppleness of mind and morals. Their mutual, unfailing attachment and their overwhelming constancy, despite snubs, despite sarcasm and wounds.

So many passionate rivalries among them; so many sometime lovers brought to their knees by one another; affairs, painful breakups that never for a moment call into question the tenderness that binds them to those they've betrayed, supplanted, left, made suffer, and who constitute part of the circle. It is their affection, their long, indomitable intimacy, their trials, and a rare elegance that bind them to one another, forever.

Often they all gathered at Charleston for a peaceful weekend, or in London at one person's house or another, in restaurants, at parties organized by Karin Stephen, Lydia Keynes, Vanessa, and others; some were to be found at the home of the elegant Ottoline Morrell. They would cause or experience great pain and suffering because of each other, without ever weakening their bonds.

They will grow old together.

Only death will be able to separate them.

Here are Clive and Vanessa, never divorced. Duncan Grant and Clive Bell and Roger Fry remain fast friends. Clive long accompanied by Mary Hutchinson—and Virginia laughing: "No, says Mary; and I dont want to hear any more. If Virginia's going on like this about her house, as well as—I mean if we've got to admire 52 Tavistock Square [Virginia's address at the time] and the WC [bathroom] and the basement, as well as the dress, the genius, the face, the charm, the shoes, the stockings, the wit, the letters, the character, the temper, the manners, the shoe laces, the finger nails, the way she comes in, and the way she goes out—then, my dear Mr Bell, says Mary, I say your sister in law's high at the price."[10]

Here, part of the swarm we have already witnessed around the singular Duncan: Maynard Keynes, who struggled so hard to win and keep him, only to lose him. Maynard, later married to Lydia Lopokova, the tall and very slender star of the Ballets Russes. A union Virginia and Vanessa eagerly predict will be a disaster; later they have to acknowledge, disappointedly, the durability of their idyllic romance. Keynes, indispensable, assiduous, whom they all love to detest and whom they have been ready to exclude, Virginia remarks, for twenty-five years.

Lytton—long in love with Duncan, whom he has also courted and lost—lives a condensed version of all of Bloomsbury's romantic entanglements, by Dora Carrington's side.

Carrington, captivating, unique, as daring as she is shy. Considered a primitive painter by those more educated. A moving intelligence and imagination; a passionate, timid young woman who, in photographs, appears to be the most modern of our group. Lacking the erudition and culture of the Stracheys and Bloomsbury (or so she claims), she soaks in the knowledge, emotions, experiences that Lytton transmits to her. They first met at the home of Ottoline Morrell (with whom Carrington had had an affair).

Dora (she didn't like her first name) . . . Carrington, with her many lovers, among them Gerald Brenan, with whom she sporadically maintains passionate, overtly sexual relations, or the painter Mark Gertler, suffering artist, who later commits suicide and of whom Virginia, overwhelmed, wrote: "We have been talking about Gertler to Gertler for some 30 hours."[11]

Carrington, who passionately adores Lytton, and Lytton, who gently protects and is greatly attracted to her. But, most importantly, when Ralph Partridge (one of the Woolfs' always temporary slaves at Hogarth Press) falls in love with her, Carrington marries him; Strachey is very much in love with him. A guarantee, a bond. The three of them live together in Lytton's house, Ham Spray, each free to have other partners. And Frances Marshall, who then works in Bunny Garnett's bookstore, falls in love with Ralph. At first conflicted, he settles on living with her in London and spending weekends at Ham Spray, often accompanied by Frances.

Carrington to Duncan, declaring that she loves Frances very much but disapproves of her conduct: "But you dont understand, Duncan. She was passionately in love—is still—with R [Ralph Partridge]. So when it came to the point—I mustn't come this week end—one shade of pressure from him—how could she resist it?"[12]

Virginia, less generous, jokes about her jealousy with regard to Carrington, so exquisite, but whom she compares to a cook who does not take Sundays off. The conversations with Lytton recorded by Virginia in her diary recall those earlier ones with Clive: "'I believe I'm sometimes jealous—' 'Of her? That's inconceivable—' 'You like me better, dont you?' He said he did; we laughed; remarked on our wish for an intimate correspondent [sic]; but how to overcome the difficulties? Should we attempt it? Perhaps."[13]

Carrington is captivated by Virginia: "I have a queer love for Virginia with fills me with emotion when I see her," but she is sure she likes "the Woolves far more than they like me."[14]

And they are constantly found in London, at the country houses, at the Memoir Club; they are forever running into one another, crossing paths. And endlessly commenting on those encounters, watching one another captivated, laughing together, dramatizing, plotting, maligning, encouraging, irritating, blaming, suffering, and all sobbing at Lytton's death, Nessa in Duncan's arms, the Woolfs beside a fire, then all four together, Clive weeping with them.

Lytton held them in suspense for weeks, ill with undetected cancer. One day out of danger, the next day worse than before, the following day close to recovery, then lost, then stronger, then. . . . The countless Stracheys, in despair, reading detective novels or doing crossword puzzles in the adjoining inn. Carrington, of whom they vaguely disapprove, wandering about distraught, and they are afraid that she will kill herself if Lytton dies.

Which does happen—the day after a visit from the Woolfs, during which she appears as welcoming as she is overcome with grief, and Virginia is overwhelmed, powerless: "I held her hands. Her wrists seemed very small. She seemed helpless, deserted, like some small animal left." In Lytton's room, which the Stracheys refuse (it would be morbid) to preserve as his, Carrington collapses and sobs in Virginia's arms: "There is nothing left for me to do. I did everything for Lytton. But I've failed in everything else." Virginia doesn't contradict her: "I did not want to lie to her—I could not pretend that there was not truth in what she said." But she hadn't failed, dear Virginia! Virginia concurs with Carrington: "I said life seemed to me sometimes hopeless, useless, when I woke in the night & thought of Lytton's death."[15]

Carrington serves them lunch, laughs a bit, kisses Virginia, and talks about Lytton Strachey for the last time: these are her last exchanges. "People say he was very selfish to me. But he gave me everything. . . . He taught me everything I know. He read poetry & French to me." Virginia continues: "She said he had been silly with young men. But that was only on the top. She had been angry that they had not understood how great he was." (Virginia agrees, "I said I had always known that.") "She said I made too much of his young friends . . . Roger [Senhouse] was very high spirited & liked going to Rome, & rather liked Lytton reading aloud to him—but they couldn't talk. And this last year Lytton made up his mind to be middle aged. He was a realist. He faced the fact that Roger could not be his love. . . ." "And we were going to Malaga & then he was going to write about Shakespeare. . . . He said things like Lear when he was ill."[16]

As the Woolfs are leaving, she offers them a small box, a souvenir from Paris, with the Arc de Triomphe engraved on the lid. The Stracheys have forbidden her to give away anything that belonged to their brother: "But this is all right. I gave it him."[17]

Very affected by Lytton's death, Leonard would consider the young woman's suicide to be "histrionic: the real thing is that we shall never see Lytton again."[18]

Carrington shoots herself with a rifle without killing herself immediately. Before dying three hours later, she tries to convince her husband, Ralph, who rushes there from London, that she slipped while shooting rabbits.

"Lord how I suffer!" Virginia would write in the weeks that follow. "Cant make things dance; . . . wonder how a year or 20 perhaps to be endured. Think, yet people do live; cant imagine what goes on behind faces. All is surface hard; myself only an organ that takes blows, one after another . . . Lytton's death; Carrington's; a longing to speak to him; all that cut away, gone . . . Nessa's children; society; . . . buying clothes; how I hate Bond Street. . . . And my eyes hurt; & my hand trembles."[19]

Something Leonard said comes back to her; as they were strolling along a "silent blue street" in London one evening, he stopped suddenly:

"'Things have gone wrong somehow.' It was the night Carrington killed herself."[20]

But life picks up again at Rodmell, around the Woolfs; at Charleston, around Nessa and Duncan, around Duncan Grant, so good at letting himself adore, share, and who, until then, has been particularly in love with Adrian, it seems.

Duncan, whom Nessa seems to have stolen from them all; the only one among them who now lives in terror of seeing him leave; and Duncan, in the end, established, happy at Charleston, where he will die a very old man. He lives there, surrounded by their former lovers, always available to him, cherishing his regrets with regard to Nessa and watching his daughter grow up as if she were not his.

Trials and tribulations, new works follow one after another, and festivities as well: how to forget Leonard returning from a costume ball with Virginia one night and solemnly taking sides with a street prostitute against the police, whom he confronts under the dumbfounded gaze of everyone, including the police and the prostitute: he is still dressed up as a gardener from *Alice in Wonderland*, wearing a wig and overalls, equipped with enormous scissors.[21]

How to forget *Freshwater*, the play written on a whim, to be performed by family and friends before family and friends, which will enchant them all, even after arduous rehearsals?[22]

A digression here, a leap in time to demonstrate the freshness, the impact of Virginia Woolf at her centenary in 1982. Asked by the British Council and the Pompidou Center to organize her commemoration, I had the idea to perform *Freshwater* with other writers as an homage to Virginia Woolf.

Eugene Ionesco (and his wife Rodica), Michel Deguy, Florence Delay, Guy Dumure, Alain Jouffroy, Jean-Paul Aron, and myself (and later, Nathalie Sarraute, Alain Robbe-Grillet, Joyce Mansour) took the roles formerly played by Vanessa, Adrian, Leonard, Duncan, Julian, and Angelica. I had Simone Benmussa direct the production, which had been Virginia's responsibility.

In the Pompidou Center's large theater hall, a roaring success. The audience was laughing to the point of tears, won over by Virginia Woolf's humor and charm. Angelica Garnett and Quentin Bell attended; she had played the role of the leading lady, he had been part of the audience. This was the first performance of the play since its creation in 1935.

Another performance followed in the Rond-Point Theater in Paris, then in New York (where Tom Bishop played a . . . penguin), in London, and in Italy at the Spoleto Festival.

I engaged writers from all countries to pay the same homage to Virginia. And thus to bring Bloomsbury back to life.

❊ ❊ ❊

Having digressed, let us return to the true Bloomsbury of its time. The Bloomsbury that does not formally exist.

Was T. S. Eliot part of it? He is a regular visitor especially at Rodmell, first with his wife, the lovely Vivien (or Vivienne, depending), who would eventually go insane and spend the last nine years of her life in an asylum, without one visit from her husband. Widowed, he would marry his secretary.

The Woolfs discovered the poet early on. He had published only one poem in the review the *Egoist*, when the Woolfs themselves printed his *Poems* in 1919, and then *The Waste Land* in 1923. "I have just finished setting up the whole of Mr Eliots poem [*The Waste Land*] with my own hands. You see how my hand trembles. Don't blame your eyes. It is my writing," Virginia writes to a friend.[23] The Woolfs and other of Eliot's friends try to help him escape his clerk's position. He would eventually win the Nobel Prize, already reeling under all his awards.

At first disappointing, stiff, he warms up and soon impresses and charms Virginia: "But what about Eliot? Will he become 'Tom'? What happens with friendships undertaken at the age of 40?" Leonard elaborates: "When we first got to know Tom, we liked him very much, but we were both a little afraid of him." Once or twice, Virginia will allude to what might have happened if . . . and will wonder what effect lipstick might have on the imperturbable Tom.[24]

Who, over time, will become increasingly more puritan, more strictly religious. And Virginia will describe him as "behaving . . . like an infuriated hen, or an old maid who has been kissed by the butler." Politically? It was hearing him eulogize Mussolini that led Vivienne, in order to win him back, to join a league of fascists! He is anti-Semitic (to the extreme) and Leonard will defend him on this point after World War II. Sarah recites an excerpt from *The Waste Land* in *The Years*, when she rails against the city upon the arrival of her neighbor Abrahamson: "'Polluted city, unbelieving city, city of dead fish and worn-out frying pans.'"[25]

With or without the Bloomsbury stamp, a number of men and women who surrounded Virginia, and whose lives can be followed with hers year after year, sometimes remained unknown, as, for example, Saxon Sydney-Turner, an Apostle and great friend of Thoby and Leonard at Cambridge. Turner, as mad about opera as he was weak in character, a musician who never tried to accomplish anything. Defeated by life and delighted by that. A member of the circle who had once accompanied Adrian and his sister to Bayreuth and who was in love with Barbara Hiles, as was his friend and rival, Nicholas Begenal. For a long time, the young woman wavers; the two men are in anguish, especially Saxon.

Her decision? We learn it with Vanessa, from Virginia, who writes to her in 1918, with bombing nearby: "Dearest, I now begin another letter, partly that should I die tonight you may know my last thoughts were of you. Not that you care—but think of all the gossip you'd miss—yes, that touches one sensitive spot. My chief item—Barbara—is stale by this time. I daresay you've written her an expressive letter in your best style. She burst in this morning saying she was going to be married on Friday. With consummate presence of mind I exclaimed 'Then you've chosen the right man!' I hadn't the least notion which. She said, 'Yes, its Nick.' So I said 'Of course Nick's the right man,' and she said, 'Yes, he's the right man to marry, but Saxon is very wonderful as a friend. And it's not going to make the least difference to any of us. We've all discussed it, and we're agreed, and we're going to Tidmarsh [Lytton Strachey's house at the time] for the honeymoon, and Carrington and Lytton'll be there—which makes it all the nicer.' I cant say I altogether understand the young; I'm not sure, I mean that I dont see a reversion to the devoted submissions of our grandmothers," Virginia ends, perplexed.[26]

But this marriage would make a difference: Saxon will not be content to accompany Barbara Bagenal for the rest of his life, humble and resigned, or her marriage and her children.

Barbara, whom Virginia accuses Nessa of leading astray: "Theres Barbara, condemned by you to have three children and decorate her house; and now—all thanks to you and Duncan—the poor woman has moved into a caravan, where she sits all day on the ladder, shelling peas. Somehow she thinks this is in the Bloomsbury manner."[27]

But Virginia has always guessed at the hidden distress of the timid Saxon and endlessly endeavors, without him detecting it (as with Jacques

Raverat) to cheer and comfort him, to assure him of an admiration based solely on his former promise, before he had so willingly renounced it.

On the other hand (with the exception of Eliot—if he is part of it), Bloomsbury remains impenetrable to Virginia's peers, who are not, whatever their virtues, the likes of Forster or Strachey. First and foremost, James Joyce comes to mind. Also, less unequivocally, T. E. and D. H. Lawrence, and also the giant Ludwig Wittgenstein, who lives nearby and often crosses paths with the Woolfs at Cambridge, but is hardly mentioned.

Joyce? Between them, a single messenger, Miss Weaver, appears in the Woolfs' life, carrying a heavy brown package, the manuscript of *Ulysses*. It is Tom Eliot who sends them both Miss Weaver and the manuscript: could the Hogarth Press publish this text rejected for "indecency" by all the publishers, and especially by the printers, whom English law punishes just as severely as the publishing houses when forbidden books appear?[28]

Miss Weaver, editor of the *Egoist*, the avant-garde review for which Ezra Pound is editor-in-chief, is devoted to the work of Joyce, for whom she is a patron; she has published *Portrait of the Artist as a Young Man* as a series in her journal (and as a book at her own expense).

April 18, 1918, the Woolfs curiously await this audacious and subversive woman. Alas: "almost instantly Harriet Weaver appeared. Here our predictions were entirely at fault. I did my best to make her reveal herself, in spite of her appearance, all that the Editress of the Egoist ought to be, but she remained inalterably modest judicious & decorous. Her neat mauve suit fitted both soul & body." When she left, Leonard put the manuscript, that "piece of dynamite," in a desk drawer in the sitting room.[29]

According to her version, they read the manuscript and decided to publish it on the condition that they could find a printer who would agree to take charge of the printing. None did, but it was clearly not so simple. A letter from Virginia to Lytton reveals her first (and decisive) reaction: "We've been asked to print Mr Joyce's new novel, every printer in London and most in the provinces having refused. First there's a dog that p's—then there's a man that forths, and one can be monotonous even on that subject—moreover, I don't believe that his method, which is highly developed, means much more than cutting out the explanations and putting in the thoughts between dashes. So I don't think we shall do it."[30] A few months later the manuscript is returned to Miss Weaver with a letter of regret.

It's true that Hogarth had only been in existence then for two years, and with scant resources, as we know. It's surprising that a project of such scope could have been considered at all.

Thus, no encounter of any kind, but at Joyce's death, two months before her own, Virginia, stunned, remembers (and forgets): "Then Joyce is dead—Joyce about a fortnight younger than I am. I remember Miss Weaver, in wool gloves, bringing Ulysses in type script to our tea table at Hogarth House. Roger [Fry] I think sent her [it was really Tom Eliot]. Would we devote our lives to printing it? The indecent pages looked so incongruous: she was spinsterly, buttoned up. And the pages reeled with indecency. I put it in the desk drawer of the inlaid cabinet. One day Katherine Mansfield came, & I had it out. She began to read, ridiculing: then suddenly said, But theres some thing in this: a scene that should figure, I suppose in the history of literature. . . . He [Joyce] was about the place, but I never saw him. Then I remember Tom [Eliot] in Ottoline [Morrell]'s room at Garsington saying—it was published then—how can anyone write again after achieving the immense prodigy of the last chapter? He was for the first time in my knowledge, rapt, enthusiastic. I bought the blue paper book, & then read it here one summer I think with spasms of wonder, of discovery, & then again with long lapses of intense boredom. . . . That goes back to a pre-historic world. And now all the gents are furbishing up opinions, & the books, I suppose, take their place in the long procession."[31] As following his death, those of Bergotte, in Proust—which she read.

Virginia Woolf's sadness thinking of James Joyce's death, so shortly before her own: the only element, along with their demon, writing, that brought them together.

But this testimonial reveals that she actually only read *Ulysses* after it was already published, never in its entirety in manuscript. If reasons and circumstance prevented its publication, the Woolfs must not have tried very hard to overcome them. Virginia in particular, according to John Lehmann.

Eliot's enthusiasm served to cool her own, as did rivalry. The work too, but not for its "indecency": she loved using crude language, no doubt even more because she led a chaste life. Being the editor of this "daring" book would certainly have delighted her.

The work is antinomic to her because in this revolutionary novel existence goes without saying. In an ordinary work, that would hardly matter.

Whereas, once Joyce postulates existence, he proceeds with explorations and operations of wholly original audacity; a new, explosive penetration into the individual. An author organized to disorganize, deconstruct, penetrate; who draws up plans never before imagined, and completes them. But if he accomplishes his project with new means that shift, disturb, and deepen narration, he still relies upon it. Upon the display, the exposition of what he has already elaborated, beginning from this world as a given, already established, certainly underexploited by literature and which Joyce discovers, analyzes more audaciously than ever before. But the value of that process itself, unfaltering as it is, stands between Virginia Woolf and this important text, so different from her own interrogations.

And her work, in comparison? Stunned, displaced, exiled but eager, uncertain and searching not so much for ways of rendering or even for proofs of existence as for its emergence, rising beyond the silence, tangible, integral in its transience, grasped in that flight itself. A presence that immediately seizes hold, charged with absence, loss, and desire, pulsing with exactitude, maintained in indiscernible architectures, adapted each time. In pages pierced through with what is not said there.

Virginia Woolf will not have read *Finnegans Wake*, Joyce's next work, unique at the time; there he does not appropriate language but becomes it, engenders its existence. He becomes one with it, moves about in it, plays, laughs and makes laughter burst through each space, between two letters, two syllables; the words violate one another, cutting across multiple, freed, abundant meanings. A language that creates rather than submitting to meaning, unlimited. Joyce, a vast and cunning demiurge, here at the height of the comic, the root of the tragic.

Armed with a more traditional language, Finnegan and Joyce return toward the end (as Woolf does) to the father. To the terrible father, in abeyance: "O bitter ending! I'll slip away before they're up. They'll never see. Nor know. Nor miss me. And it's old and old it's sad and old it's sad and weary I go back to you, my cold father, my cold mad father, my cold mad feary father."[32]

But before such a return, before her "bitter ending" as World War II begins, Virginia seems to have experienced, in the course of some twenty years, one and the same day marked by events always in the same order, a few griefs, passionate hope. Most importantly, a single day filled with attentiveness, fervor, obstacles, "horrors" relating to the books that follow one after another; a day in which she is forever surrounded and ever more exiled, isolated and struggling not to be, to be accepted like the others, to remain different.

To stand fast, she will always have to toe the line with real life, with intimate friends and strangers steeped in convention, all of whom pique her curiosity. In fact, are exchanges with forerunners of her day actually useful? Or desirable, intrusive as they are? Moreover, aside from Joyce, among English writers at that time she has no equal.

Well, there is that D. H. Lawrence fellow she spots twice from a distance, in a St. Ives shop and at the Roman train station, on a platform opposite hers. They exchanged two letters . . . regarding the sale of a house.

It's not (or not only) a question of social class that separates them, each snubbing the other: Lawrence is a stranger to Cambridge and any other university, which Bloomsbury considers inexpiable, and Bloomsbury enjoys "bourgeois" privilege, which Lawrence abhors, although he was Ottoline Morrell's lover nonetheless—as were Roger Fry and Bertrand Russell, among others—before he caricatured her in *Women in Love*. On the occasion of the writer's death, Virginia, indignant: "Not a first rate genius. No . . . my word, what a cheap little bounder he was, taking her money, books, food, lodging and then writing that book."[33]

No literary affinities: she always read him (or not) "without pleasure"; she would have rejected his mysticism. In a review of a Lawrence novel for the *Times Literary Supplement*, after citing some passages she admires, Virginia claims to have truly hoped for a certain originality from the author:

> We were wrong. . . . Details accumulated; the picture of life in Woodhouse was built up . . . we adopted a fresh attitude and read Mr. Lawrence as one reads Mr. Bennett—for the facts, and for the story. Mr. Lawrence shows indeed something of Mr. Bennett's power of displaying by any means of immense industry and great ability a section of the hive beneath the glass. . . . And then again the laborious process continues of building up a model of life from saying how d'you do, and cutting the loaf, and knocking the cigarette ash into the ash tray, and standing the yellow bicycle against the wall. Little by little Alvina disappears beneath the heap of facts recorded about her, and the only sense in which we feel her to be lost is that we can no longer believe in her existence.[34]

But, three months after Lawrence's death, she reads *Sons and Lovers* and is amazed: "Now I realise with regret that a man of genius wrote in my time and I never read him. Yes, but genius obscured and distorted I think: the fact about contemporaries (I write hand to mouth) is that they're doing the same thing on another railway line."[35]

Of the writers then living, only one dazzles her, scares, discourages her, renders her "suicidal," and fulfills her:

> My great adventure is really Proust. Well—what remains to be written after that? I'm only in the first volume, and there are, I suppose, faults to be found, but I am in a state of amazement; as if a miracle were being done before my eyes, how, at last, someone solidified what has always escaped—and made it too into this beautiful and perfectly enduring substance? One has to put the book down and gasp. The pleasure becomes physical—like sun and wine and grapes and perfect serenity and intense vitality combined.[36]

She continues: "Oh if I could write like that! I cry. And at the moment such is the astonishing vibration and saturation and intensification that he procures—theres something sexual in it—that I feel I *can* write like that, and seize my pen and then I *can't* write like that. Scarcely anyone so stimulates the nerves of language in me: it becomes an obsession."[37]

As for one of the world's greatest thinkers, Ludwig Wittgenstein, who lived in Cambridge, imagine the exchanges they could have had. Two poets, each of whom rejects any peremptory given. Wittgenstein: "If someone says 'I have a body,' he can be asked 'Who is speaking here with this mouth?'" And here, very close to Virginia: "It is not *how* things are in the world that is mystical, but *that* it exists." And these lines, undoubtedly the last written by Ludwig Wittgenstein: "Someone who, dreaming, says 'I am dreaming,' even if he speaks audibly in doing so, is no more right than if he said in his dream 'it is raining,' while it was in fact raining. Even if his dream were actually connected with the noise of the rain." To end a logician's life with the sound of falling rain![38]

The meeting will not take place; it is Lytton and above all Keynes whom Wittgenstein befriends. He and the Woolfs seem hardly to notice one another. Leonard Woolf notes only "the aggressive cruelty," reported by Bertrand Russell, that Wittgenstein demonstrates when he is living with the Keyneses and makes Lydia cry.[39]

Virginia mentions him after Keynes snubs Julian Bell when he tries to talk to him about the philosopher (no doubt because the young man satirized Keynes in a piece published in a student newspaper). He appears only one other time, when she teases Saxon Sydney-Turner: "nothing said half so clever, I daresay, as what you said to Wittgenstein—the fame of that interview has gone round the world. How you talked without ceasing, some say in an obscure Austrian dialect, of the soul, and matter, till W. was moved to offer himself to you as bootboy at Hogarth House, in order to hear you still talk."[40]

The truth is, with regard to her forays into thinking and writing, where she remains most herself, or where she does not abandon herself but struggles to return to herself, Leonard is her closest accomplice, all the more so for being respectful of that space; he doesn't intervene there, but senses it, recognizes it.

In another domain entirely, he writes as much as she does, and publishes more in his lifetime.[41] Essays, mostly political, in which she takes polite interest, enough for the author, who does not share her need for it.

But they are in almost perfect harmony over the texts they publish together—especially Virginia's, which he only sees finished, but which she confidently writes in his proximity, because he knows what he must know of those hours, and she knows he knows.

In those spaces, their visions can emerge side by side. Long walks at Rodmell. Intimacy. Intelligence. They know how to read, to listen together, and each of them can think peacefully near the other. Leonard's intrusions are oppressive, harmful, but not in this domain. The space where Virginia operates is never invaded. She reigns there. . . . A Room of One's Own.

The quotidian space is another matter. There Leonard's fussiness grows, increases, unabated.

If Leonard is upset when Virginia, without rejecting him, swoons over Vita Sackville-West, he never shows it but remains dogged in his obsession. As she leaves to spend her first weekend with Vita alone at her home in Kent, he gives her a letter for her hostess: "I enclose Virginia & hope she will behave. The only thing I ask is that you will be adamant in sending her off to bed not 1 minute later than 11 P.M. She ought not to talk for too long a stretch at a time. It is good of you to have her."[42] No comment!

Virginia is bewitched, enflamed, tortured. Her litanies: "Vita Vita Vita" in her letters, her diary, and when Vita travels with her husband or joins him (rarely) at some foreign post: "I have missed you. I do miss you. I shall miss you." Or, "Honey dearest, don't go to Egypt please. Stay in England. Love Virginia. Take her in your arms."[43]

Returning, Vita prompts an atmosphere of vaudeville that is finally distressing: "Heaven knows what excuse I can make for staying that night [at Sissinghurst]. Can you invent one?" And in a panic as the summer ends: "Its the last chance of a night before London's chastity begins." She lives in constant desire, longing, sensuality as well, as reflected in the diary, but never specified: Leonard sometimes reads it. She suffers without Vita, whom she doesn't see often.[44]

"I do adore you—every part of you from heel to hair. Never will you shake me off, try as you may."[45] But she will. And Virginia, tortured, senses that Vita, still close, is drawing away from her as a lover; so it's something of the Scheherazade syndrome that gives rise to *Orlando*. A game. An attempt at seduction. An offering openly meant for Vita, delighted to be its hero/heroine. Orlando, man or woman according to the century, sets out through history with a patrician air suitable to Vita, an air of legend, from a castle similar to Knole, which she can't inherit because she is a woman.

Having become a woman, Orlando is the target of a lawsuit: "The chief charges against her were 1) that she was dead, and therefore could not hold any property whatsoever; 2) that she was a woman, which amounts to much the same thing."[46]

It pleases Virginia to accompany Vita throughout these pages, and to amuse herself with a book that she nevertheless fears is "too long for a joke, & too frivolous for a serious book."[47] A writer's holiday, but it addresses the condition of women before *A Room of One's Own*, so full of charm, and *Three Guineas*, so serious. In *Orlando*, humor reigns.

The charm will not work as it did for Scheherazade. Imperceptibly, elegantly, always with spirit, the two women will cease to be lovers, Virginia brokenhearted; but in pure Bloomsbury style, they will always remain bound by affection, complicity, and their interest in each other. No clean break. For Virginia, a fissure, and imperceptibly as always, resignation.

A few years and . . . the effect of those years on the Vita of pearls and cashmere, of long legs and slender figure, confirms her loss: "I cant really forgive her for growing so large: with such tomato red cheeks and thick black moustache—Surely that wasn't necessary: and the devil is that it shuts up her eyes that were the beaming beauty I first loved her for. . . . You'd never say she could turn a phrase; only whip a dog."[48]

And Vanessa: "She has simply become Orlando the wrong way round—I mean turned into a man, with a thick moustache. . . . How have you done it?"[49]

Virginia often dreamed of women, as here, over a cup of tea with Mary Hutchinson: "Yesterday I had tea in Mary's room & saw the red lighted tugs go past & heard the swish of the river: Mary in black with lotus leaves round her neck. If one could be friendly with women, what a pleasure—the relationship so secret & private compared with relations with men. Why not write about it? truthfully?"[50]

When she was younger, a passionate, unstable friendship with Katherine Mansfield had blossomed with their first encounter: "I was fascinated, and she respectful, only I thought her cheap, and she thought me priggish; [but] she had a quality I adored, and needed; I think her sharpness and reality—her having knocked about with prostitutes and so on, whereas I had always been respectable—was the thing I wanted then."[51] Virginia herself had printed *Prelude*, which appeared when Hogarth Press was in its infancy. She had then hated, despised another long short story, *Felicity*, as she had continued alternately to love and despise Katherine.

But soon after, January 1923:

Katherine has been dead a week & how far am I obeying her "to not quite forget Katherine" which I read in one of her old letters? . . . Nelly said in her sensational way at breakfast on Friday "Mrs Murry's dead! It says so in the paper!" At that one feels—what? A shock of relief?— a rival the less? Then confusion at feeling so little—then, gradually, blankness & disappointment; then a depression which I could not rouse myself from all that day. When I began to write, it seemed to me there was no point in writing. Katherine wont read it. Katherine's my rival no longer. . . . Sometimes we looked very steadfastly at each other, as though we had reached some durable relationship, independent of the changes of the body, through the eyes. Hers were beautiful eyes— rather doglike, brown, very wide apart, with a steady slow rather faithful & sad expression. . . . She looked very ill—very drawn, & moved languidly, drawing herself across the room, like some suffering animal . . . she was inscrutable. Did she care for me? Sometimes she would say so—would kiss me—would look at me as if (is this sentiment?) her eyes would like always to be faithful . . . she said she would send me her diary to read, & would write always. . . . She never answered my letter.

Yet I still feel, somehow that friendship persists. Still there are things about writing I think of & want to tell Katherine.[52]

Katherine became a distant memory.

Less ethereal, so much older, Ethel Smyth would come to play as important a role as Vita, although platonic, when she burst in on Virginia, enthralled after reading *A Room of One's Own*. Ethel, a suffragette who was once imprisoned for throwing stones at the prime minister's window, now defended the cause of just one woman: herself. Alarmed, Virginia receives this septuagenarian who is in love with her, a composer, orchestra conductor, forever passionate, who declares that she considers herself the most interesting person she knows. She is odious and magnificent, magisterial, ridiculous. Their letters are so many eruptions of fury and confidence. Just looking at Ethel's at the New York Public Library, in the Berg Collection, one is overcome with the desire to flee or to rip them up, the writing is so aggressive, their pages so teeming with dramas that give way in half an hour to a new letter and new dramas. But how alive she is! How vigorous and determined. In ecstasy before her victim. And most importantly, she takes Virginia seriously, she believes in her. She talks to her about her and listens to her free of all prejudice, and Virginia can remain just as she is before this hypergifted, hyperactive, hyperenthusiastic or indignant woman. Hyperexasperating as well: "You've got to listen to me—You've got to listen."[53]

But Virginia finds herself listened to, respected, understood. To Ethel: "I scribble to you as I scribble in my diary." She can speak to her without fear of "such caverns of gloom and horror open round me I daren't look in." Thanks to her friend, she can bear her solitude a little better, more calmly, level-headedly, within her circle. Without bitterness, she remarks that "Because everyone I most honour is silent—Nessa, Lytton, Leonard, Maynard: all silent; and so I have trained myself to silence; induced to it also by the terror I have of my own unlimited capacity for feeling. . . . But to my surprise, as time went on, I found that you are perhaps the only person I know who shows feeling and feels." And then, most importantly: "What you give me is protection. . . . Its the child crying for the nurses hand in the dark." However, "she is so old, so violent and sly," she complains to Quentin Bell, as horrified as Leonard. "An old woman of seventy one has fallen in love with me. It is at once hideous and horrid and melancholy-sad. It is like being caught by a giant crab."[54]

Ethel, more restless, with so much more character, plays something of the role of Violet Dickinson, many years earlier and long since forgotten. Virginia, now the author of an authentic body of work. "Don't go on reading my works. Give it up," Virginia had written to Violet, after a remark about them that had displeased her.[55] Virginia Woolf, who now moves in other circles and around whom Virginia Stephen's earlier witnesses are no longer welcome.

Nevertheless, in 1936 when Violet contacts her and proposes sending her her early letters, a rather excited Virginia cheerfully accepts. But when she receives them, handsomely bound, a forgotten Hyde Park Gate springs back to life and the shock overwhelms her: "At points I became filled with such a gust from her tragic past, I couldn't read on. . . . All I beg of you is dont let anybody else read those letters."[56] She is moved to thank Violet for her support back then. Nevertheless, she doesn't see her again.

Twenty-eight years earlier, Vanessa too had reacted with horror when she became aware of *Reminiscences*, that first account of their childhood and adolescence written by Virginia when she was twenty-five. Rediscovering that "awful underworld of emotional scenes" had terrified her: "It seems to me almost too ghastly and unnatural now ever to have existed."[57]

What stronger bond than that underworld they secretly endured together, those troubled, painful times they formerly shared? Than that memory inhabiting them still, sometimes tender and joyous, sometimes salting the wound of their grief? Than that freedom achieved in tandem, and even the betrayals that had followed! They never truly left each other; they would not let each other go, faithful in their jealousy, their rancor, their alliance. Not a single man to love them entirely, these two audacious women, so beautiful, feminine, condemned to chastity. And who could laugh together. Could keep each other from crying.

"I put my life blood into writing, & she had children." Virginia's leitmotif, which doesn't stop her from admiring her sister, her relationship with Duncan: "Nessa and Duncan are so quiet always that when they go, it isn't the noise that is less, but the substance."[58]

From Charleston, the less indulgent Vanessa sighs to (and, as always, after) Duncan: "Leonard has gone today and Virginia will go tomorrow, when I hope we shall return to normal existence. . . . Yesterday, Vita came to lunch . . . Virginia held forth in her usual style which you know and I cannot describe, very amusing but also most uneasy, at least to my mind. The whole evening afterwards was spent in her mock apologies for having

talked too much. It is brilliant of course and I suppose one sounds like cur-
mudgeonly for finding any fault, but one simply gets exhausted and longs
for some quiet talk." Then comes the inevitable: "I wonder what you've
decided about going to Bunny's and when you'll come here."[59]

Virginia has no such anxieties; if she cannot manage without Leonard,
Vanessa remains the one most dear to her, for better—their alliance—and
for worse—their betrayals. Actually, so many of her intimates are indispensable to her, who could themselves do without her, like her sister who,
although always available, remains inaccessible, reticent. We know what
distress and fears Vanessa harbors and hides. What pride and mistrust
make her withdraw into herself. Only grieving will allow her to express
her sorrow, to break down without restraint and reveal, even expose her
suffering, which is then redoubled. Angelica would remember her mother
wailing for entire days and nights at the death of Roger Fry.

Unspeakable sorrow, much more than redoubled when Julian Bell,
enlisted in the Spanish Civil War despite his mother's pleas, is killed in
Spain. Julian, who had "some queer power" over his mother, of "the lover
as well as the son"; of a son who told her what she wanted to hear: that he
could never love any other woman as he did her.[60] Of a son who desperately tried to flee the grip of that mother, so frustrated in other respects.
Going to teach in China had not been enough. In Spain, his wish would
be granted.

Virginia, appalled, "the great cat is playing with us once more," throws
herself into saving Nessa, devotes herself to ensuring her survival. And she
achieves it.[61]

Now equally unrestrained, she too can give her spirit free rein, reveal
her tenderness toward her sister: "I'd rather think I'm more nearly attached
to you than sisters should be." She sees her every day, writes to her as soon
as she returns to Rodmell and claims that attentiveness as a privilege for
"your singe,[62] who adores you, and cant stay away from you." "Oh why
are you the only person I never see enough of?" "You shant be rid of me
for long." And it *is* a privilege for Virginia to be able to express without
restraint what she must ordinarily repress, for fear of awakening Nessa's
irony and distrust, Nessa always aware of the latent dispute that Virginia
is forever trying to erase.[63]

The "unbelievable nightmare" must be eased. Virginia tries to keep
Nessa awake and warm, to entertain her with one thing or another, life
around them, always coming back to their childhood. It is to Vanessa, the

shattered pietà, that she recalls Nessa, the little girl: "I've been always in love with her since I was a green eyed brat under the nursery table, and so shall remain in my extreme senility."[64]

But if "no-one has penetrated the cave where Dolphin[65] lies couched, like some proud sea monster," this time Nessa responds.[66] Overcome, ruined, sick, apparently lost forever, she comes back to life, begins to paint again, altered but saved, largely by Virginia. Whereas, emblematically, Vanessa will never speak to her sister of this period; she will direct Vita to tell Virginia (overwhelmed) that she knows what she owes her and thanks her for it.

"And dear old Clive," Julian's father, was not absent, "—he is such a pathetic, and always honest, man. cracking his jokes. to try and make us all laugh—wh. I admire."[67]

Clive and Virginia had never completely stopped feeling something for each other, a certain emotion, Clive occasionally attentive, Virginia enjoying his visits: "He comes on Wednesdays; jolly, & rosy, & squab: a man of the world; & enough of my old friend, & enough of my old lover, to make the afternoons hum."[68]

Bloomsbury! The feelings!

Time passes.

✳ ✳ ✳

It passes for Virginia but remains immutable for Virginia Woolf when she is working; the course of her work doesn't age. All her ardor, her solitude, the song that goes through it, and not her anger but her fury would go into an essay, *Three Guineas*, that would encounter hostility from Bloomsbury, the exceptional cold reception from Leonard. It would cause a scandal but find its audience.

Virginia Woolf gives herself over to it wholly, as never before. Drawing on inner resources and thinking as yet unrevealed in all their rigor—not even in her diary or her letters. A power of indignation, of political thinking that no one knew she had, that she did not permit herself, permeates it entirely. At Bloomsbury, it will not be recognized, it will not be acknowledged as such, with such a tone.

It is the question of women.

As in two of the earlier books. But where in *Three Guineas* does one find the gentle grace of *A Room of One's Own*? The impulsive imagination of *Orlando*? Virginia, who knows so well how to transcribe silence and disturb language—who knows how to say and to make heard so much that she does not say—goes straight to the facts here, with the supporting figures. She goes straight to the roots of the problem: this world, of which she is an inhabitant, has been spirited away from her; men have usurped it, they occupy and control the territory. Virginia doesn't get lost in idealistic reveries: their ends, their means are economic. The reason for this usurpation, which they call supremacy: exploitation. Men, who are the owners of the world, intend to remain so.

She describes the long oppression of daughters by their fathers, the right of sons to the family inheritance, the right of husbands over their wives' destinies.

She describes the signs, codes, official decrees, unwritten laws, invisible obstacles that deny women free access to the world, to action, a right of way, independence, a viable relationship to their own bodies. In everything and everywhere, they must have an intermediary, a man, to win even—maybe—a chance to act.

"She wrote that book tongue in cheek," Quentin Bell told me, but he also claimed . . . the opposite: "If I compare *A Room of One's Own* to *Three Guineas*, I'm sure that *A Room of One's Own* is better, as a work of art as well, because Virginia remains good humored in it, she's witty. In *Three Guineas*, there's anger and anguish. Moreover, she was really suffering at the time. She wasn't thinking straight."[69]

Or inside the box, actually.

One can certainly prefer one of these books over the other, one's charm to the other's unforeseen power. But Quentin only acknowledges the good-humored Virginia, what a sign! What better proof of the book's thesis!

According to him, suffering undermines her credibility. Pleasant, cheerful, undisturbing when she is only somewhat critical, then she is acceptable, maybe even charming. But indignation is denied her. Resistance? Better not to mention it.

The solitude of women in a world impossible to read. The solitude of the writer who knows how to read the world beyond the translations provided, and who perceives what flows (and how it flows) under the mountains of images heaped upon us. A world undressed. The king has nothing on, there is no queen; the realm is in ruin. She considers at length the photographs of a Spain strewn with bodies from the Civil War (among them Julian's). She evokes the figure of the Duce, the Führer, recalls, ironically, the men outfitted in uniforms covered in knickknacks disguised as decorations, and wonders if women must join their parade. She is alone in this view, because the few women before her who have struggled so hard to obtain so little have done it to achieve the status of men.

No sexism, no utopia for her. Women, different from men, are not, for all that, perfect; she doesn't even call them better. She doesn't imagine a matriarchal paradise, a society of amazons, and doesn't want a struggle against men, or even a separation from them: "A common interest unites us: it is one world, one life."[70]

But, excluded by men, women are less trapped than men in the male system, in their world of hierarchy and exploitation; in 1938, they do not bear direct responsibility. They have a chance to begin differently; must they be denied it in a world where there are still, in fact, no women? Only the nullification of women by men, who reign as mournful conquerors over a mutilated world.

And, in a world staggering under the Spanish War, Nazism and Fascism at their height, she recalls an earlier tyranny heard in the news on the radio:

As we listen to the voices we seem to hear, an infant crying in the night, the black night that now covers Europe, and with no language but a cry, Ay, ay, ay, ay. . . . But it is not a new cry, it is a very old cry. Let us shut off the wireless and listen to the past. We are in Greece now; Christ has not been born yet, nor St. Paul either. But listen:

"Whomsoever the city may appoint, that man must be obeyed, in little things and great, in just things and unjust . . . disobedience is the worst of evils . . . We must support the cause of order, and in no wise suffer a woman to worst us . . . They must be women, and not range at large. Servants, take them within." That is the voice of Creon, the dictator. To whom Antigone, who was to have been his daughter, answered, "not such are the laws set among men by the justice who dwells with the gods below." But she had neither capital nor force behind her. And Creon said: "I will take her where the path is loneliest, and hide her, living, in a rocky vault." And he shut her not in Holloway or in a concentration camp, but in a tomb. And Creon we read brought ruin on his house, and scattered the land with the bodies of the dead. It seems, Sir, as we listen to the voices of the past, as if we were looking at the photographs again, at the pictures of dead bodies and ruined houses that the Spanish Government sends us almost weekly. Things repeat themselves it seems. Pictures and voices are the same today as they were 2,000 years ago.[71]

The voice one hears here is political, but it is the voice of a woman whose husband, Leonard Woolf, claims "was the least political animal that has lived since Aristotle invented the definition." And everyone smiles, Virginia first among them. The Angel in the House is never completely exterminated! Even in the one who, alone, very much alone, writing in her diary, already senses not only "the faces & the voice" but one of the *sounds* of the coming war and the horror on its way: a horror for the horror, conscious, planned.[72]

And that war is approaching. Yet another encounter: with Freud.

This time the decision to translate and publish him was Leonard's, fifteen years earlier in 1924. Virginia's less lucid remarks at the time: "I'm rather alarmed at the productivity of the Hogarth press this autumn—having laid out 800 pounds in the works of Freud, which will sell they say because he has cancer; but I doubt any book selling that isn't Berta Ruck."[73]

A single encounter, time for a cup of tea and the gift of a flower when Virginia goes to see him as co-editor with Leonard. But once the flower (a narcissus!) is presented to Mrs. Woolf, Freud will only address Leonard, who recounts this meeting:

> The Nazis invaded Austria on March 11, 1938, and it took three months to get Freud out of their clutches. He arrived in London in the first week in June. . . . I made discreet enquiries to see whether he would like Virginia and me to come and see him. The answer was yes, and in the afternoon of Saturday, January 28, 1939, we went and had tea with him. . . . Nearly all famous men are disappointing or bores, or both. Freud was neither; he had an aura, not of fame, but of greatness. The terrible cancer of the mouth which killed him only eight months later had already attacked him. It was not an easy interview. He was extraordinarily courteous in a formal, old-fashioned way—for instance, almost ceremoniously he presented Virginia with a flower. There was something about him as of a half-extinct volcano, something somber, suppressed, reserved. He gave me the feeling which only a very few people whom I have met gave me, a feeling of great gentleness, but behind that gentleness, great strength.[74]

And then, an incident: strangely enough, Leonard is surprised to see Freud turn bitter (and nonetheless amused) when he tells him about the trial of a man accused of stealing books, one of Freud's among them. At the end of the trial, the judge said he wanted to punish the thief by condemning him to read Freud's book. "His books, he said, had made him infamous, not famous," remarks Leonard. Freud must have taken the story seriously and must have stewed over it, been obsessed by it, because three days later he writes to Leonard (not to Virginia): "Handicapped in the use of your language I think I could not give full expression to my satisfaction of having met you and your lady. The condemnation delivered by the Norwegian judge I take to be a misrepresentation or a bad joke by a malicious journalist."[75]

Was it really necessary for Leonard to launch into that anecdote during such a brief visit?

Their excellent editorial relations with Freud become difficult only when he simultaneously sells the U.S. rights to his works to two publishers, one of which is Hogarth.

However, psychoanalysis doesn't get good press in Bloomsbury. Alix Strachey, Lytton's sister-in-law, wife of James Strachey, with whom she translated the Freudian opus and who was one of the first psychoanalysts to practice in England, confirmed this in 1973, when I visited the beautiful woodland home that she and James had designed. She was living there alone, widowed, elderly, in great style, surrounded by canvases by Duncan Grant, Carrington, Vanessa Bell, among the portraits and busts of Lytton.

She and James had been analyzed in Vienna by Freud right before their marriage in 1920. The first (and last) case of a wife and husband analyzed together by Freud. The couple had remained very discreet, according to Alix: "If I thought certain things, I would not say them," she claimed innocently. Alix, an analyst who "never discussed James's decisions" and evidently could not think "certain things" about him![76]

Freud decided not to treat them as patients: "Instead of doing nothing but listen and interpret, he spoke to us of analytical theories and taught us. That was not a good idea, he realized later."[77] All methods he would renounce, like inviting these "patient-students" to tea with his family.

James and Alix return to London dubbed. "In those early times, Freud was rather an autocrat. He just simply declared us members of a British or Austrian psychoanalyst society. He simply said: 'I want these two people to be members,' and we entered by the front door with no effort."[78]

Did Freud's work have much influence on the Bloomsbury group? "No, none," and Alix Strachey, a little bitter, says: "I don't think the Bloomsbury people wanted to be bothered by what could change their approach, for example, to psychology. After we returned from Vienna, things were never the same between them and us. Never as lively. Adrian also became a psychoanalyst, and that cut him off from the others. Nothing disagreeable happened, but they were never again as intimate."[79]

It's true that Virginia takes a dim view of her brother's (late) conversion to psychoanalysis, depressed as he was until then. Witnessing his practice: "I creep up and peer into the Stephen's dining room where any afternoon, in full daylight, is to be seen a woman in the last agony of despair, lying on a sofa, burying her face in the pillow, while Adrian broods over her like a vulture, analyzing her soul—"[80]

George Duckworth, by his very naïveté, would prove to be most open-minded; so touching, moving, when he exclaims spontaneously and with great feeling: "Oh but does that mean you'll be able to cure poor Laura?"[81] Laura, so long forgotten.

Unless the very idea was enough to worry him.

An often-asked question: why wasn't Virginia analyzed? Countless answers from her contemporaries. Too dangerous, according to some; according to others, for someone considered manic-depressive like Virginia, psychoanalysis could do nothing at the time, focused as it was on psychosis. Or this: Leonard did not want a third party to come between them. Leonard, who joked about making a speech in a suit and tie before hundreds of psychoanalysts: "I found it an intimidating experience, partly because they would know (1) what I was thinking, (2) that I was not thinking what I thought I was thinking, (3) what I was really thinking when I was not thinking what I thought I was thinking."[82]

Moreover, Virginia would have been opposed to it, afraid of losing her identity as a writer, of the effects on her ability to write. Perhaps a sign of withdrawal, fear, rejection: she read nothing by Freud before their meeting. A few months later she dove into his work "to enlarge the circumference. To give my brain a wider scope: make it objective; to get outside. Thus defeat the shrinkage of age." Soon, she is devouring it ("I'm gulping up Freud"). At his death, announced by the newspaper hawkers on September 23, 1939, she remarks that only such "little facts" offer a break from the monotony of war—declared just twenty days earlier![83]

The specific horrors of that war Leonard had foreseen well before it was declared, and here we find them described in all their brutality:

> Jews were hunted down, beaten up, and humiliated everywhere publicly in the streets of towns. I saw a photograph of a Jew being dragged by storm troopers out of a shop in one of the main streets in Berlin; the fly buttons of the man's trousers had been torn open to show that he was circumcised and therefore a Jew. On the man's face was the horrible look of blank suffering and despair which from the beginning of human history men have seen under the crown of thorns on the faces of their persecuted and humiliated victims. In this photograph what was even more horrible was the look on the faces of respectable men and women, standing on the pavement, laughing at the victim.[84]

With that war, the long fruitful day spent removed from those horrors, the day that lasted more than twenty years for Virginia, would come to an end. The time of hostilities would mark her last battle before the "embrace" of death, as Mrs. Dalloway calls it.[85]

Part 5

"ALL the walls, the protecting & reflecting walls, wear so terribly thin in this war." And soon: "No audience. No echo. Thats part of one's death." Especially as her solitude with Leonard increases and the rampart formed by the public, friends, others gradually dissolves.[1]

But at first, after they leave London to take permanent refuge at Monk's House, there will be the happiness of days that ring "from one simple melody to another," and Virginia will have "never had a better writing season." For months, she will be seized with a passionate desire to live despite the pact we know about, her joint suicide pact with Leonard, should England be invaded. She will still cast herself entirely into a future time, under bombardment at Rodmell and its surroundings every evening, located in the air corridor between continental Europe and London.[2]

Around her, friends like Kingsley Martin, editor of the *New Statesman & Nation*, discuss possible suicides. "I dont want to die yet," she says to Leonard, hearing the bombs. But in her pocket, morphine provided by Adrian. Morphine, the garage, the suicide envisioned by Leonard if the Nazis. . . . And she has book projects for at least ten years "if Hitler doesn't drop a splinter into my machine." The vanquished continent of Europe belongs almost entirely to the Nazis.³

Virginia sighs: "Yes, I was thinking: we live without a future." Even Marie Woolf finally dies in July 1939, after holding out against old age like "a cricketer doing a record score." Anti-Semitism is no longer in fashion. The Bloomsbury crowd has dispersed; the gasoline shortage prevents them from getting together often. Virginia searches the ruins of the London apartment, destroyed during a bombing raid, to find her diaries and her parents' letters. Hogarth Press is partly moved out of town; John Lehmann (to whom Virginia sold her shares while still retaining her role at the publishing house) takes over the day-to-day operations. Leonard only goes to London once or twice a week. He and Virginia are still selling books to the bookstores in 1940.⁴

But gradually time grinds to a halt, and Virginia, far from everyone, insidiously neglected by Leonard, slips into a fatal isolation: "Those familiar circumvolutions—those standards—which have for so many years given back an echo & so thickened my identity are all wide & wild as the desert now. I mean, there is no 'autumn' no winter. . . . I cant conceive that there will be a 27th June 1941."⁵ For her, there won't be one.

After having worked, struggled, as in every moment of her life, but this time struggling against the worst threats with the worst weapons, Virginia Woolf in isolation would founder.

Alone, confined, adrift.

"The play was over, the strangers gone."⁶ Nearly every page of *Between the Acts* utters a calm, inexorable farewell, to what is no more than the territory of farewell. But a farewell that she is still observing, without preparing herself for it.

Whatever makes her capsize, this work is not to blame. On the contrary, it exorcises its content. Despite the havoc of the war, Virginia feels productive again, as hungry for books as when she was a child, and finds herself "a little triumphant about the book. I think its an interesting attempt in a new method. I think its more quintessential than the others. . . . I've enjoyed writing almost every page."⁷ She has five months left to live.

But she notes that she must write those pages in the intervals left by "the drudgery of Roger."⁸ That disaster.

Roger's family, in league with the rest of Bloomsbury, traps her into writing the dead painter's biography. Virginia resists, then acquiesces, and we can only think bitterly of the pack that makes her waste her powers on such useless labor. She feels hounded by those who had known Fry, who seem to be reading over her shoulder; nervously she watches herself confronting her "hero," whose schizophrenic wife was institutionalized shortly after their marriage and spent the rest of her life that way. Virginia struggles under Roger Fry's voluminous papers, articles, bills, manuscripts, agendas, under the letters he wrote and received, among them intimate exchanges with Nessa . . . who advises her sister to publish all of it and adds, "I hope you wont mind making us all blush."[9] But Virginia refuses to mention anything that involves lovers, Roger's private life; so many things must not be said, or only alluded to. A process of censorship.

And martyrdom above all. "An experiment in self suppression," she complains. And it's true![10] A serious one. She persists, entrenched in it since before the war; it will take two years. Two wasted years. The book will be uninteresting.

One Sunday in March 1940, during a walk in the fields around Rodmell, Leonard, who has just read the proofs, criticizes Virginia's work for the first and only time, and violently. It is the editor who speaks, but it is the wife who suffers: "It was like being pecked by a very hard strong beak. The more he pecked the deeper, as always happens. At last he was almost angry that I'd chosen 'what seems to me the wrong method. Its merely anal[ysis], not history. Austere repression. In fact dull to the outside. All those dead quotations.'"[11] He's right, despite his blows from such a cruel—and virile—beak.

But no matter, since, reading it, Vanessa breaks down in tears over the life of her former lover, forever her dear friend: "I'm crying cant thank you." And Virginia, ecstatic: "Lord to have given back Nessa her Roger. . . ."[12]

But that isn't all. Virginia had played with taking Roger from Nessa, and through this dead man, we see her return to the time when she stole Clive from her sister. Her discomfort with Roger Fry's memory, her rejection of his emotions and private life, stem in part from her fantasies about him and herself. No doubt she once envied his passionate love for Vanessa, who, once burned and distrustful, had kept her lover as far from her sister as possible. Perhaps he is still too much alive for her to reveal herself publicly, to show any sign of her distress.

And suddenly: "What a curious relation is mine with Roger at this moment—I who have given him a kind of shape after his death." The shape of a ghost to carry within and fulfill her: "I feel very much in his presence at the moment; as if I were intimately connected with him; as if we together had given birth to this vision of him: a child born of us."[13]

That deeply rooted frustration, those vain cries and hopes through the years! Only a phantom to answer them, who doesn't have the power to refuse that birth, or perhaps the embrace, the union that preceded it. "He had no power to alter it. And yet for some years it will represent him."[14] As Leonard's children would have represented him had he not refused them. Or as Clive's children represent him, born of Vanessa. As this child conceived with Vanessa's lover represents Roger Fry.

An ongoing obsession, children, now paired with the ever-present obsession of the war, which reawakens in her Septimus's awareness that "millions lamented; for ages they had sorrowed," and now they are more real than ever. Obsession with her confinement at Rodmell under bombardment: the planes coming every day, flying so close. Every evening, waiting to hear where the bombs drop. "If it doesn't kill me its killing someone else," writes Virginia.[15]

When Leonard thinks it's too risky to cross the garden, they lie flat on their bellies under a tree. "Don't close yr teeth," he advises Virginia. Each evening the Nazi planes threaten, but each evening they spend bowling, Virginia's passion, and she imagines a prosaic and peaceful death mid-game on a lovely summer evening. The planes swoop over the villages; you can see their swastikas. Vita telephones from Sissinghurst, frantic as the bombs drop around her house: "Can you hear that? . . . Thats another. Thats another." Virginia listens horrified to the voice of a friend who could be killed while talking to her—pressure, horror, danger, she concludes.[16]

Spluttering, whistling, the sound of something like a saw overhead, raids every night, death held in suspense, and for Virginia, the frantic desire to survive:

> Last night a great heavy plunge of bomb under the window. So near we both started. . . . I said to L.: I don't want to die yet. The chances are against it. . . . Oh I try to imagine how one's killed by a bomb. I've got it fairly vivid—the sensation: but cant see anything but suffocating nonentity following after. I shall think—oh I wanted another ten years—not this—& shant, for once, be able to describe it. It—I mean death; no, the scrunching & scrambling, the crushing of my bone shade in on my very active eye & brain: the process of putting out the

light,—painful? Yes. Terrifying. I suppose so—then a swoon; a drum, two or three gulps attempting consciousness—& then, dot dot dot.[17]

But worse than the bombs, the past is going to swoop down on her, the past of Hyde Park Gate, inexorable, its path cleared by her disbanded circle of friends, the many missing, sometimes frivolous diversions that kept her occupied or allowed her to channel the memory and sublimate it into her work.

Leonard doesn't compensate for those absences. On the contrary. They know how to live together, but their lives run parallel and never meet. Privately, they have constructed a kind of mutual, harmonious existence. But Virginia's character cannot confide in Leonard's, as she confides in Vanessa, Ethel, many of her other friends. And Leonard cannot confide in anyone since the years in Ceylon.

Each is grounded in an adjacent but self-contained world: "L. saw a grey heraldic bird: I only saw my thoughts."[18]

He is always judging her according to the same criteria. In his eyes, Virginia is continually threatened by madness, a madwoman under reprieve, renowned, a partner he's used to. He has himself suffered from so many tacit judgments because of his family's social status, his Judaism.

He remains calm, fairly withdrawn. Even if he writes articles, political essays, gives lectures, participates in antifascist activities, and, as a journalist, holds important positions, even if he still directs the Hogarth Press, he lives at Rodmell for the present and devotes himself mostly to raising his dogs, tending his garden; in his autobiography he proudly remembers one afternoon, as he was planting irises, Virginia called to him from the sitting room window: "Hitler is making a speech," and in answer he shouted: "I shan't come. I'm planting iris and they will be flowering long after he is dead."[19] And then, noting in his memoir that they are still flowering twenty-one years after Hitler's suicide, he does not mention the twenty-five years since Virginia's.

Virginia enjoys periods of remission, like that day "almost too—I wont say happy: but amenable. The tune varies, from one nice melody to another. All is played (today) in such a theatre. Hills & fields; I cant stop looking." She savors it: "One things 'pleasant' after another: breakfast, writing, walking, tea, bowls, reading, sweets, bed. . . . The globe rounds again. Behind it—oh yes."[20]

Already quite despondent in November 1940, she nevertheless writes to Vita: "Look, Vita . . . You *must* come here instantly. Not to see me. To see the flood. A bomb burst the Banks. We are so lovely—all sea, up to the gate. I've never seen anything more visionary lovely than Caburn upside down in the water."[21] She has twenty ideas for books all buzzing around in her head.

At the start of the war, she is not just writing two works, *Roger Fry* and *Between the Acts*; as we have seen, she is also working on a third, which will become *A Sketch of the Past* well after her death. We have seen it open the floodgates for disturbing, devastating memories, allowing us to know Virginia Stephen better. And we have seen Virginia Woolf tormented by her own memory, transcribing the cruelty, placing side by side the reality of the present war with the disasters of a bygone childhood, its destructive griefs, its perverse aftermaths. The personal horror inscribed in the general horror.

Virginia revels in these memories erupting in their terrible freshness; she undoubtedly thinks she can rid herself of them by writing them out. But, once invoked, the ghosts will claim her and won't let go. In particular, the ghost of her father.

She can't talk about her family to Leonard, hurt by his wife's snobbery with regard to the Woolfs and jealous of the endless attention she lavishes on the Bells, their importance to her, which he considers excessive. The two sisters often joked about his occasional reluctance to visit Charleston and his bitterness "imagining," according to them, Virginia's preference for the Bells over the Woolfs. Which was hardly "imagined," and they knew that very well. . . .

At present, Leonard is not, cannot be, aware of what is going to transpire and is content with supervising his wife's diet and activities, reassured by Rodmell's isolation and calm, which for her, on the contrary, will prove fatal.

She is still a passionate conversationalist, but encounters and gatherings are rare. There's a party for Angelica at Charleston, where a meeting of the Memoir Club will take place. There are letters. Virginia receives a long letter from Benedict, or rather from Ben Nicolson, twenty-seven years old, one of Vita's sons. He criticizes Bloomsbury's elitism, the importance given to their poets, who should have been political activists and gotten involved. She answers with an even longer letter and remarks:

Aren't you taking what you call "Bloomsbury" much too seriously? . . .
What puzzles me is that people who had infinitely greater gifts than
any of us had—I mean Keats, Shelley, Wordsworth, Coleridge and so
on—were unable to influence society. They didn't have anything like
the influence they should have had upon 19th century politics. And so
we drifted into imperialism and all the other horrors that led to 1914.
Would they have had more influence if they had taken an active part
in politics? Or would they only have written worse poems?[22]

Thinking is in itself political. As ever, Virginia devotes herself to her work:
"Thinking is my fighting."[23]

For a time she works on all three projects at once; one of them will
reach the very core of presence, our presence, in a world that remains
indifferent to us. "They were all caught and caged; prisoners; watching a
spectacle. Nothing happened."[24]

She does not "reach" that core: she *is* there.

It is *Between the Acts*.

Leonard read the finished manuscript, without reading the signs indicating where Virginia was then, or found herself: on the verge of departure.
. . . But it was already so late, and it's easy to say this long after the fact,
knowing what happened next. Virginia herself was taking delight in writing what she drew from within, neither analyzing nor decoding it. Not
writing in the first person no doubt let her extract but also extricate herself
from what haunted her, fatally—by distributing it among the characters
she created; by making other players act it out, by transcribing it in living
signs throughout her pages.

So there is Isa, with an unquenchable desire for water throughout the
book, who wonders: "'What wish should I drop into the well?' . . . 'that
the waters should cover me . . . of the wishing well.'" And there is a pond
about which we are told for no reason that "it was in that deep centre, in
that black heart, that the lady had drowned herself." And again, when the
time punctually announces itself for Isa: "The church bells always stopped,
leaving you to ask: Won't there be another note? Isa, half-way across the
lawn, listened. . . . Ding, dong, ding. . . . There was not going to be another
note." And Isa remarks that the show given near her manor by the villagers
had drawn a larger crowd than in other years, "but then last year it rained,"
and she murmurs: "This year, last year, next year, never," and repeats it later
in the evening.[25]

Meanwhile, outside, the performance over, the audience mingling, and the actors scattered, Miss LaTrobe, the author, experiences a fleeting moment of fulfillment: "You have taken my gift! Glory possessed her—for one moment . . . her gift meant nothing. If they had understood her meaning; if they had known their parts. . . . 'A failure,' she groaned." She leans against a tree and looks at the ground, which is nothing more than ground, not some remarkable territory. "This is death, death, death, death, she noted in the margin of her mind; when illusion fails."[26]

And Miss LaTrobe, the creator, the sot, the marginalized lesbian, takes refuge in a bar, its hubbub, the smell of rancid beer. "What she wanted . . . was the darkness in the mud; a whisky and soda at the pub; and coarse words descending like maggots through the waters." When she gets her drink, "she raised her glass to her lips. And drank. And listened. Words of one syllable sank down into the mud. She drowsed; she nodded. . . . Words without meaning—wonderful words."[27]

The words for the next performance. Issued from the mud at the bottom of the water.

That fascinating clear or muddy water with its menacing charms, which runs through all the work, the letters, the diary of Virginia. The water that Julia, her mother, "exhausted swimmer," would never manage to cross. The water that Virginia asks to be left "to go deeper and deeper in" in *Moments of Being*. Also the water of the great lake of melancholy: "And so I pitched into my great lake of melancholy. Lord how deep it is! . . . The only way I keep afloat is by working. . . . Directly I stop working I feel that I am sinking down, down. And as usual, I feel that if I sink further I shall reach the truth." Unless she lets herself slip "tranquilly off into the deep water of my own thoughts navigating the underworld," or into "some continuous stream, not solely of human thought, but of the ship, the night &c, all flowing together."[28]

A never-ending metaphor. In 1931, ten years before drowning herself, she wrote to John Lehmann: "If I live another 50 years I think I shall put this method to some use, but in 50 years I shall be under the pond, with the gold fish swimming over me." In 1925, she wrote to Gerald Brenan that "one ought to sink to the bottom of the sea, probably, and live alone with ones words." There are countless examples, forever pointing to the River Ouse.[29]

But, just as alarming, the mountains are now emerging and with them, the specter of Leslie. Solitude with Leonard, the solitude of Rodmell, authorizes the past to haunt Virginia, without the former safeguard of a dazzling, public, and abundantly full life; of an audience and an array of activities that formed a barrier against certain obsessions.

With no more barriers, the grief of the past descends upon her, in the present; suffering never extinguished nor even wholly realized. The enigma of what "was impossible to say aloud" assails her and remains forever forbidden: the suspicions of incest regarding the father.[30] Hyde Park Gate returns, morbid, corrupted. And more immediately, there is the war.

"I plunged into the past this morning; wrote about father."[31] She goes through his papers, rereads his books, renews her love for him; but above all, she advances alone into the harrowing account of what she hides within, unleashing the most disturbed, least healthy part of herself, which pours forth in this steadily deteriorating time of war, asphyxiation awaiting her in the garage, or morphine: the suicide planned by Leonard in case of defeat, which she dreads.

"How beautiful they were, those old people—" she marvels, lost in the letters of her parents, which she sees free of "mud" . . . whereas at the same time she describes the suspect atmosphere surrounding them, evoking or insinuating the ambiguous discomfort, the libidinous cloud around Leslie Stephen, widowed.[32]

Throughout the diary, mention of the father, or even of mountains, which symbolize him, often anticipates a depressive episode. Symptoms are usually mentioned within a few pages of such allusions.

At the moment, Leslie is never far away. Remember that she wrote, "[I] turn toward my father," upon learning of a war-related disaster. On a March day in 1940, trying to overcome her depression, Virginia takes heart, as she often does, in making plans: she will take books around to the bookstores with Leonard; they will have tea, window shop at antique stores; there will be beautiful farms, green lawns; she will bowl, buy a notebook, rearrange the furniture in her room, occasionally make a cake, write a book of prose poetry. "For in Gods name I've done my share, with pen & talk, for the human race. I mean young writers can stand on their own feet. Yes, I deserve a spring—I owe nobody nothing." And as the primary cure she adds, "Now being drowned by the flow of running water, I will read Whymper till lunch time."[33]

Water. But also, going by the name of Whymper, the mountain. Edward Whymper: the first alpinist to scale Mont Cervin (the Matterhorn), a climb that caused a scandal: four members of the roped party, among them Oscar Wilde's brother, died there, falling into a crevasse. Whymper was suspected of cutting the rope to save his own life. Most importantly, Whymper's is a world of glaciers, summits, peaks, alpenstocks, guides . . . and suspicion.

"I plunged into the past," and for her next book, Virginia thinks of "taking my mountain top—that persistent vision—as a starting point." Which requires the presence of a ghost, her father.[34]

Twenty-eight days before her suicide, on the back of a rough draft of *Between the Acts*, she will write a short sketch: "The Symbol."[35]

And the symbol is a mountain.

A woman seated on a hotel balcony . . . facing the mountain writes: "The mountain is a symbol." She looks through binoculars at "the virgin height" that the first version (crossed out) describes as "a menace: something cleft in the mind like two parts of a broken disk: two numbers: two numbers that cannot be added: a problem that is insoluble."[36]

Today she has the impression of having observed the mountain as she stared at her mother in her death throes, succumbing to cancer, and she recalls having been impatient for her to come to the end of it, wishing her dead in order to be free, to be able to marry. Virginia, beside Leslie, had suffered the same impatience.

But the mountain, complains the woman, the mountain "never moves . . . it would need an earthquake to destroy that mountain." Since the symbol mountain can't be removed, this woman, this girl, in "the most absurd dreams," aspires to climb it, no doubt reaching its summit: "If I could get there, I should be happy to die. I think there, in the crater . . . I should find the answer." The peak. The crater. The cavity. The mountain also contains a place to pitch oneself, like the "great lake of melancholy"—to reach the truth, or because of course there is none.[37]

Virginia has already wondered "if shadows could die, and how one buried them."[38] But, like the mountain once hidden by clouds, they are not gone. They are there, all around. Leslie, and Stella, and Thoby avoiding saying Stella's name after her death, *Stella*, the name of a ship that had just sunk; and Thoby dead, and Virginia and Adrian deciding together to repeat his name often; and the elusive Julia, her corpse and Dr. Seton and Jack Hill and St. Ives, and . . . Laura, and even Roger, now surround Virginia Woolf, who yields to them and staggers, spellbound.

Leonard doesn't see her succumb, alone, adrift; he doesn't see her letting herself be sucked in by the lines she draws. For him, it's normal to find her scrubbing floors to ease her anxiety. He doesn't see her languish, isolated with him, cut off from her circle. On the contrary, he insists on maintaining the calm and isolation forced upon them by the war.

It was Leonard, the pillar, the rock, who proposed, if necessary, their joint suicide. "All the walls, the protecting & reflecting walls, wear so terribly thin in this war."[39]

He doesn't see her, only watches over her, holding to his old theories; the liturgical glass of milk remains a part of their routine. She has no support. Leonard pursues the life that she made possible for him, that he's good at, that fulfills him, and that he has pursued faithfully at her side, at a propitious distance until now. But now he no longer sees her, seems tired of her.

And then . . . and then . . . Virginia Woolf's prestige no longer protects her, without the publicity, without the audience, or at least the perceived audience, she had before. It has dispersed, the circle that allowed the brilliant woman to sparkle (under Leonard's reproving but impressed gaze) and to assert herself, to command everyone's respect, safeguarded by them. The rampart of the public, of Bloomsbury, has disappeared. She is alone with her husband and seems to blur in his eyes. In a sense, she is mastered; no more escapades at Ottoline Morrell's or other thrilling scenes, no more circle of friends who heighten her successes. Who keep her in focus.

More than anyone else, Leonard recognizes the value of the work. But for him it's the product of his wife's "genius," and since he links genius to madness, that work doesn't protect her.

The unthinkable: in January 1941, *Harper's Bazaar* returns to Virginia Woolf a short story they had commissioned from her. Rejected. "A battle against depression, rejection (by Harper's of my story & Ellen Terry) routed today (I hope) by clearing out kitchen; by sending an article (a lame one) to N.S. [*New Statesman*]: & by breaking into PH[40] 2 days, I think, of memoir writing. This trough of despair shall not, I swear, engulf me. The solitude is great." And even now, words she will repeat to Leonard in three months' time: "We live without a future . . . our noses pressed to a closed door."[41]

The solitude is great. . . .

A visit to Cambridge in February slightly relieves the despondency, the pervasive sadness. "[It] felt as if we'd had a hot bath—it was so clean warm and civilised." Virginia is ecstatic, and that speaks volumes about what Rodmell has become for her. She thanks one of her hosts for the "extraordinarily happy evening you gave us. . . . It remains like an oasis, last Wednesday, not a mirage—in the desert."[42]

Returning to that "desert," she loses her footing again. As the months go by, her distress becomes increasingly perceptible, the isolation desolate. Around others, she bears up well, her gaiety restored for those ever rarer encounters or in her letters, as when she thanks Vita for her gift of butter, then so precious: "Please congratulate the cows from me, and the dairy maid, and I would like to suggest that the calf should be known in the future (if it's a man) as Leonard if a woman as Virginia."[43]

She continues to write to Ethel Smyth, at length, confiding in her as never before. March 1, 1941—by March 28 Virginia Woolf will be dead: "Do you feel, as I do, when my head's not this impossible grindstone, that this is the worst stage of the war? I do. I was saying to Leonard, we have no future. He says that's what gives him hope. He says the necessity of some catastrophe pricks him up."[44]

Difficult to follow the exchange. But where does Leonard's response come from? Why this hope in the absence of a future, a future Virginia refutes? What is the "necessary catastrophe" that seems inevitable—and exciting—to him? Is he just expressing his attitude toward the war, or has something unconscious escaped here?

In four weeks' time, Virginia will drown herself.

* * *

Octavia Wilberforce entered the scene a few months earlier; Octavia, whose role in this disaster has not been examined.

Octavia Wilberforce, a doctor, a pioneer in that profession in her youth. A former suffragette. Some sort of distant cousin to Virginia. The lover of an old actress, Elizabeth Robins, who remembered a "vicious" Julia and lived for some time in the United States.[45] Octavia has a practice at Brighton, where she attends Virginia.

A decent enough woman, Octavia Wilberforce. Leon Edel, who knew her a bit later, describes her as "robust and round-faced"; "literature was obviously a mystery to her." She occupied herself with medicine and animal husbandry. The last time he saw her, "she sat on her little tractor and meandered triumphantly through the pastures, ruling her bovine empire and wearing her little crown of artificial flowers on her off-the-face hat."[46]

But Virginia, so alone now, throws herself upon her, a woman six years her junior who treats her almost like a child. A pathetic, emaciated Virginia. An Octavia petrified by the great writer to whom Elizabeth Robins has already introduced her, terrified of not being equal to the task, although at each visit, Virginia begs her to stay.

An Octavia Wilberforce who, like Leonard, provides milk! Her power over the couple: each week when she comes for tea, she brings them milk and cream from her cows. Virginia soon nicknames her "leech Octavia," but she's the one who begs for the leech's presence. "I rather think I've a new lover," she writes in fun to Ethel and especially to Vita, "a doctor, a Wilberforce, a cousin." Above all, someone to hang onto.[47]

She hardly mentions her in her diary or elsewhere in her letters; she writes a few letters to Octavia, and the opening of one of them is inauspicious: "You've reduced me not to silence quite, but to a kind of splutter."[48] With gratitude this time for the products of the Devonshire cows. Octavia then proposes a trade: for the milk, a book.

A book in exchange for milk. Milk, forever the obstacle in Virginia's path.

Milk, even Devonshire milk, is hardly fair trade for a book, Octavia continues, albeit unconvinced. And Virginia: "I never heard of a more absurd 'business proposition' as you call it. A month's milk and cream in return for an unborn and as far as I can tell completely worthless book." And this cry: "I've lost all power over words, cant do a thing with them." Which she doesn't write anywhere else, and which is inaccurate. But the injury, the terror are not.[49]

She proposes apples instead of a book and goes on: "I cant, as you see, make my hand cease to tremble."[50] Her hands at present are always icy, stalactites, says Octavia, who sometimes takes them into her own while she repeats idiotic theories comparing mental suffering to appendicitis.

And it is Virginia's right hand that trembles continuously now, like Leonard's.

Virginia lets herself go a little around this woman whom she dominates, who doesn't not really count, but serves as a lifeline—and who is tortured by her inability to help the writer for whom Devonshire milk, she confesses, doesn't seem to do much good. "Don't go yet," is Virginia's refrain, who insists: "You don't know how much I need it."[51]

Leonard sometimes takes tea with them and returns to his work, despite his wife's attempts to retain him as well. Alone with Octavia, Virginia can then speak of Leslie, whose love letters to his wife she is classifying, enraptured. "Poor Leonard is tired out by my interest in my family and all it brings back." And Wilberforce listens as she spills the thousand versions of that fixation with a father who, Virginia repeats to her, leaned too heavily on his children at the death of their mother, demanded too much emotionally from them, ruined her life and, she says, deadened her physical responses. She reevaluates what she wrote elsewhere. Octavia understands what she can of it, strangely convinced that George Duckworth was evidently adored by his half-sister. "Did you know him?" she asks Elizabeth Robins.[52]

Virginia Woolf is at her wit's end, jumpy, thin as "a razor," with no one to turn to but this powerless woman who listens to her, rarely understands her, and despairs at not being able to "save" her.[53]

She feels useless. The village doesn't even want her for night watches during air raids, though they asked Leonard. She can no longer work for long stretches, never after tea. When she is too desperate, she goes to the kitchen to make cakes.

Miss Robins is able to start writing again thanks to a letter from Virginia. She cables Octavia, "Virginia's letter sets me to work again." Delighted to hear the news, Virginia asks Octavia excitedly to "Say it again!" And when Octavia obeys: "Yes, but tell me again the exact words."[54]

Octavia's last visit, March 21, and Virginia, as always: "Don't go yet," and Octavia torn, because a patient is waiting. Virginia asks her if she can give her something to do.... Catalogue her library? Flattered, considering it sufficient to "buck up" Virginia, Wilberforce repeats her refrain: "there's nobody in England I'd like, *adore* more to help." Which sounds laughable ... but she is the only one who can say that.[55]

Leonard worries about his wife much less now than he did before, when she was doing fine. Now he no longer notices her. Nothing in Virginia's behavior corresponds to the list of red flags he has established, calls for "tak[ing] steps" he considers panaceas: drinking milk, eating better, getting more sleep, insignificant remedies amounting to superstitions.[56]

As always, he justifies himself in his memoir: he began to worry toward the end of January; Virginia was doing better until then. Her depression stemmed from completing *Between the Acts*: the fatigue, having cut "the umbilical cord" and sent the manuscript to the printer.[57] The breakdown occurred suddenly, without warning, according to him.

She has hung on for months. Now she starts losing ground. During the first half of March, Virginia returns from a walk soaked, distraught; she claims to have slipped in a stream. No doubt a first attempt. But no one to rally around her. Leonard, terrified, seems to withdraw still further. Wilberforce is upset, of course, but mainly because the writer's fame intimidates her and she's afraid of making a bad impression. The others have dispersed. Virginia struggles alone.

❊ ❊ ❊

Alone? Not completely. Vanessa pays her a visit on March 20; upset, genuinely worried, she writes to her immediately upon returning to Charleston. A lethal letter. Which could have arisen instinctively from the old dispute, now closed. Or from stupidity.

With this letter she would have the last word. In it we can also hear how the one who falters is discredited. "Once you fall, Septimus repeated to himself, human nature is on you."[58]

Vanessa: "You *must* be sensible. Which means you must accept the fact that Leonard and I can judge better than you can. . . . You're in the state when one never admits what's the matter—but you must not go and get ill just now. What shall we do when we're invaded if you are a helpless invalid—"[59] The death blow.

She adds that both she and Leonard (as opposed, that is, to Virginia) have always had reputations for good sense and honesty. So her sister must "believe in" them.[60]

But what is there to believe in, which she is rejecting? Leonard has nothing to offer. He is always talking of "tak[ing] steps," but goes in circles, not knowing what those measures are.[61] In any case, it's too late now, but he never considered asking Virginia, talking to her, listening to her. For him, his wife's difficulties are physical in nature, and he considers her to inhabit a different sphere from his when she becomes sick. There's no question of exchange or understanding, only of authority. He digs in his heels, alone, powerless, clueless, superior, dominant: Virginia's only chance, he insists, is to yield.

Yield to what? He must convince her that she's very sick. Increase her anxiety about her condition, terrify her. Corner her. And make her drink milk.

On February 25, she accompanied him to Brighton again, where he was giving a talk. In the restroom at the Sussex Grill, "p—ing as quietly as I could," she listens to the women chatting as they powder their faces, and a short story takes shape, the last one after the mountain-symbol story, this time about a coastal town that reeks of fish, even in the restrooms.[62]

In a Brighton bakery, she observes, horrified, a fat woman with her "large white muffin face," heavily made-up old women stuffing themselves: "something scented, shoddy, parasitic about them. Then they toted up cakes. . . . Where does the money come from to feed these fat white slugs? Brighton a love corner for slugs." And then in Rodmell, "infernal boredom."[63]

The journal is silent until March 8, and then Brighton again, "shell encrusted old women, rouged, decked, cadaverous at the tea shop," and then immediately a jump; Virginia Woolf defends herself: "No: I intend no introspection. I mark Henry James's sentence: Observe perpetually. Observe the oncome of age. Observe greed. Observe my own despondency. By that means it becomes serviceable. Or I hope so. I insist upon spending this time to the best advantage. I will go down with my colours flying."[64]

A final entry in the diary, March 24, four days before going down. She observed much, with great care, and begins: "She had a nose like the Duke of Wellington & great horse teeth & cold prominent eyes. When we came in she was sitting perched on a 3 cornered chair with knitting in her hands. An arrow fastened her collar . . . two of her sons had been killed in the war. This, one felt, was to her credit. . . . I tried to coin a few compliments. But they perished in the icy sea between us. And then there was nothing."[65]

Nevertheless, a few more lines: "This windy corner. And Nessa is at Brighton, & I am imagining how it wd be if we could infuse souls."[66]

✳ ✳ ✳

She makes dates for April with Tom Eliot, Ethel Smyth; writes to Vita, whose parakeets are dying in great numbers: "If we come over [to Sissing-hurst], may I bring her [Louie, the housekeeper] a pair if any survive? Do they die all in an instant? When shall we come? Lord knows—"[67]

She writes to John Lehmann. He has just read the manuscript of *Between the Acts*, to mediate between Leonard, who is enthusiastic, and Virginia, who no longer believes in it. He sides passionately with Leonard. They decide on its publication, but Virginia protests: "Dear John, I'd decided, before your letter came, that I cant publish that novel as it stands—its too silly and trivial." She plans to revise it, to see if she can make something of it; she had not realized that it was so bad. And she humbly apologizes, apologizes again "profoundly" to John Lehmann.[68]

So many mental, physical, cerebral, technical "acts" required by her work over so long a time . . . she had come so far, she was exhausted. And all that time having also borne the burden of living, just existence itself.

There is no writer, no authentic thinker, who is not burdened with bitter knowledge: the eternally unknown language of the world in which we are the actors in our own disappearances.

Virginia Woolf had acquired yet another kind of knowledge: the ability to capture what whispers within the silence. There's great danger in saying, even through old Lucy Swithin, that "we haven't the words—we haven't the words."[69]

❊ ❊ ❊

And on March 27 Leonard is more frightened than ever, finding "the terrifying decision which I had to take then once more faced me. It was essential for her to resign herself to illness and the drastic regime which alone could stave off insanity." That tedious regime: milk, food, sleep! But above all, "I had to urge her to face the verge of disaster in order to get her to accept the misery of the only method of avoiding it." Her only chance, once again, is to yield.[70]

Urgently he turns to Octavia Wilberforce, who—although there's no proof of her competence, especially in this area—impresses him just as George Duckworth once did. "A remarkable character. Her ancestors were the famous Wilberforces of the anti-slavery movement; their portraits hung on her walls. . . . She was large, strong, solid, slow growing, completely reliable, like an English oak. Her roots were in English history and the English soil of Sussex."[71] What better proof!

She is also a timid woman, not very intelligent; an unassertive, compliant doctor.

She is in bed, very sick with the flu and a bad fever, and the telephone rings: Leonard, in a panic, is calling for her help. She is too sick, can't come; he begs her to see them. He adds that Virginia doesn't want to see her. Later he will write that together they had agreed upon this visit.

And it is a horror.

The women spoke together, he writes, had a conversation. No. He gave Wilberforce control; she accepted and suddenly took herself very seriously. Here is Virginia, Virginia Woolf, dragged against her will to an incompetent doctor, humiliated before the woman who had supported her, who had been proud to know her; she sees herself at Octavia's mercy. And she is. Quite pleased with herself, Octavia Wilberforce plays doctor. She forgets her cough: a battle is under way, "a battle of—not wits but *minds*," she dares to call it.[72]

That great mind is indignant. Virginia Woolf seems to resist her questions: "[she] wouldn't answer my questions frankly . . . and was generally resistive." So Wilberforce treats her as though she were lying, or at least "gently and firmly [I] told her that I knew her answer wasn't true"; whatever the true answer is, she thinks Virginia Woolf is withholding it.

She orders her to undress, which serves no purpose in this instance. As though "sleep-walking," Virginia obeys, then stops and asks Octavia to promise not to order her a rest cure. Octavia answers evasively and the examination continues. Virginia resists at each step, "like a petulant child."[73]

"God knows if I did her a penn'orth of good," confesses the stupid Octavia to Elizabeth. She took Virginia's ice-cold hands in her own, reaffirmed that, in all of England, Virginia was the person she'd like most to help, but Virginia must "collaborate." "All you have to do is to reassure Leonard," she concludes. Whom she joins in the next room, leaving Virginia alone to wait while they discuss her.[74]

This is Virginia Woolf, the writer. She is not allowed to speak. Papa, Mama are taking charge of her. "Once you fall. . . ."[75]

While she is waiting docilely in her corner, a plane rumbles over, a loud din above the roof; bombs explode nearby. Absorbed in their conversation, Wilberforce and Leonard take no notice. It's only on the drive home that Leonard will remember and make note of it. But Virginia, left alone, offended, waiting by herself while bombs are dropping? Laboriously, Wilberforce arrives at "her" prescription: Virginia is not to work for a certain amount of time, Virginia consumes too many books. Rationed, she will be fine.

All that for only that.

Leonard is satisfied. Returning home with Virginia, he hopes that the words of Wilberforce, "the oak," have had some effect on her.[76]

They have. The next day she will drown herself.

The last person to see her is Louie Maier, the housekeeper.

The morning of March 28, Leonard brings her Virginia, who is not doing well: "'Louie, will you give Mrs Woolf a duster so that she can help you clean the room?' I gave her a duster, but it seemed very strange. I had never known her want to do any housework with me before."[77]

And Louie taught the writer, terrified by the idea of no longer being able to write books, how to clean them. (I watched her repeat that epic lesson for a film. Majestically, slowly and solemnly, she opened, shook out, flapped and closed each volume.) "After a while Mrs Woolf put the duster down and went away. I thought that probably she did not like cleaning the study and had decided to do something else."[78] Yes, exactly.

To get from Monk's House to the River Ouse, you must first cross through a romantic, lopsided cemetery adjacent to the garden. Then comes a long path leading through a bare, very flat landscape offering no reference points or recourse. You must be very determined, as Virginia was. Forget Ophelia with her wreath of flowers, even if she too was led "from her melodious lay/to muddy death."[79] There's nothing pastoral about the River Ouse; it runs through an industrial district. It's a setting out of Zola, where the desperate come from the surrounded villages to commit suicide.

Virginia left three letters. One to Vanessa, thanking her for hers! Two testimonials for Leonard, written a few days apart. One of them prior to her first attempt, perhaps. She confirms that she's hearing voices again, that she's afraid of being mad forever and that he has been perfect for her. She repeats what Rachel says to her fiancé in *The Voyage Out*, even though they obviously never managed to love each other: "I don't think two people could have been happier than we have been." Leonard will be better without her: "I know that I am spoiling your life, that without me you could work." He has been so patient with her, done all that could be done. And she adds each time . . . "everybody knows it."[80]

What was Virginia Woolf denied? Respect.

As were Vincent Van Gogh and Antonin Artaud, Gérard de Nerval and Giordano Bruno, Friedrich Nietzsche and Edgar Allan Poe, Charles Baudelaire as well, so many others, Camille Claudel. . . . Many of them, judging themselves through the eyes of others, found themselves guilty and took their own lives.

They remain, "colours flying."[81]

* * *

A few months before sinking into the River Ouse, her pockets weighted with stones, Virginia Woolf wrote: "All frost. Still frost. Burning white. . . . What is that phrase I always remember—or forget. Look your last on all things lovely."[82]

ABBREVIATIONS

Works by Virginia Woolf

BA   *Between the Acts*. New York: Harcourt, 1941.

CSF   *The Complete Shorter Fiction*. Ed. Susan Dick. Orlando: Harcourt, 1989.

D.i-v   *The Diary of Virginia Woolf: 1915–1941*. Vol. 1–5. Ed. Anne Olivier Bell. New York: Harcourt Brace Jovanovich, 1977–84.

MB   *Moments of Being*. Ed. Jeanne Schulkind. San Diego: Harcourt, 1985.

MD   *Mrs. Dalloway*. Orlando: Harcourt, 1925.

O   *Orlando*. San Diego: Harcourt, 1928.

PA   *A Passionate Apprentice: The Early Journals: 1897–1909*. Ed. Mitchell A. Leaska. London: Hogarth Press, 1990.

TG   *Three Guineas*. New York: Harcourt, 1938.

TL   *To the Lighthouse*. Oxford: Oxford University Press, 1992.

VO   *The Voyage Out*. London: Hogarth Press, 1957.

W   *The Waves*. Orlando: Harcourt, 1931.

Y   *The Years*. London: Hogarth Press, 1951.

Supplementary Works

HL   Lee, Hermione. *Virginia Woolf*. London: Chatto & Windus, 1996.

LW.i   Woolf, Leonard. *Sowing: An Autobiography of the Years 1880–1904*. London: Hogarth Press, 1960.

LW.ii Woolf, Leonard. *Growing: An Autobiography of the Years 1904–1911*. London: Hogarth Press, 1970.

Abbreviations

LW.iii	Woolf, Leonard. *Beginning Again: An Autobiography of the Years 1911–1918.* London: Hogarth Press, 1964.
LW.iv	Woolf, Leonard. *Downhill All the Way: An Autobiography of the Years 1919–1939.* London: Hogarth Press, 1968.
LW.v	Woolf, Leonard. *The Journey Not the Arrival Matters: An Autobiography of the Years 1939–1969.* London: Hogarth Press, 1969.
SLS	Stephen, Leslie. *Sir Leslie Stephen's Mausoleum Book.* London: Clarendon Press, 1977.
WV	Woolf, Leonard. *The Wise Virgins.* New Haven: Yale University Press, 2007.

Letters

Letters are identified with the writer's name followed by the recipient's name, then the date written. Frequent correspondents are identified by their initials:

CB	Clive Bell
ES	Ethel Smyth
LS	Lytton Strachey
LW	Leonard Woolf
OW	Octavia Wilberforce
VB	Vanessa Bell
VD	Violet Dickinson
VS	Virginia Stephen
VS-W	Vita Sackville-West
VW	Virginia Woolf

Selections of letters are abbreviated as follows:

CDL	*Carrington: Letters and Extracts from Her Diaries.* New York: Holt, Rinehart and Winston, 1970.
L.i-vi	*The Letters of Virginia Woolf: 1888–1941.* Ed. Nigel Nicolson and Joanne Trautmann. New York: Harcourt Brace Jovanovich, 1975–79.
LSL	*The Letters of Lytton Strachey.* Ed. Paul Levy and Penelope Marcus. New York: Farrar, Straus & Giroux, 2005.
LWL	*Letters of Leonard Woolf.* Ed. Frederic Spotts. San Diego: Harcourt Brace Jovanovich, 1989.
VBL	*Selected Letters of Vanessa Bell.* Ed. Regina Marler. London: Moyer Bell, 1998.
VH	*Vita and Harold: The Letters of Vita Sackville-West and Harold Nicolson.* Ed. Nigel Nicolson. New York: G. P. Putnam's Sons, 1992.

NOTES

Part 1

1. Virginia Woolf, *The Waves* (Orlando: Harcourt, 1931), 114.
2. Virginia Woolf, *The Complete Shorter Fiction*, ed. Susan Dick (London: Hogarth Press, 1989), 87.
3. February 27, 1926. *D.iii*, 62.
4. Virginia Woolf, *Mrs Dalloway* (Orlando: Harcourt, 1925), 184.
5. How is one: April 28, 1897. Virginia Woolf, *A Passionate Apprentice: The Early Journals: 1897–1909*, ed. Mitchell A. Leaska (London: Hogarth Press, 1990), 77. Very very . . . day: *MD*, 8. I feel: November 1, 1940. *D.v*, 335.
6. Virginia Woolf, *Moments of Being*, ed. Jeanne Schulkind (San Diego: Harcourt, 1985), 72.
7. O le sale monde: LW to LS, July 30, 1905. *LWL*, 98. Why one: LW to LS, October 11, 1904. *LWL*, 47. Did he invent: LW to LS, July 23, 1905. *LWL*, 97. The saddest: LW to LS, September 29, 1907. *LWL*, 132–33.
8. *LW.iii*, 74, as cited in Hermione Lee, *Virginia Woolf* (London: Chatto & Windus, 1996), 301.
9. The crash: LW to LS, September 27, 1904. *LWL*, 44. A battered usher: LW to LS, September 27, 1904. *LWL*, 44.
10. Very yellow and silent: LW to LS, September 29, 1904. *LWL*, 45. Oh no, no: LS to LW, September 30, 1904. *LWL*, 45.
11. LS to LW, November 20, 1904. *LSL*, 35.
12. LW to LS, July 15, 1905. *LWL*, 95.
13. The Goth: nickname for Thoby Stephen, Virginia's older brother.

14. I feel that: LW to LS, October 11, 1904. *LWL*, 48. It was always: LW to LS, January 26, 1905. *LWL*, 75. You can't exist: LW to LS, December 16, 1904. *LWL*, 67.
15. LW to LS, November 17, 1907. *LWL*, 134.
16. LW to LS, September 14, 1909. *LWL*, 150.
17. I sometimes wonder: LW to LS, March 21, 1906. *LWL*, 115. Damn damn: LW to LS, April 21, 1906. *LWL*, 118.
18. LS to LW, September 9, 1904. *LSL*, 32.
19. LS to LW, September 9, 1904. *LSL*, 32.
20. Oh but the Goth!: LS to LW, October 23, 1905. *LSL*, 84. The Gothic: LS to LW, October 23, 1905. *LSL*, 84. Rather wonderful: LS to LW, December 21, 1904. *LSL*, 43.
21. LW to LS, March 4, 1906. *LWL*, 114.
22. LW to LS, October 2, 1908. *LWL*, 137.
23. LW to LS, September 29, 1907. *LWL*, 133.
24. appalling: LW to LS, September 29, 1907. *LWL*, 133. My only news: LW to Saxon Sydney-Turner, March 10, 1907. *LWL*, 125.
25. Adrian Stephen to Duncan Grant, July 1911. As cited in Jean MacGibbon, *There's the Lighthouse: A Biography of Adrian Stephen* (London: James & James, 1997), 84.
26. He has ruled: VS to Lady Robert Cecil, June 1912. *L.i*, 504. confession: VS to VD, June 4, 1912. *L.i*, 500. A penniless: VS to VD, June 4, 1912. *L.i*, 500.
27. *Marcel Proust, Selected Letters: 1904–1909*, ed. Philip Kolb (New York: Oxford University Press, 1989), 221.
28. LW to LS, July 13, 1902. *LWL*, 24.
29. degraded debauch: LW to LS, October 1, 1905. *LWL*, 102. these degradations: LW to LS, February 1, 1909. *LWL*, 145.
30. among other: LW to LS, May 19, 1907. *LWL*, 128. nonetheless: LW to LS, May 19, 1907. *LWL*, 128. cancerous kiss: LW to Saxon Sydney-Turner, June 12, 1910. *LWL*, 151. dead man's lips: LW to LS, February 1, 1909. *LWL*, 146.
31. Would you: LW to LS, July 7, 1907. *LWL*, 130. a half naked: LW to LS, July 7, 1907. *LWL*, 130. Most women: LW to LS, November 25, 1908. *LWL*, 142.
32. VS to VD, May 13, 1908. *L.i*, 331.
33. Am I to: VS to VB, August 10, 1908. *L.i*, 348. I have heard: VS to VB, August 14, 1908. *L.i*, 354.
34. Marriage is: VS to VB, July 21, 1911. *L.i*, 469. What am I: VS to VD, March 1907. *L.i*, 289.
35. Adrian Stephen to Duncan Grant, July 1911. In MacGibbon, *There's the Lighthouse*, 84.
36. VS to VB, June 8 (?), 1911. *L.i*, 466.
37. *MB*, 188.
38. VS to LW, May 1, 1912. *L.i*, 496.
39. The final: LW to LS, February 1, 1909. *LWL*, 145. It certainly: LW to LS, February 1, 1909. *LWL*, 145. on the principle: LW to LS, February 1, 1909. *LWL*, 145. I don't: LW to LS, February 1, 1909. *LWL*, 145. Do you: LW to LS, February 1, 1909. *LWL*, 144.
40. October 17, 1924. *D.ii*, 317.

41. greater or less: LS to LW, February 19, 1909. *LSL*, 173. You would: LS to LW, February 19, 1909. *LSL*, 174. copulated: LS to LW, February 19, 1909. *LSL*, 174.

42. LW to LS, September 14, 1909. *LWL*, 149.

43. You must: LS to LW, August 21, 1909. *LWL*, 148. young, wild: LS to LW, August 21, 1909. *LWL*, 149. the opportunity: LS to LW, August 21, 1909. *LWL*, 149.

44. the one: LW to LS, September 14, 1909. *LWL*, 149. The horrible: LW to LS, September 14, 1909. *LWL*, 150. As cited in Lee, *Virginia Woolf*, 298.

45. From the perspective: Recorded as part of a series of programs broadcast by France Culture. These broadcasts were transcribed and taken up again by Maurice Nadeau in a 1973 supplement of the *Quinzaine Littéraire*. France Culture, 1973; program transcribed 1973, Maurice Nadeau, *Quinzaine Littéraire*.

46. France Culture, 1973.

47. VW to Roger Fry, May 27, 1927. *L.iii*, 386.

48. *TL*, 165.

49. *TL*, 165.

50. And as usual: June 13, 1923. *D.ii*, 247. An attempt: *MD*, 184.

51. Excitement: *HL*, 331: Gerald Brenan to Rosemary Dinnage, November 4, 1967. *LWL*, 162. Ça lui dit trop: VS-W to Harold Nicolson, August 17, 1926. *VH*, 159.

52. I want: June 13, 1923. *D.ii*, 247. Leonard told me: *HL* 331–332: Gerald Brenan to Rosemary Dinnage, November 4, 1967. *LWL*, 162.

53. ghastly: *HL*, 304. LW to LS, September 14, 1909. *LWL*, 150. preliminary: LW to LS, September 14, 1909. *LWL*, 150.

54. *HL*, 331: Gerald Brenan to Rosemary Dinnage, November 4, 1967. *LWL*, 162.

55. her attacks: *HL*, 331: Gerald Brenan to Rosemary Dinnage, November 4, 1967. *LWL*, 162. excitement: Victoria Glendinning, *Leonard Woolf: A Biography* (New York: Free Press, 2006), 143.

56. VW to LS, July 25, 1916. *L.ii*, 107.

57. horrible: LW to LS, September 14, 1909. *LWL*, 150. ghastly: LW to LS, September 14, 1909. *LWL*, 150.

58. Why do: VW to Katherine Cox, September 4, 1912. *L.ii*, 6. I might: VW to Katherine Cox, September 4, 1912. *L.ii*, 7. Don't marry: VW to Katherine Cox, March 18, 1913. *L.ii*, 20.

59. The W.C.: VW to LS, September 1, 1912. *L.ii*, 5. Several times: VW to LS, September 1, 1912. *L.ii*, 5.

60. *TL*, 146.

61. Virginia Woolf, *The Waves* (Orlando: Harcourt, 1931), 57.

62. Love between: *MD*, 89. How Shakespeare: *MD*, 88.

63. VS-W to Harold Nicolson, August 17, 1926. *VH*, 158.

64. VS-W to Harold Nicolson, August 17, 1926. *VH*, 159. As cited in *HL*, 326.

65. I do hope: Harold Nicolson to VS-W, July 7, 1926. *VH*, 150n. It's a relief: Harold Nicolson to VS-W, September 2, 1926. As quoted in *Portrait of a Marriage: Vita Sackville-West and Harold Nicolson*, ed. Nigel Nicolson (New York: Atheneum, 1973), 229.

66. VW to VS-W, December 8, 1926. *L.iii*, 306–7.

67. VW to VS-W, December 5, 1927. *L.iii*, 442–43.
68. Talking to Lytton: VW to VS-W, March 23, 1927. *L.iii*, 352–53. I do feel: VW to LS, March 21, 1927. *L.iii*, 351.
69. *LW.iii*, 18–19.
70. Vanessa was: *LW.iii*, 27. the form: *LW.iii*, 27. some resemblance: *LW.iii*, 27.
71. I always: LW to LS, July 30, 1905. *LWL*, 97. You think: LW to LS, July 30, 1905. *LWL*, 98.
72. Leonard had already described his first vision of the two sisters, in keeping with the general opinion: "In white dresses and large hats, with parasols in their hands, their beauty literally took one's breath away, for suddenly seeing them one stopped astonished and everything including one's breathing for one second also stopped as it does when in a picture gallery you suddenly come face to face with a great Rembrandt or Velasquez. . . . It was almost impossible for a man not to fall in love with them. . . . It must, however, be admitted that at that time they seemed to be so formidably aloof and reserved that it was rather like falling in love with Rembrandt's picture of his wife, Velasquez's picture of an Infanta, or the lovely temple of Segesta." (In white dresses: *LW.i*, 183 and 186.)

    a very different: *LW.iii*, 28. She was, as: *LW.iii*, 28. when she was: *LW.iii*, 28. when, unexcited: *LW.iii*, 28. painful: *LW.iii*, 28.
73. *LW.iii*, 28.
74. strange: *LW.iii*, 28. ridiculous: *LW.iii*, 28–30. would go into: *LW.iii*, 29.
75. *LW.iii*, 29.
76. May 26, 1924. *D.ii*, 301.
77. *LW.iii*, 52.
78. On March 28: *LW.iv*, 157. I must return: *LW.iv*, 157. At 7:30: *LW.iii*, 83. whistling through: *LW.iii*, 83.
79. November 23, 1926. *D.iii*, 118.
80. His first novel, *The Village in the Jungle*, met with great success.
81. utterly vulgar: LS to LW, June 20, 1905. *LSL*, 68. how many: LS to LW, June 20, 1905. *LSL*, 69. Your Jewish: LW to LS, July 16, 1905. *LWL*, 95.
82. July 11, 1930. *Harold Nicolson: Diaries and Letters, Vol. 1, 1930–1939*, ed. Nigel Nicholson (London: Collins, 1966). As quoted in Glendinning, *Leonard Woolf*, 236.
83. *LWL*, 470, citing Quentin Bell.
84. Virginia Woolf, *Between the Acts* (New York: Harcourt, 1941), 219.
85. In the beginning: Leonard Woolf, *The Wise Virgins* (New York: Harcourt, 1914), 1. jealous for the: *WV*, 2.
86. *BA*, 219.
87. Are you in your stall, brother: June 14, 1925. *D.iii*, 30. I said to: VS to VB. October 8, 1938. *L.vi*, 286.
88. As quoted in Glendinning, *Leonard Woolf*, 294.
89. Morocco is here code for homosexuality. LW to LS, November 1, 1911. *LWL*, 167.
90. pure, often: *LW.iii*, 35. in love with: *LW.iii*, 52.
91. I only: "Volume I" in Quentin Bell, *Virginia Woolf: A Biography* (New York: Harcourt Brace Jovanovich, 1972), 186. the strength: VS to LW, May 1, 1912.

L.i, 496. Again, I want: VS to LW, May 1, 1912. *L.i*, 496. being half: VS to LW, May 1, 1912. *L.i.*, 496. As cited in *HL*, 311.

92. VS to VD, June 4, 1912. *L.i*, 500.

93. LW and VS to LS, June 6, 1912. *Congenial Spirits: The Selected Letters of Virginia Woolf*, ed. Joanne Trautmann Banks (San Diego: Harcourt Brace Jovanovich, 1989), 72.

94. Virginia always referred to her mother-in-law as Mrs. Woolf. When used here, "Mrs. Woolf" never refers to Virginia but to Marie Woolf.
       How I hated: VW to ES, August 2, 1930. *L.iv*, 195. immense vitality: VW to ES, August 2, 1930. *L.iv*, 196. They can't die: VW to ES, August 2, 1930. *L.iv*, 196.

95. January 4, 1915. *D.i*, 6.

96. *WV*, 59. As cited in *HL*, 313.

97. *LW.iii*, 70.

98. Marie Woolf to LW, August 7, 1912. *LWL*, 178.

99. VS to VD, October 9, 1912. *L.ii*, 9. As cited in *HL*, 334.

100. VW to ES, March 17, 1930. *L.iv*, 151.

101. a world of good: *LW.iii*, 82. I am rather: VB to LW, January 22, 1913. Vanessa Bell, *Selected Letters of Vanessa Bell*, ed. Regina Marler (London: Moyer Bell, 1998), 134. They confirmed: LW.iii, 82.

102. France Culture, 1973.

103. O dearest Gwen: VW to Gwen Raverat, March 11, 1925. *L.iii*, 171. To think: VW to Gwen Raverat, March 11, 1925. *L.iii*, 171. My own: September 5, 1926. *D.iii*, 107. As cited in *HL*, 329.

104. *MD*, 99.

105. VW to VB. June 2, 1926. *L.iii*, 271.

106. Bell, *Virginia Woolf*, 8.

107. As with many: *LW.iv*, 56–57. The mother wants: *LW.iv*, 58.

108. VS to Duncan Grant, August 8, 1912. *L.i*, 508.

109. *HL*, 314.

110. May 14, 1912, CB to Molly McCarthy, Charleston Papers, University of Sussex. As cited in *HL*, 321.

111. CB to Mary Hutchinson, January 21, 1915, Harry Ransom Humanities Research Center, The University of Texas at Austin. Washington State: Manuscripts, Archives, and Special Collections, Holland Library, Washington State University. As cited in *HL*, 308.

112. [The dictator]: Virginia Woolf, *Three Guineas* (New York: Harcourt, 1938), 156–57. Common interest: *TG*, 217.

113. October 13, 1937. *D.v*, 114.

114. *W*, 58.

115. VS to VD, April 5, 1905. *L.i*, 184.

116. the richest: VW to Quentin Bell, December 12, 1933. *L.v*, 258. gloves, hat: VW to Quentin Bell, December 12, 1933. *L.v*, 258. didn't like: VW to Quentin Bell, December 12, 1933. *L.v*, 258.

117. Virginia and the Jew: John Maynard Keynes to VB, July 28, 1917. Garnett Collection, Northwestern University Library, Evanston, Ill. As quoted in Alex Zwerdling,

Virginia Woolf and the Real World (Berkeley: University of California Press, 1986), 116. but no Jew: John Maynard Keynes to VB, January 31, 1918. Garnett Collection, Northwestern University Library, Evanston, Ill. As quoted in Zwerdling, *Virginia Woolf and the Real World*, 116.

118. What is: VW to Jacques Raverat, September 4, 1924. *L.iii*, 130. I make: VW to Jacques Raverat, July 30, 1923. *L.iii*, 58.

119. A sandwich: VS to Janet Case, June 1912. *L.i*, 502–3. Work and love: VS to VD, June 1912. *L.i*, 502.

120. 10 Jews: VW to ES, February 28, 1932. *L.v*, 23. I do nothing: VW to Ottoline Morrell, October 31, 1933. *L.v*, 240. these dull plain: September 3, 1928. *D.iii*, 195. I am so: VW to ES, September 28, 1930. *L.iv*, 222–23.

121. To be: September 3, 1928. *D.iii*, 195. How many: September 29, 1930. *D.iii*, 321.

122. Angel of: Virginia Woolf, "Professions for Women," in *Collected Essays, Volume 2* (New York: Harcourt and Brace, 1967), 286–87. to want: *TL*, 165.

123. VW to Quentin Bell, October 28, 1930. *L.iv*, 237–38.

124. VW to Julian Bell, October 25, 1935. *L.v*, 436.

125. VW to ES, January 11, 1934. *L.v*, 269.

126. Belonged to: Marcel Proust, *In Search of Lost Time, vol. IV: Sodom and Gomorrah*, trans. Terence Kilmartin and C. K. Scott Moncrieff (London: Chatto & Windus, 1992), 121. One can: Proust, *In Search of Lost Time*, IV:121.

127. VW to ES, August 8, 1934. *L.v*, 321.

128. My Jew had: VW to Katherine Cox, November 1912. *L.ii*, 11. a good: VW to VB. June 2, 1926. *L.iii*, 269.

129. VW to ES, August 28, 1930. *L.iii*, 204.

130. Virginia Woolf, *The Years* (London: Hogarth Press, 1951), 365.

131. like a drowned sailor: *MD*, 93. The depths: *TL*, 168.

132. *Y*, 365–66.

133. Abrahamson was Marie Woolf's cousin, Sir Martin Abrahamson, whom her mother-in-law sometimes invited when Virginia came to visit, as she mentions in her diary.

134. *Y*, 366.

135. *Y*, 366.

136. *Y*, 367.

137. an odious: April 2, 1937. *D.v*, 75. It was: November 3, 1936. *D.v*, 29.

138. Very tired: November 3, 1936. *D.v*, 29. into one: November 3, 1936. *D.v*, 30. The miracle: November 5, 1936. *D.v*, 30.

139. *LW.iv*, 155.

140. we are Jews: VW to Margaret Llewelyn Davies, April 28, 1935. *L.v*, 388. our Jewishness: VW to ES, April 26, 1935. *L.v*, 386.

141. France Culture, 1973.

142. *LW.v*, 46.

143. This morning: May 15, 1940. *D.v*, 284–85. No, I dont: May 15, 1940. *D.v*, 285. its all bombast, this war: May 15, 1940. *D.v*, 285.

144. March 24, 1940. *D.v*, 274.

145. our waiting while: June 27, 1940. *D.v*, 299. I will continue: June 9, 1940. *D.v*, 292–93.
146. VW to Margaret Llewelyn Davies, April 28, 1935. *L.v*, 388.
147. VW to Margaret Llewelyn Davies, April 28, 1935. *L.v*, 388.
148. *MB*, 39.
149. *MD*, 184.
150. There is a: *LW.v*, 95. The long: *LW.v*, 95.
151. April 8, 1941. VS-W to Harold Nicolson. Reproduced in Harold Nicolson, *The War Years: Diaries and Letters 1939–1945* (New York: Atheneum, 1967), 159.
152. LW, note found after his death. *LWL*, 165.
153. June 10, 1919. *D.i*, 280.
154. John Lehmann, *Thrown to the Woolfs* (New York: Holt, Rinehart and Winston, 1979), 10.
155. Lehmann, *Thrown to the Woolfs*, 17.
156. France Culture, 1973.
157. VW to CB, January 28, 1931. *L.iv*, 283.
158. Glendinning, *Leonard Woolf*, 294.
159. France Culture, 1973.
160. LW to Trekkie Ritchie, June 1, 1944. *Love Letters: Leonard Woolf and Trekkie Ritchie Parsons (1941–1969)*, ed. Judith Adamson (London: Chatto & Windus, 2001), 128.
161. Caption of lithograph produced by Trekkie of Leonard. See *LWL*, 480n2.
162. VB to Angelica Garnett, December 25, 1944. *VBL*, 484.
163. Quentin Bell, introduction to *D.i*, xvi.
164. LW to Trekkie Ritchie, June 15, 1944. Adamson, ed., *Love Letters*, 144.

Part 2

1. *MB*, 84.
2. *MB*, 124.
3. As quoted in *HL*, 112.
4. The world has: *MD*, 14. my wings still: *MB*, 124.
5. *MB*, 83.
6. How difficult it: *MB*, 87. What would: *MB*, 36.
7. *TL*, 68.
8. *TL*, 146.
9. *TL*, 146.
10. May 4, 1928. *D.iii*, 183.
11. Sir Leslie Stephen, *Leslie Stephen's Mausoleum Book* (London: Clarendon Press, 1977), 40.
12. *SLS*, 41.
13. very quick: *MB*, 83. the sad: *MB*, 83. All life: Quentin Bell, *Virginia Woolf: A Biography* (New York: Harcourt Brace Jovanovich, 1972), 13. an exhausted: *MB*, 39.
14. *MB*, 32.
15. *MB*, 83.

16. *MB*, 82.
17. omnibus expert: *MB*, 121. shabby cloak: *MB*, 36. Your feet: *MB*, 37. excited many instincts: *MB*, 42–43. would insist: *MB*, 43. that passive: *MB*, 96. Old Cow: *MB*, 97. almost canine: *MB*, 96.
18. tease: *MB*, 114. with pretty: *MB*, 114. as she came: *MB*, 82. I was playing: *MB*, 82.
19. *MB*, 82.
20. one, two: *MB*, 66. Vanessa and I: *MB*, 68. It was like being: *MB*, 95.
21. *MB*, 40.
22. Hold yourself: *MB*, 84. She always liked: *MB*, 92. It's nice that: *MB*, 92.
23. Italics are my own.
24. I think of: November 23, 1940. *D.v*, 341. All this afternoon: VW to Lady Tweedsmuir. March 21, 1941. *L.vi*, 483.
25. his pale eyes: *MB*, 107. Whats to: June 20, 1940. *D.v*, 297. Today the dictators: *MB*, 107. I sit: *MB*, 107.
26. was impossible: *MB*, 108. How deep they: *MB*, 108.
27. Quite naturally: *MB*, 45. almost welcome: *MB*, 45. the sharp pang: *MB*, 45. Recognizable: *MB*, 45. hideous as it was: *MB*, 45.
28. *SLS*, 92.
29. see *SLS*, 12, for example.
30. my darling Minny: *SLS*, 9. her beautiful: *SLS*, 18n. She was a poem: *SLS*, 19.
31. Her Ladyship: As quoted in *HL*, 102. backward: *SLS*, 44.
32. besides the: *MB*, 182. a vacant-eyed: *MB*, 182.
33. Letter, Leslie Stephen to Julia Stephen, April 29, 1881. The Henry W. and Albert A. Berg Collection, New York Public Library, as cited in *HL*, 102.
34. *SLS*, 92.
35. VW to VB. November 13, 1921. *L.ii*, 492.
36. not only had: *MB*, 184. incarcerated with: *MB*, 184.
37. VS to VD. December 6, 1904. *L.i*, 164.
38. VW to VB. May 4, 1934. As cited in *HL*, 104.
39. *SLS*, 47.
40. There is a touch: *SLS*, 36. Unqualified . . . lover: *SLS*, 36–37.
41. in those days: *MB*, 106. choked us: *MB*, 45.
42. any comfort: *MB*, 45. Whatever comfort: *MB*, 41. suddenly she: *MB*, 41.
43. darling Julia: *SLS*, 36. She found that: *MB*, 48.
44. *MB*, 108.
45. she gave indiscriminately: *MB*, 45. his right: *MB*, 45. could not give: *MB*, 48.
46. Leslie Stephen to Stella Hills, April 10, 1897. Leslie Stephen, *Selected Letters of Leslie Stephen, Volume 2*, ed. John W. Bicknell (Columbus: Ohio State University Press, 1996), 474.
47. Old Cow: *MB*, 97. often one: *MB*, 94.
48. Leslie Stephen to Stella Hills, April 13, 1897. Stephen, *Selected Letters of Leslie Stephen, Volume 2*, 475.
49. impossible to: *MB*, 108. One of the consequences: *MB*, 45.
50. *MB*, 107.

51. Italics are my own.

52. illicit: *MB*, 145. illicit need: *MB*, 145. stirred in him: *MB*, 146.

53. *MB*, 136.

54. other words: *MB*, 56. an extraordinary: *MB*, 144. Have you no: *MB*, 144. unbound contempt: *MB*, 144.

55. VS to VD. Early October 1903. *L.i*, 98.

56. *MB*, 145.

57. *MB*, 108.

58. illicit: *MB*, 145. chronic state: *MB*, 45.

59. strange: *MB*, 146. whatever: *MB*, 145.

60. violent: *MB*, footnote ‡ on 145. illicit: *MB*, 146.

61. dependence: *MB*, 145. to sympathize: *MB*, 145.

62. the horror: *MB*, 144. It was like: *MB*, 116.

63. next victim: *MB*, 56. tasked Stella's: *MB*, 55.

64. Another lion appears in *To the Lighthouse* in the form of Mr. Ramsay, through the eyes of the prudish Lily Briscoe: "he was like a lion seeking whom he could devour, and his face had that touch of desperation, of exaggeration in it which alarmed her, and made her pull her skirts about her" (*To the Lighthouse*, 233). *MB*, 116.

65. *MB*, 146.

66. *MB*, 111.

67. his honesty: *MB*, 110. his attractiveness: *MB*, 111.

68. replaced the beauty: *MB*, 56. very small: *MB*, 111. in league: *MB*, 111.

69. I remember: *MB*, 112. Slowly he would: *MB*, 157. feeling proud: *MB*, 158.

70. *MB*, 46.

71. VS to VD. March 4, 1904. *L.i*, 131.

72. VW to V-SW. March 2, 1926. *L.iii*, 245.

73. Do I love: *PA*, xliv n 61. Quoted from the holograph version of *The Years*, Vol. VII, August 5, 1934. I think: January 21, 1918. *D.i*, 110.

74. the thing that exists: October 30, 1926. *D.iii*, 114. Mr. Ramsay: *TL*, 105.

75. *Y*, 49.

76. leered at her: *Y*, 28. as if to stop her: *Y*, 28. he did not stretch: *Y*, 29.

77. Breakdown: Bell, *Virginia Woolf*, 44. madness: Bell, *Virginia Woolf*, 44.

78. Italics are my own.

79. Bell, *Virginia Woolf*, 44.

80. vitally important: Bell, *Virginia Woolf*, 44. To know that . . . the cure of death: Bell, *Virginia Woolf*, 44.

81. black and: *MB*, 100. for it was: *MB*, 50. Stella and Mr Hills: *MB*, 50. Blushing: *MB*, 50. she was: *MB*, 101. Did mother: *MB*, 101.

82. My Joy: *MB*, 83. the blow: *MB*, 50. clumsy, cruel: *MB*, 106.

83. bluer: *MB*, 105. incandescence: *MB*, 105. something of moonlight: *MB*, 105.

84. Leslie Stephen to Charles Norton, January 10, 1897. Harvard. As quoted in *HL*, 137.

85. very white: April 10, 1897. *PA*, 68. in her sleep: April 10, 1897. *PA*, 68. It was half: April 10, 1897. *PA*, 68.

86. April 10, 1897. *PA*, 68.
87. *MB*, 136.
88. April 28, 1897. *PA*, 77.
89. frightening: April 29, 1897. *PA*, 77. No getting rid: April 29, 1897. *PA*, 77. Macauley: April 29, 1897. *PA*, 77.
90. Pleased . . . happy: April 30, 1897. *PA*, 78–79. still more . . . cheerful: June 6, 1897. *PA*, 96.
91. That old cow: *PA*. Mr. Henry James: *PA*, 54.
92. Hyde St: June 2, 1897. *PA*, 94. I managed: May 9, 1897. *PA*, 83. had the pleasure: May 12, 1897. *PA*, 85.
93. funny stories: May 27 , 1897. *PA*, 91.
94. the greatest: May 1, 1897. *PA*, 79. 'Ginia is devouring: *SLS*, 103.
95. so bad for Stella: July 7, 1897. *PA*, 112. that old: July 9, 1897. *PA*, 112–13.
96. big chair: July 11, 1897. *PA*, 113. We talked: July 11, 1897. *PA*, 113.
97. July 15, 1897. *PA*, 114.
98. July 24, 1897. *PA*, 116.
99. *MB*, 69.
100. *MB*, 171.
101. VW to Emma Vaughn. August 8, 1901. *L.i*, 43.
102. *MB*, 156.
103. *MB*, 168.
104. dear old Bar: VS to George Duckworth: April 22, 1900. *L.i*, 31. Nessa's . . . grateful to you: VS to George Duckworth: April 26, 1900. *L.i*, 32.
105. He paid: *MB*, 157 footnote *. How could we: *MB*, 157.
106. I vividly: *SLS*, 35. I think that: *SLS*, 35.
107. has a calm: VS to VB, July 25 (?) 1911. *L.i*, 472. Whew: VS to VB, July 25 (?) 1911. *L.i*, 472.
108. that gigantic: VW to VB, February 20, 1922. *L.ii*, 505. I am going: VW to VB, February 20, 1922. *L.ii*, 505. Dont you: VW to VB, February 20, 1922. *L.ii*, 505.
109. VW to LS, September 8, 1925. *L.iii*, 206.
110. carpet of duckweed: August 18, 1899. "Extract from the Huntingdonshire Gazette: Terrible Tragedy in a Duckpond," in Virginia Woolf, *PA*, 151; and Virginia Woolf, "A Terrible Tragedy in a Duck Pond," in *A Cezanne in the Hedge and Other Memories of Charleston and Bloomsbury*, ed. Hugh Lee (Chicago: University of Chicago Press, 1993), 178. the green shroud: August 18, 1899. "Extract from the Huntingdonshire Gazette" in Virginia Woolf, *PA*, 151. The angry waters: August 18, 1899. "Extract from the Huntingdonshire Gazette," in Virginia Woolf, *PA*, 151. The corpses, however: Virginia Woolf, "A Terrible Tragedy in a Duck Pond," in Lee, ed., *A Cezanne in the Hedge*, 182.
111. I sank & sank: Virginia Woolf, "A Terrible Tragedy in a Duck Pond," in Lee, ed., *A Cezanne in the Hedge*, 183. hair & body: Virginia Woolf, "A Terrible Tragedy in a Duck Pond," in Lee, ed., *A Cezanne in the Hedge*, 185.
112. February 22, 1930. *D.iii*, 293.
113. Did you go: VW to VB, May 4, 1934. *L.v*, 299. the batting: May 2, 1934, *D.iv*, 211.
114. *MB*, 57.

Part 3

115. a stupid: *MB*, 57. modified, confused: *MB*, 58. little plans: *MB*, 58.
116. VW to VB, November 13, 1921. Joanne Trautmann Banks, ed., *Congenial Spirits: The Selected Letters of Virginia Woolf* (San Diego: Harcourt Brace Jovanovich, 1989), 138.
117. *MB*, 108.
118. *MB*, 108.
119. Virginia Woolf, *Between the Acts* (New York: Harcourt, 1941), 219.

Part 3

1. November 1, 1940. *D.v*, 335.
2. VW to Jacques Raverat, March 8, 1924. *L.i*, *ii*, 93.
3. There is nothing: VS to VD, August 1905. *L.i*, 204. I sometimes: VS to VD, April 30, 1903. *L.i*, 75. Wonderful strength: VS to VD, December (?) 1903. *L.i*, 117. If only: VS to VD, December 25, 1903. *L.i*, 118. I know: VS to VD, February 1904. *L.i*, 124. We have: VS to Janet Case, February 1904. *L.i*, 124.
4. November 28, 1928. *D.iii*, 208.
5. VS to Thoby Stephen, May 1903. *L.i*, 76.
6. A place to: VS to Emma Vaughan, April 25, 1904. *L.i*, 138. Geralds figure: VS to VD. March 1904. *L.i*, 134.
7. *MB*, 92.
8. *MD*, 14.
9. VS to CB, September 4, 1910. *L.i*, 434.
10. *MD*, 67.
11. No crime: *MD*, 67. the trees waved: *MD*, 69. Men must not: *MD*, 24.
12. *MD*, 91.
13. among the orchids: *MD*, 70. But I am: *MD*, 70. Now . . . fascinated him: *MD*, 66.
14. *MD*, 70.
15. *MD*, 98.
16. My food is: VS to VD, June 30, 1903. *L.i*, 83. I went to: VB to VS, December 7, 1904. *VBL*, 27.
17. VS to VD, October/November 1902. *L.i*, 60.
18. VS to VD, July 7, 1903. *L.i*, 85.
19. Would you like: VS to VD, late September 1903. *L.i*, 96. Who thinks: VS to VD, December 5, 1906. *L.i*, 257. I wish you: VS to VD, June 4, 1903. *L.i*, 79.
20. VS to VD, September 22 (?), 1904. *L.i*, 142.
21. Jane Dunn, *A Very Close Conspiracy: Vanessa Bell and Virginia Woolf* (London: Jonathan Cape, 1990), 54.
22. *MB*, 195.
23. satisfied: see for example, November 7 (?), 1906. VW, *L.i*, 239. "irritation caused by": VS to VD, November 9 (?), 1906. *L.i*, 241.
24. February 7, 1931. *D.iv*, 10.
25. My Violet: VS to VD, December 2, 1906. *L.i*, 255. Dear old Thoby: VS to VD, November 29, 1906. *L.i*, 253. Thoby slept better: VS to VD, November 30 (?), 1906.

L.i, 254. He is not: VS to VD, December 2, 1906. *L.i*, 256. A great many: VS to VD, December 10, 1906. *L.i*, 259.

26. We are really: VS to VD, July 23, 1903. *L.i*, 86. I am the happiest: VW to ES, April 7, 1931. *L.iv*, 303.

27. Almost on the: December 1906 edition of *The National Review I.* As quoted in *L.i*, 266n1. You must think: VS to VD, December 18, 1906. *L.i*, 266.

28. Dunn, *A Very Close Conspiracy*, 54.

29. elderly and prosaic: VS to VD, February 1907. *L.i*, 279. a heavy hand: VS to VD, July 7, 1903. *L.i*, 85.

30. think very: VS to Madge Vaughan, December 17, 1906. *L.i*, 265. clever, and: VS to Madge Vaughan, December 17, 1906. *L.i*, 265. When I think: VS to VD, December 30 (?), 1906. *L.i*, 273. It will really be: VS to VD, October 15 (?), 1907. *L.i*, 316. Tawny and jubilant: VS to VD, January 3, 1907. *L.i*, 275. I did not: VS to VD, January 3, 1907. *L.i*, 276.

31. VS to Madge Vaughan, February 15, 1907. *L.i*, 283.

32. Poor little boy: VS to VD, December 22, 1906. *L.i*, 269. The old despair: December 3, 1923. *D.ii*, 277.

33. As cited by Jean MacGibbon, *There's the Lighthouse: A Biography of Adrian Stephen* (London: James & James, 1997), 49.

34. We perish: *TL*, 140. I beneath: *TL*, 140. Here, Virginia echoes the last verse of William Cowper's poem "The Castaway" (1799).

35. *Hyde Park Gate News*, September 9, 1892. As quoted in *HL*, 33.

36. Virginia's body was not found until three weeks after she drowned.

37. Adrian Stephen to VB, April 1941, as cited by MacGibbon, *There's the Lighthouse*, 152.

38. I begin to: VS to VD, December 25, 1904. *L.i*, 169. When I see: VS to Lady Cecil McGibbons, December 22, 1904. *L.i*, 168. the writer of: VS to VD. July 7, 1907. *L.i*, 299. I cant help: VS to Madge Vaughan. December 1, 1904. *L.i*, 162.

39. I could be wed: VS to VD, December 16, 1906. *L.i*, 263. Now do you know: VS to VD, December 16, 1906. *L.i*, 264.

40. I have been: VS to VD, September 22, 1907. *L.i*, 311. Who was: VS to VB, August 4, 1908. *L.i*, 342. dreadful weariness: September 19, 1907. *PA*, 374.

41. We both very: VW to Margaret Llewelyn Davies, December 31, 1918. *L.ii*, 313. You've given: VW to VB, March 15, 1940. *L.vi*, 385.

42. It is like: VB to CB, June 1910. Tate Gallery London (Charleston). As quoted in Dunn, *A Very Close Conspiracy*, 124. I always: December 22, 1927. *D.iii*, 168.

43. VW to VB, February 20, 1922. *L.ii*, 506.

44. my affair: VW to Gwen Raverat, March 22, 1925. *L. iii*, 172. turned more of: VW to Gwen Raverat, March 22, 1925. *L. iii*, 172.

45. a permanent: Angelica Garnett, *Deceived with Kindness: A Bloomsbury Childhood* (London: Pimlico, 1984), 28. Aloud: *MB*, 108.

46. VS to VD, May 13, 1908. *L.i*, 331.

47. VS to CB, April 15, 1908. *L.i*, 325.

48. The main point: VS to CB, May 1908. *L.i*, 334. Why do you: VS to CB, May 6, 1908. *L.i*, 329. Ah—such: As cited by Dunn, *A Very Close Conspiracy*, 116. I wished: CB

to VS, May 7, 1908. University of Sussex Library, as quoted in Frances Spalding, *Vanessa Bell* (New Haven and New York: Ticknor & Fields, 1983), 73.

49. Dont forget: *HL*, 250. Your wife gave: VS to CB, December 25, 1908. *L.i*, 376.

50. Ah! there's: VS to VB, August 10, 1909. *L.i*, 406. Shall you kiss: VS to VB, August 14 1908. *L.i*, 354.

51. VS to CB, November 14 (?), 1910. *L.i*, 439.

52. VW to ES, August 15, 1930. *L.iv*, 200.

53. VS to CB, August 19, 1908. *L.i*, 356.

54. VS to CB, February 7, 1909. *L.i*, 383.

55. *Tout va bien:* CB to VS, August 7, 1908. University of Sussex Library, as quoted in Spalding, *Vanessa Bell*, 74. I sometimes: CB to VS, August 3, 1908. University of Sussex Library, as quoted in Spalding, *Vanessa Bell*, 74.

56. CB to VS, February 5 (?), 1909. "Appendix D" of "Volume I" in Quentin Bell, *Virginia Woolf: A Biography* (New York: Harcourt, Brace Jovanovich, 1972), 208.

57. To give more: CB to VS, February 5 (?), 1909. "Appendix D" of "Volume I" in Bell, *Virginia Woolf*, 209. It seemed to: CB to VS, February 5 (?), 1909. "Appendix D of "Volume I" in Bell, *Virginia Woolf*, 209.

58. VS to CB, February 7, 1909. *L.i*, 383.

59. VW to LS, February 26, 1915. *L.ii*, 61.

60. VW to CB, July 24, 1917. *L.ii*, 167.

61. CB to LW, "Appendix D of "Volume I" in Bell, *Virginia Woolf*, 212.

62. VB to VS, August 11, 1908. *VBL*, 66–67.

63. VS to VB, August 12, 1908. *L.i*, 350–51.

64. Dunn, *A Very Close Conspiracy*, 54.

65. June 20, 1928. *D.iii*, 186.

66. VB to VS, August 11, 1908. *VBL*, 67.

67. like an elephant: VB to VS, August 11, 1908. *VBL*, 67. Has Hilton Young: VB to VS. August 13, 1908. *VBL*, 68. No answer: VS to VB, August 12 1908. *L.i*, 351. Nothing from H.Y.: VS to VB, August 14, 1908. *L.i*, 354. all the lovers: VS to VB, August 20, 1908. *L.i*, 357.

68. I'm only: VS to Emma Vaughan, August 1908. *L.i*, 359. till the: VS to Emma Vaughan, August 1908. *L.i*, 360.

69. VS to Madge Vaughan. November 19, 1908. *L.i*, 373.

70. VS to LS, February 1, 1909. *L.i*, 382.

71. VB to VS, February 7, 1909. The Henry W. and Albert A. Berg Collection, New York Public Library. As quoted in Dunn, *A Very Close Conspiracy*, 122.

72. VS to CB, April 13, 1909. *L.i*, 391.

73. VB to Margery Snowden, May 10, 1909. Monk's House Papers. As quoted in "Volume I" of Bell, *Virginia Woolf*, 144.

74. There are 6: April 18, 1918. *D.i*, 140. Oh Roger, how horribly: VB to Roger Fry, July 5, 1911. *VBL*, 105. Oh Roger, it was delicious: VB to Roger Fry, October 12, 1912. *VBL*, 129.

75. Do you really: VB to CB, October 11, 1911. *VBL*, 108–9. Are you: VB to CB, January 15, 1912. *VBL*, 115.

76. *TL*, 165.

77. David Garnett to LS, December 25, 1918. British Library, Manuscript Department. As quoted by Spalding, *Vanessa Bell*, 177.

78. DG to Bunny, May 6, 1915. As quoted in Spalding, *Vanessa Bell*, 141.

79. Duncan Grant, journal, as quoted in Spalding, *Vanessa Bell*, 172.

80. My visit to: August 16, 1918. *D.i*, 182. The rather: January 3, 1918. *D.i*, 94. Without sympathy: January 3, 1918. *D.i*, 94.

81. VB to DG, July 29, 1919. *VBL*, 233–34.

82. Duncan Grant, journal, as quoted in Frances Spalding, *Vanessa Bell* (New York and New Haven: Ticknor & Fields, 1983), 172.

83. Duncan Grant, journal, as quoted in Spalding, *Vanessa Bell*, 172–73.

84. Please don't: VB to DG, February 7, 1930: *VBL*, 352. But the fact: VB to DG., February 13, 1930. Henrietta Cooper. As quoted in Spalding, *Vanessa Bell*, 238.

85. VB to DG, February 5, 1930. *VBL*, 350.

86. I have now: August 19, 1929. *D.iii*, 242–43. You and: VW to VB, April 14, 1927. *L.iii*, 363.

87. VB to VW, February 5, 1927. *VBL*, 313.

88. VB to CB, December 27, 1912. *VBL*, 132.

89. could not dispel: *MD*, 31. like a nun: *MD*, 31. It was all over: *MD*, 47.

90. cancer of the mind: "Volume I" in Bell, *Virginia Woolf*, 44. corruption of the spirit: "Volume I" in Bell, *Virginia Woolf*, 44.

91. *W*, 159.

92. *LW.iii*, 172–73.

93. *LW.iii*, 81.

94. As quoted in *HL*, 72.

95. Vincent to Theo van Gogh, March 24, 1889. Letter #752 Br. 1990: 756 | CL: 581 (*Brieven 1990* 756, *Complete Letters* 581).

96. *LW.iii*, 158.

97. It was primitive: *LW.iii*, 153. Nothing could: *LW.iii*, 153.

98. *LW.iii*, 155

99. *LW.iii*, 157.

100. *LW.iii*, 158–59.

101. *LW.iii*, 73.

102. *LW.iii*, 74–75.

103. *LW.iii*, 91.

104. June 14, 1925. *D.iii*, 30.

105. I've not: VW to LW, August 3, 1913. *L.ii*, 33. I do believe: VW to LW, August 4, 1913. *L.ii*, 34. I have been: VW to LW, August 5, 1913. *L.ii*, 34. To begin: VW to LW, December 4, 1913. *L.ii*, 35.

106. VW to LW, December ? 1913. *L.ii*, 35.

107. always running: VW to LW, September 28, 1928. *L.iii*, 539. Poor Mandrill: VW to LW, September 25, 1928. *L.iii*, 535. We adore: VW to LW, September 28, 1928. *L.iii*, 539.

108. Virginia Woolf, *The Voyage Out* (London: Penguin, 1992), 6.

109. On a dark: *VO*, 7. There was a book: *VO*, 9–10.
110. He's dead: *VO*, 9. There was a theory: *VO*, 9. A screw loose: *VO*, 9. Accumulations of a lifetime: VO, 10.
111. The great white: *VO*, 15. The white: *VO*, 16. Grew dimmer: *VO*, 20.
112. *VO*, 244.
113. *VO*, 199.
114. Flung into the: *VO*, 281. I'm a mermaid: *VO*, 281.
115. *VO*, 322.

Part 4

1. VW to ES, October 16, 1930. *L.iv*, 231.
2. VW to ES, October 16, 1930. *L.iv*, 231.
3. VW to ES, October 16, 1930. *L.iv*, 231.
4. VW to ES, October 16, 1930. *L.iv,* 231.
5. an hour's complete: *MD*, 120. insisting that: *MD*, 99.
6. With the exceptions of *Three Guineas* (wrongly) and the Roger Fry biography (rightly).
7. *Les Nouvelles Révélations de l'être.* Antonin Artaud, Oeuvres complètes VII (Paris: Gallimard, 1967), 120.
8. France Culture, 1973.
9. They will: February 20, 1937. *D.v*, 58. The long: February 20, 1937. *D.v*, 58. A physical: March 1, 1937. *D.v*, 63. I'm: March 2, 1937. *D.v*, 65.
10. VW to Mary Hutchinson, January 9, 1924. *L.iii*, 504.
11. September 23, 1918. *D.i*, 198.
12. February 3, 1932. *D.iv*, 71.
13. December 12, 1917. *D.i*, 89–90.
14. *Carrington: Letters and Extracts from Her Diaries*, ed. David Garnett (New York: Holt, Rinehart and Winston, 1970), 261.
15. I held her: March 12, 1932. *D.iv*, 82. There is nothing: March 12, 1932. *D.iv*, 82. I did not: March 12, 1932. *D.iv*, 82. I said life: March 12, 1932. *D.iv*, 82.
16. March 12, 1932. *D.iv*, 82.
17. March 12, 1932. *D.iv*, 82.
18. March 17, 1932. *D.iv*, 83.
19. May 25, 1932. *D.iv*, 102–103.
20. May 25, 1932. *D.iv*, 103.
21. See VW to CB, January 18, 1930. *L.iv*, 129.
22. Performed at VB's studio at 8 Fitzroy Street on January 18, 1935. *D.iv*, 273–74.
23. VW to Barbara Bagenal, July 8, 1923. *L.iii*, 56.
24. But what about: March 13, 1921. *D.ii*, 100. when we first: *LW.iii*, 243.
25. behaving . . . like: VW to Roger Fry, September 16, 1925. *L.iii*, 209. Polluted city: *Y*, 366–67.
26. VW to VB, January 29, 1918. *L.ii*, 213.

27. VW to VB, May 9, 1928. *L.iii*, 496.

28. See Alec Craig, *The Banned Books of England* (London: Allen & Unwin, 1962), 98, as quoted in *HL*, 400.

29. almost instantly: April 18, 1918. *D.i*, 139–40. piece of dynamite: As cited in Victoria Glendinning, *Leonard Woolf: A Biography* (New York: Free Press, 2006), 202.

30. VW to LS, April 23, 1918. *L.ii*, 232.

31. January 15, 1941. *D.v*, 352–53.

32. James Joyce, *Finnegans Wake* (New York: Penguin, 1976), 627.

33. VW to VS-W, November 8 (?), 1932. *L.v*, 121.

34. VW, *Times Literary Supplement* 795, December 2, 1920.

35. VW to ES, April 20, 1931. *L.iv*, 315.

36. VW to Roger Fry, October 3, 1922. *L.ii*, 565.

37. VW to Roger Fry, May 6, 1922. *L.ii*, 525.

38. If someone: Ludwig Wittgenstein, *On Certainty,* trans. Denis Paul and G. E. M. Anscombe, ed. G. E. M. Anscombe and G. H. von Wright (New York: Harper & Row, 1969), 244:32e. It is not: Ludwig Wittgenstein, *Tractatus Logico-Philosophicus*, ed. D. F. Pears and B. F. McGuinness (London: Routledge & Kegan Paul, 1921), 6.44:149. Someone who: Wittgenstein, *On Certainty*, 90e.

39. *LW.v*, 48.

40. VW to Saxon Sydney-Turner, September 20, 1925. *L.iii*, 212.

41. Virginia Woolf's opus includes a considerable number of posthumous works, among them her diary (five volumes), her letters (six volumes), and many other titles.

42. LW to V S-W, December 16, 1925. *LWL*, 228.

43. Vita Vita Vita: VW to V S-W, December 23, 1925. *L.iii*, 225. I have missed: VW to V S-W, January 26, 1926. *L.iii*, 231. Honey dearest: VW to V S-W, July 18, 1927. *L.iii*, 398.

44. Heaven knows: VW to V S-W, July 15, 1927. *L.iii*, 397. Its the: VW to V S-W, September 25, 1927. *L.iii*, 423.

45. VW to V S-W, January 31, 1928. *L.iii*, 453.

46. *O*, 168.

47. March 22, 1928. *D.iii*, 177.

48. VW to ES, November 26, 1935. *L.v*, 447.

49. VB to VW, April 27, 1935. *VBL*, 385.

50. November 1, 1924. *D.ii*, 320.

51. VW to VS-W, August 1931, *L.iv*, 366.

52. January 16, 1923. *D.ii*, 225–26.

53. VW to VB, May 23, 1931. *L.iv*, 334.

54. I scribble: VW to ES, December 24, 1940. *L. vi*, 453. Such caverns: VW to ES, December 29, 1931. *L.iv*, 422. Because everyone: VW to ES, December 29, 1931. *L.iv*, 422. What you give: VW to ES, April 1, 1931. *L.iv*, 302. she is: VW to Quentin Bell, May 14, 1920. *L.iv*, 170. An old woman: VW to Quentin Bell, May 14, 1920. *L.iv*, 170.

55. VW to VD, June 23, 1925. *L.iii*, 191.

56. VW to VD, December 6, 1936. *L.vi*, 90.

57. VB to VW, April 20, 1908, as cited in Jane Dunn, *A Very Close Conspiracy: Vanessa Bell and Virginia Woolf* (London: Jonathan Cape, 1990), 145.

58. I put: November 30, 1937. *D.v*, 120. Nessa and: VW to Edward Sackville-West, February 12, 1928. *L.iii*, 458.

59. VB to DG, December 27, 1925. *VBL*, 287–88.

60. August 17, 1937. *D.v*, 108.

61. December 18, 1937. *D.v*, 121.

62. A version of Ape, one of Nessa's nicknames for Virginia.

63. I rather think: VW to VB. August 17, 1937. *L.vi*, 158. your singe: VW to VB, August 3, 1937. *L.vi*, 152. Oh why: VW to VB, August 8, 1937. *L.vi*, 155. You shant: VW to VB, August 1937. *L.vi*, 156.

64. VW to VB, August 5, 1937. *L.vi*, 153.

65. Nessa's nickname.

66. VW to VB, April 3, 1925. *L.iii*, 176.

67. VW to V S-W, July 26, 1937. *L.vi*, 151.

68. March 12, 1922. *D.ii*, 171.

69. France Culture, 1973.

70. *TG*, 217.

71. *TG*, 215–16.

72. was the least: *LW.iv*, 27. the faces: September 13, 1938. *D.v*, 169.

73. Berta Ruck, author of popular sentimental novels, is indignant, and her husband even more so, when Virginia, in complete innocence, names a character in *Jacob's Room* Bertha Ruck . . . whom she has die, no less! Threat of a lawsuit. Reconciliation. Invitation to a Bloomsbury event. Berta then makes a conquest of Virginia by singing: "Never allow a sailor an inch above the knee." VW to Roger Fry, September 22, 1924. *L.iii*, 132.

74. *LW.iv*, 168–69.

75. His books: *LW.iv*, 169. Handicapped: Sigmund Freud to LW, January 31, 1939. *LWL*, 244.

76. If I thought: France Culture, 1973. Never discussed: France Culture, 1973.

77. France Culture, 1973.

78. France Culture, 1973.

79. France Culture, 1973.

80. VW to VB, May 22, 1927. *L.iii*, 381.

81. VW to VB, May 13, 1921. *L.ii*, 468.

82. *LW.v*, 118.

83. to enlarge: December 2, 1939. *D. v*, 248. I'm gulping: December 8, 1939. *D. v*, 249. little facts: September 24, 1939. *D.v*, 238.

84. *LW.v*, 14.

85. *MD*, 184.

Part 5

1. All the: July 24, 1940. *D.v*, 304. No audience: June 9, 1940. *D.v*, 293.
2. from one: September 29, 1940. *D.v*, 325. never had: October 6, 1940. *D.v*, 327.
3. I don't: October 2, 1940. *D.v*, 326. If Hitler: VW to ES, September 12, postscript to letter dated September 11, 1940. *L.vi*, 431.
4. Yes, I was: January 26, 1941. *D.v*, 355. A cricketer: VW to ES, 9 January 1939. *L.vi*, 309.
5. June 27, 1940. *D.v*, 299.
6. *BA*, 144.
7. November 23, 1940. *D.v*, 340.
8. November 23, 1940. *D.v*, 340.
9. VB to VW, October 14, 1938. *VBL*, 450.
10. VW to ES, August 16, 1940. *L.vi*, 417.
11. March 20, 1940. *D.v*, 271.
12. I'm crying: March 20, 1940. *D.v*, 271–72. Lord to have: March 20, 1940. *D.v*, 272.
13. July 25, 1940. *D.v*, 305.
14. July 25, 1940. *D.v*, 305.
15. millions lamented: *MD*, 70. If it doesn't: VW to Benedict Nicolson, August 13, 1940. *L.vi*, 414.
16. Don't close: August 16, 1940. *D.v*, 311. Can you: August 31, 1940. *D.v*, 314.
17. October 2, 1940. *D.v*, 326.
18. February 11, 1940. *D.v*, 267.
19. *LW.iv*, 254.
20. October 12, 1940. *D.v*, 328–29.
21. VW to VS-W, November 15, 1940. *L.vi*, 446.
22. VW to Benedict Nicolson, November 15, 1940. *L.vi*, 421.
23. May 15, 1940. *D.v*, 285.
24. *BA*, 120.
25. What wish: *BA*, 71. it was in: *BA*, 30–31. The church: *BA*, 140. but then: *BA*, 145. This year: *BA*, 145.
26. You have taken: *BA*, 142. This is death: *BA*, 122.
27. What she: *BA*, 138. she raised: *BA*, 144.
28. exhausted swimmer: *MB*, 39. to go deeper: *MB*, 39. And so I: June 23, 1929. *D.iii*, 235. tranquilly off: June 27, 1925. *D.iii*, 33. some continuous: June 18, 1927. *D.iii*, 139.
29. If I live: VW to John Lehmann, September 17, 1931. *L.vi*, 381. one ought: VW to Gerald Brenan, June 14, 1925. *L.iii*, 189.
30. *MB*, 108.
31. November 15, 1940. *D.v*, 338.
32. December 22, 1940. *D.v*, 345.
33. I turn: *MB*, 107. For in Gods: March 29, 1940. *D.v*, 276.
34. I plunged: November 15, 1940. *D.v*, 338. taking my: November 23, 1940. Virginia Woolf, *D.v*, 341.
35. *CSF*, 312.

36. The mountain: "The Symbol," *CSF*, 288. the virgin: "The Symbol," *CSF*, 289. a menace: Deleted portions of the holograph version of "The Symbol" included in "Notes and Appendices," *CSF*, 312.

37. never moves: "The Symbol," *CSF*, 290. the most/If I could: Deleted portions of "The Symbol" included in "Notes and Appendices," *CSF*, 312–13. great lake: June 23, 1929. *D.iii*, 235.

38. "The Mysterious Case of Miss. V," *CSF*, 32.

39. July 24, 1940. *D.v*, 304.

40. Initials of *Point'z Hall*, the working title for *Between the Acts*.

41. A battle: January 26, 1941. *D.v*, 355. We live: January 26, 1941. *D.v*, 355.

42. felt as if: VW to Philippa Strachey, February 17, 1941. *L.vi*, 473. extraordinarily: VW to George Rylands, February 19, 1941. *L.vi*, 473.

43. VW to VS-W, November 29, 1940. *L.vi*, 448.

44. VW to ES, March 1, 1941. *L.vi*, 474.

45. Elizabeth Robins. *D.iii*, 183.

46. robust and round-faced: Leon Edel, "Some Memories of Octavia Wilberforce," in *A Cézanne in the Hedge*, ed. Hugh Lee (Chicago: University of Chicago Press, 1993), 117. literature was obviously: Edel, "Some Memories of Octavia Wilberforce," 119. she sat on: Edel, "Some Memories of Octavia Wilberforce," 121.

47. leech: November 29, 1940. *D.v*, 342. I rather: VW to VS-W, January 19, 1941. *L.vi*, 462. a doctor: VW to Ethel Smyth, February 1, 1941. *L.vi*, 465.

48. VW to OW, February 23, 1941. *L.vi*, 474.

49. VW to OW, December 31, 1940. *L.vi*, 456.

50. VW to OW, December 31, 1940. *L.vi*, 456.

51. OW to Elizabeth Robins, March 30, 1941. Herbert Marder, *The Measure of Life: Virginia Woolf's Last Years* (Ithaca: Cornell University Press, 2000), 362.

52. Poor Leonard: OW to Elizabeth Robins, December 23, 1940. Marder, *The Measure of Life*, 350. Did you: OW to Elizabeth Robins, March 14, 1941. Marder, *The Measure of Life*, 356.

53. a razor: OW to Elizabeth Robins, February 28, 1941. Marder, *The Measure of Life*, 354.

54. OW to Elizabeth Robins, December 23, 1940. Marder, *The Measure of Life*, 349.

55. Don't go: OW to Elizabeth Robins, March 30, 1941. Marder, *The Measure of Life*, 362. Buck up: OW to Elizabeth Robins. Marder, *The Measure of Life*, 335. there's nobody: OW to Elizabeth Robins, March 27, 1941. Marder, *The Measure of Life*, 358.

56. See *LW.v*, 79 and 86.

57. *LW.v*, 79.

58. *MD*, 98.

59. VB to VW, March 20, 1941. *VBL*, 473–74.

60. VB to VW, March 20, 1941. *VBL*, 474.

61. See *LW.v*, 79 and 86.

62. February 27, 1941. *D.v*, 357.

63. large white: February 26, 1941. *D.v*, 357. Something scented: February 26, 1941. *D.v*, 357. infernal: February 26, 1941. *D.v*, 357.

64. shell encrusted: March 8, 1941. *D.v*, 357. No. I: March 8, 1941. *D.v*, 357.
65. March 24, 1941. *D.v*, 358.
66. March 24, 1941. *D.v*, 358.
67. VW to VS-W, March 22, 1941. *L.vi*, 484.
68. VW to John Lehmann, March 27, 1941. *L.vi*, 486.
69. *BA*, 38.
70. *LW.v*, 91.
71. *LW.v*, 80.
72. OW to Elizabeth Robins, March 27, 1941. Marder, *The Measure of Life*, 358.
73. OW to Elizabeth Robins, March 27, 1941. Marder, *The Measure of Life*, 358.
74. OW to Elizabeth Robins, March 27, 1941. Marder, *The Measure of Life*, 358.
75. *MD*, 98.
76. *LW.v*, 80.
77. Joan Russell Noble, *Recollections of Virginia Woolf* (New York: William Morrow, 1972), 160.
78. Noble, *Recollections of Virginia Woolf*, 160.
79. Shakespeare, *Hamlet* (Oxford: Oxford University Press, 1987), 4.7, 319.
80. VW to LW, March 18, 1941. *L.vi*, 481.
81. March 8, 1941. *D.v*, 357.
82. January 9, 1941. *D.v*, 351.

WORKS CITED

Adamson, Judith, ed. *Love Letters: Leonard Woolf and Trekkie Ritchie Parsons (1941–1969)*. London: Chatto & Windus, 2001.

Artaud, Antonin. *Oeuvres Completes*. Paris: Gallimard, 1967.

Banks, Joanne Trautmann, ed. *Congenial Spirits: The Selected Letters of Virginia Woolf*. San Diego: Harcourt Brace Jovanovich, 1989.

Bell, Quentin. *Virginia Woolf: A Biography*. Orlando: Harcourt Brace, 1972.

Bell, Vanessa. *Selected Letters of Vanessa Bell*. Ed. Regina Marler. London: Moyer Bell, 1998.

Carrington, Dora. *Carrington: Letters and Extracts from Her Diaries*. Ed. David Garnett. New York: Holt, Rinehart and Winston, 1970.

Dunn, Jane. *A Very Close Conspiracy: Vanessa Bell and Virginia Woolf*. London: Jonathan Cape, 1990.

Garnett, Angelica. *Deceived with Kindness: A Bloomsbury Childhood*. Oxford: Oxford University Press, 1984.

Glendinning, Victoria. *Leonard Woolf: A Biography*. New York: Free Press, 2006.

Joyce, James. *Finnegans Wake*. New York: Penguin, 1976.

Lee, Hermione. *Virginia Woolf*. London: Chatto & Windus, 1996.

Lee, Hugh, ed. *A Cézanne in the Hedge and Other Memories of Charleston and Bloomsbury*. Chicago: University of Chicago Press, 1993.

Lehmann, John. *Thrown to the Woolfs*. New York: Holt, Rinehart and Winston, 1979.

MacGibbon, Jean. *There's the Lighthouse: A Biography of Adrian Stephen*. London: James & James, 1997.

Marder, Herbert. *The Measure of Life: Virginia Woolf's Last Years*. Ithaca, N.Y.: Cornell University Press, 2000.

Nicolson, Harold. *The War Years: Diaries and Letters 1939–1945*. New York: Atheneum, 1967.

Nicolson, Nigel, ed. *Portrait of a Marriage: Vita Sackville-West and Harold Nicolson*. New York: Atheneum, 1973.

——, ed. *Vita and Harold: The Letters of Vita Sackville-West and Harold Nicolson*. New York: G. P. Putnam's Sons, 1992.

Noble, Joan Russell. *Recollections of Virginia Woolf*. New York: William Morrow, 1972.

Proust, Marcel. *In Search of Lost Time, Vol. IV: Sodom and Gomorrah*. Trans. Terence Kilmartin and C. K. Scott Moncrieff. New York: Random House, 1993.

——. *Selected Letters: 1904–1909*. Trans. Terence Kilmartin. Ed. Philip Kolb. New York: Oxford University Press, 1989.

Shakespeare, William. *Hamlet*. Oxford: Oxford University Press, 1987.

Spalding, Frances. *Vanessa Bell*. New Haven and New York: Ticknor & Fields, 1983.

Stephen, Leslie. *Selected Letters of Leslie Stephen*. Ed. John W. Bicknell and Mark A. Reger. Columbus: Ohio State University Press, 1996.

——. *Sir Leslie Stephen's Mausoleum Book*. London: Clarendon Press, 1977.

Strachey, Lytton. *The Letters of Lytton Strachey*. Ed. Paul Levy and Penelope Marcus. New York: Farrar, Straus & Giroux, 2005.

Wittgenstein, Ludwig. *On Certainty*. Trans. Denis Paul and G. E. M. Anscombe. Ed. G. E. M. Anscombe and G. H. Von Wright. New York: Harper & Row, 1969.

——. *Tractatus Logico-philosophicus*. Ed. D. F. Pears and B. F. McGuinness. London: Routledge & Kegan Paul, 1921.

Woolf, Leonard. *Beginning Again: An Autobiography of the Years 1911–1918*. London: Hogarth Press, 1964.

——. *Downhill All the Way: An Autobiography of the Years 1919–1939*. London: Hogarth Press, 1967.

——. *Growing: An Autobiography of the Years 1904–1911*. London: Hogarth Press, 1970.

——. *The Journey Not the Arrival Matters: An Autobiography of the Years 1939–1969*. London: Hogarth Press, 1969.

——. *Letters of Leonard Woolf*. Ed. Frederic Spotts. San Diego: Harcourt Brace Jovanovich, 1989.

——. *Sowing: An Autobiography of the Years 1880–1904*. London: Hogarth Press, 1960.

——. *The Wise Virgins*. New York: Harcourt, 1941.

Woolf, Virginia. *Between the Acts*. New York: Harcourt, 1941.

——. *The Complete Shorter Fiction*. Ed. Susan Dick. Orlando: Harcourt, 1989.

——. *The Diary of Virginia Woolf, Volume 1: 1915–1919*. Ed. Anne Olivier Bell. New York: Harcourt Brace Jovanovich, 1977.

——. *The Diary of Virginia Woolf, Volume 2: 1920–1924*. Ed. Anne Olivier Bell. New York: Harcourt Brace Jovanovich, 1978.

——. *The Diary of Virginia Woolf, Volume 3: 1925–1930*. Ed. Anne Olivier Bell. New York: Harcourt Brace Jovanovich, 1980.

——. *The Diary of Virginia Woolf, Volume 4: 1931–1935*. Ed. Anne Olivier Bell. New York: Harcourt Brace Jovanovich, 1982.

——. *The Diary of Virginia Woolf, Volume 5: 1936–1941*. Ed. Anne Olivier Bell. New York: Harcourt Brace Jovanovich, 1984.

——. *The Letters of Virginia Woolf, Volume 1: 1888–1912*. Ed. Nigel Nicolson and Joanne Trautmann. New York: Harcourt Brace Jovanovich, 1975.

——. *The Letters of Virginia Woolf, Volume 2: 1912–1922*. Ed. Nigel Nicolson and Joanne Trautmann. New York: Harcourt Brace Jovanovich, 1976.

——. *The Letters of Virginia Woolf, Volume 3: 1923–1928*. Ed. Nigel Nicolson and Joanne Trautmann. New York: Harcourt Brace Jovanovich, 1978.

——. *The Letters of Virginia Woolf, Volume 4: 1929–1931*. Ed. Nigel Nicolson and Joanne Trautmann. New York: Harcourt Brace Jovanovich, 1979.

——. *The Letters of Virginia Woolf, Volume 5: 1932–1935*. Ed. Nigel Nicolson and Joanne Trautmann. New York: Harcourt Brace Jovanovich, 1979.

——. *The Letters of Virginia Woolf, Volume 6: 1936–1941*. Ed. Nigel Nicolson and Joanne Trautmann. New York: Harcourt Brace Jovanovich, 1979.

——. *Moments of Being*. Ed. Jeanne Schulkind. San Diego: Harcourt, 1985.

——. *Mrs. Dalloway*. Orlando: Harcourt, 1925.

——. *Orlando*. San Diego: Harcourt, 1928.

——. *A Passionate Apprentice: The Early Journals: 1897–1909*. Ed. Mitchell A. Leaska. London: Hogarth Press, 1990.

——. "Professions for Women." In *Collected Essays, Volume 2*. New York: Harcourt and Brace, 1967.

——. *Three Guineas*. New York: Harcourt, 1938.

——. *To the Lighthouse*. Oxford: Oxford University Press, 1992.

——. *The Voyage Out*. London: Hogarth Press, 1957.

——. *The Waves*. Orlando: Harcourt, 1931.

——. *The Years*. London: Hogarth Press, 1951.

Zwerdling, Alex. *Virginia Woolf and the Real World*. Berkeley: University of California Press, 1986.

INDEX

Virginia Woolf is abbreviated as VW; Leonard Woolf is abbreviated as LW. Headings and subheadings containing the term "correspondence" refer to letters as source material, and the name of the source may not actually be found on the page.

on younger writers, and desire to relax, 193. *See also A Passionate Apprentice: The Early Journals: 1897–1909* (Leaska, ed.)

Dickinson, Violet: appreciation for VW, 114–115; characteristics of, 114; correspondence with VW, 12, 14, 38, 40, 47, 49, 81, 87, 91, 110, 112, 114, 115, 117, 118, 119, 122, 123, 126, 176; cradle for infant offered by, 40; crisis following death of father, recovery at home of, 113, 114, 115; end of relationship with VW, 176; lover relationship with VW, 115; religiosity of, 119; suicide attempt by VW at home of, 95, 114; travel with VW, 117

the divine, effervescence of the moment as, 4

Dostoyevsky, Fyodor, *Crime and Punishment,* 25

Dreadnought farce, 121

duck(s), as theme in VW's life, 105–106

Duckworth, George (half-brother): correspondence with VW, 103; country house lent for VW convalescence, 106, 146–147; death of, 106–107; and death of mother, 77, 98; and Stella Duckworth, 97, 101; incestuous climate created by, and Virginia and Vanessa Stephen, 102–108, 146–147, 183, 198; LW and, 106, 146–148; marriage of, 104; nicknames of ("Bar," "Georgie"), 103; and Laura Stephen, 80, 107, 183; as supportive brother, attempts at, 80, 103–106, 107

Duckworth, Gerald (half-brother): and death of mother, 77, 98; and Stella Duckworth, 96, 97, 99, 101; as editor of VW, 106, 150; incest of Virginia Stephen by, 102, 104, 107–108; and Laura Stephen, vulnerability of, 107–108; Venice trip organized by, 112

Duckworth, Herbert (first husband of Julia Stephen): children of, 77; death of, 72–73; at death of Julia, VW as

seeing image of, 75; as eternal prince charming, 75, 78, 104; Leslie Stephen on, 82, 104

Duckworth, Stella (half-sister): and Vanessa Bell, 96–97, 99, 101–102; courtship and marriage to Jack Waller Hills, 84, 86, 93, 95–98, 100, 101–102; death of, 70, 86, 98–102, 108, 194; and death of mother, 75, 77; and incestuous climate created by Leslie Stephen, 83–86, 88–89, 91, 96; and mother, 73–74; nickname of ("Old Cow"), 74, 85, 99; physical characteristics of, 83; VW and, 85, 93, 96–97, 99, 100–102

Edel, Leon, 196–197

education: universities forbidden to women, 111; VW as volunteer educator for girls, 116

Egoist (review), 167

Eliot, T. S., 64, 165, 167, 168, 200; *Poems,* 165; *The Waste Land,* 165

Eliot, Vivien (Vivienne), 165

Empire, LW as colonialist in Ceylon, 7–9, 10–12, 13–14, 16–17, 18, 37

Fascism: T. S. Eliot sympathies and, 165; VW condemning, 46. *See also* Hitler, Adolf, and Nazism

feelings, lack of: Vanessa Bell and need for, 140; LW and need for, 39; in *Mrs. Dalloway,* 114; VW's crisis following death of father and, 112

feminism, VW and, 46, 180. *See also* women

Fisher, Commander, 121

Flaubert, Gustav, *Madame Bovary,* 6–7

Forster, E. M., 7, 64, 66, 167

fragility of VW: Quentin Bell's biography and assumption of, 6; LW as dominant guardian to protect, 23, 25–26

Freshwater, 164, 221n22; VW centenary performances (1982), 164–165

with Gwen Raverat, 42; with Jacques Raverat, 48, 109; with George Rylands, 196; with Edward Sackville-West, 176; with Vita Sackville-West, 28, 91, 170, 172–173, 178, 184, 190, 196, 197, 200; with Ethel Smyth, 38–39, 41, 49, 50, 51, 52, 56, 118, 127, 156, 171, 173, 175, 185–186, 187, 196, 197; with Ethel Smyth, nature of, 175; with Margery Snowden, 133; with Thoby Stephen, 111; with Lytton Strachey, 24–25, 28, 38, 105, 129, 132, 167; with Philippa Strachey, 196; with Lady Tweedsmuir, 76; with Emma Vaughn, 103, 112, 132; with Madge Vaughn, 119, 122, 132; with Octavia Wilberforce, 197; with Leonard Woolf, 17, 38
——works: "Am I a Snob?," 66; *Freshwater* (play), 164–165, 221n22; Roger Fry biography, 186–188, 221n6; *Harper's Bazaar* commissioning and then rejecting short story, 195; *The Hyde Park Gate News,* 74–75, 120; inherited by Trekkie Parson, 67; *Jacob's Room,* 156, 223n73; literary criticism, 116, 122, 157, 170; "The Mark on the Wall," 62, 129, 156; "The Mysterious Case of Miss. V," 194, 225n38; *Night and Day,* 155–156; "The Old Bloomsbury," 66, 80; *Orlando,* 173, 174, 178; posthumous disposition of papers, 66–67; *Reminiscences,* 76, 176; *Sketch of the Past,* 75–77, 104, 190; "The Symbol," 194; "A Terrible Tragedy in the Duck Pond," 105–106; *Three*

Guineas, 46, 56, 173, 178, 178–181, 221n6; "22 Hyde Park Gate," 66; *The Waves,* 1, 26, 117, 143; *The Years,* 52–55, 58, 91, 92, 165. *See also Between the Acts*; diary of VW; Hogarth Press; *Moments of Being* (Schulkind, ed.); *Mrs. Dalloway*; *Passionate Apprentice, A: The Early Journals: 1897–1909* (Leaska, ed.); *Room of One's Own, A*; *To the Lighthouse*; *Voyage Out, The*
Wordsworth, William, 191
World War I, 136, 137
World War II: air raids, 185, 186, 188–189, 198, 202; beginning of, 76; desire to survive, VW and, 185, 188–189; T. S. Eliot politics and, 165; end of, 66; Sigmund Freud, evacuation of, 181–182; isolation of VW and, 185, 186, 189, 190, 192–193, 195–196, 198–199; LW on future necessary catastrophe, 196; LW on treatment of Jews, 184; LW work life and, 186, 189; *Moments of Being* on, 76; Adrian Stephen and, 121, 185; suicide pact between LW and VW, 9, 57–58, 89, 185, 193; *Three Guineas* written in lead-up to, 46, 56, 173, 178, 178–181, 221n6; VW and, 185–186, 188–190, 195–196. *See also* anti-Semitism; Hitler, Adolf, and Nazism

The Years, 52–55, 58, 91, 92, 165
Young, Hilton, 15, 131, 132

Zola, Émile, 203

DATE DUE